God's Ultimatum

David E. Gardner

Jesus Is Alive! Ministries

First published 1993 by National Council for Christian Standards

This edition published 2005 by Jesus Is Alive! Ministries,
PO Box 5301
Southend-on-Sea
SS1 1TL

ISBN 1 903725 40 2

Editor: Geoffrey Barlow

Index: Jill Ford

Printed in the United States of America.

God's Ultimatum

Foreword

Throughout all generations there has been a prophetic voice, calling people to believe in and live by the standards of the Living God. Since the Gospel went out to all nations after the sacrificial death of the Lord Jesus Christ and His resurrection to glory, there have been growing numbers of preachers, proclaiming the Word of God to a needy world. Sometimes a man or woman arises in a nation to give extra emphasis to what an individual, or even the whole nation, needs to hear. At such a time, there is often a growing urgency to warn a people who have known the Word of God, but who are turning away to sin. One remembers the messages and lives of the biblical prophets who brought messages to Israel and Judah, these messages they brought still ring true for today.

Such a man was David Gardner, not the only one in his generation to warn the leaders of Britain about the decline from biblical standards and the consequences that would follow of course, but one of the highest calibre nevertheless. He devoted many years of his life to understanding the times in terms of Britain's Christian heritage and current decline, and also the outworking of biblical prophecy.

In his trilogy, *The Trumpet Sounds for Britain*, David Gardner did the people of Great Britain a great service in recalling the growth of the Christian heart of the nation so that we might remember, consider our present sinful ways, and repent before the judgement of God would cause us to reap the consequence of our sins. In this later book David expanded the horizons and scope to take in the Gospel message to all individuals, and also bring a warning to all nations. In so doing, David was conscious of the times in which we live as moving ever closer to the time of the return of the Lord Jesus Christ. He interpreted the signs of our times as pointing to this.

It is not an easy thing to maintain balance in one's message with such a scope. Yet David has achieved this. He understood the role of Israel in the purposes of God and how the history of God's dealings with Israel teaches us about His character and standards for all people. He understood that God speaks not only through the pages of Scripture but also through signs in the physical world. He was able to speak with confidence about the disasters that have befallen Britain and other nations as early warning signals of God's displeasure, and so warn of greater troubles ahead for those who will not turn fully to God. He was able to balance the message of personal salvation with the prophetic message to the nations. He was also able to balance the Gospel message with the call to obey the Laws of God.

David spoke out boldly both from the pulpit and in his writings. He also sent many warnings to the leaders of the nation. In his early days he understood the initial signs in the nation and in the world that are clear warnings from Almighty God to this generation. Generally speaking, the warnings that David and others gave have been unheeded. We are witnesses, as he also was in his lifetime, of the falling away from the ways of God throughout the nations. Now David Gardner's work is done on this earth and the baton has passed to others; but also the crisis among the nations has escalated. This particular book was first published over a decade ago, but its message is still relevant. We trust that in republishing it the warning that was given – ultimatum indeed – will stay alive even through the inevitable troubles that lie ahead in this world. We also trust that there are those who will hear this message and will heed the warning, and that those who are in a similar ministry to David today will be encouraged to hold fast to the Word of truth, the Word of witness and the Word of warning in the days ahead.

Dr Clifford Denton
Director of Cambrian Bible College

God's ultimatum for every individual
God's ultimatum for Britain. Gods ultimatum for the whole world.

By The Reverend David E. Gardner.
Author of "The Trumpet Sounds For Britain", "Sound The Trumpet Among The Nations".

BRITAIN'S EARLY CHRISTIAN HISTORY AND WHAT GOD IS SAYING AND DOING BECAUSE WE HAVE DEPARTED FROM IT.

Some of the Author's previous Predictions about the kind of Divine Judgments which could be visited upon us, and how the majority of them have already been dramatically fulfilled.

Through the Prophet Ezekiel we are admonished that he who "seeth the sword" (of judgment) come upon the land he should blow the trumpet and warn the people". If he does so, he is cleared of all responsibility; he is free from blood - guiltiness. But if he does *not* do so , God says he will require the consequences of what happens at that watchman's hands. He will hold him responsible. See Ezekiel Chapter 33 verses one to eleven.

This is a sequel, a follow-up, to my booklet entitled, "A New Government - A New Era" which was published in July 1992 and has since had to be reprinted. It bore the sub-title:- "So what is God now saying (a) About the state of the nation of Britain today? (b) As to the responsibility of its Church?" But it also raised the question, "What is God saying to the Royal House of Windsor?"

This is also a sequel to my three Volumes entitled, "The Trumpet Sounds for Britain", and to my more recent book entitled, "Sound the Trumpet Amoung the Nations" which was published in November 1991 and which also has since had to be reprinted. This is also a sequel to my other publications entitled, "The Decade of Evangelism. The Extreme Urgency of it", published in the summer of 1991, and "Whither Britannia?" published in the Winter of 1991/1992.

It was as a result of my little booklet "A Warning to the Nation", first published in 1967, and which went into over 120,000 copies that I felt constrained of God to write "The Trumpet Sounds for Britain", because so many people were writing, and phoning, asking me if I could elaborate on the points I had raised in that little booklet's message. At that time also

I was gripped with the burning and overwhelming conviction that Britain is fast heading towards an extremely severe judgment of God, the like of which she has never before experienced in any period of her long history. I therefore felt convinced, even at *that* time, that there was an urgent need, like the prophets of old, to "Sound the Trumpet and warn the people".

For instance, in the first two volumes of "The Trumpet Sounds for Britain" I set out to explain how Britain got herself into such a state. It was because:-

(1) She had forsaken God;
(2) She is now living without Him, and never so much as mentions Him in all her deliberations.
(3) She has reversed God's laws and is flying directly in the face of them;
(4) She has become a blood-guilty nation.

Furthermore, I was at great pains to point out that it is neither a heathen nor a pagan nation which is guilty of all this. That is the appalling thing about it. On the contrary, it is a nation which has had a long and rich Christian heritage; a nation which was once known throughout the world as a godly nation and a Bible-loving, missionary-hearted and God-fearing nation. A nation which had the fear of God before its peoples' eyes.

To establish all this, I indicated clearly in the first two volumes of 'The Trumpet Sounds for Britain" how there is ample evidence to assert that the hand of Almighty God has been on the history of this country *in blessing*, right from its very earliest beginnings, and how God has been at work on her behalf throughout all that time in many marvellous ways, raising her up until, at various identifiable points in her history, she had become a great nation.

I pointed out for instance, that it was due to a mighty act of God, way back in the dim, distant past, that she became an island, or group of islands, severed from the continent of Europe by a mighty oceanic surge. And it is my firm belief and conviction that that meant we should be severed from the continent of Europe for all time.

I then traced how God caused the pure, New Testament form of Christianity to come to these islands at an extremely early time - over 550 years at least before Augustine - and I provided all the evidence for that. This thus ensured that these islands were established on strong, true, Christian, and Biblical foundations. And I went to great lengths to point out how, once those foundations were firmly secured, God continued to preserve or restore them whenever they were in danger of being lost, weakened or destroyed.

I showed how God did this through Patrick, then at the Reformation, and yet again at the time of the Great Spiritual Awakening under the dynamic and anointed preaching of Whitefield and Wesley, when, as it is recorded on a plaque in Westminster Abbey, "Divine Providence exalted Great Britain to an height of prosperity and glory unknown to any former age".

I also made it clear that it was through the working of Almighty God on our history that these islands became based on Christian and Bible-based laws, during the reign of King Alfred, and even before the time of King Alfred. I quoted Winston Churchill as showing in his "History of the English - Speaking Peoples", how we, as a nation, were brought by Divine Providence to three great land marks of our history:-

(1)   When "there was no kingdom in the realm in which heathen religions and practices now prevailed. The whole Island was now Christian."

Alas! how different are things today!

(2)   How, during the twelfth century, "After years of being the encampment and battleground of an invading army, England became finally and for all time one coherent kingdom *BASED ON CHRISTIANITY*". That is what Churchill wrote in 1956, for so he then thought. (The capital letters and italics are mine.) But look what has happened now!

(3)   How God so moved by his Holy Spirit through the Reformation period, so as to cause this nation to become so Protestant Christian in its faith and beliefs, that England, under Queen Elizabeth I, became a Protestant Christian Country *by law*. Thereafter, the Christian faith, (and it needs to be stressed that it was the Protestant, New-Testament and totally Bible-Based, Christian Faith) became Britain's *constitutional* position to such an extent that it was embodied by Act of Parliament in the Coronation Oath - which commits every British Sovereign, pledged with the full support of Parliament, "to uphold to the utmost of our power the Laws of God in the realm and the True Profession of the Christian Gospel". This Christian constitutional position was also embodied in the Act of Settlement of 1701, which requires that only a *Protestant* Christian may ascend and occupy the British throne.

3

I then made plain in Volume 2 of "The Trumpet Sounds for Britain", how the hand of Almighty God can be traced all down the years of our nation's history, bringing about mighty acts of deliverance whenever this country has been in mortal danger. I recounted the amazing interventions of God from as far back as the time of King Alfred, and at the time of the Spanish Armada, and wrote about two extraordinary interventions which brought us through to victory in 1918.

Then I went on to relate in detail at least twelve of the amazing miracles which took place between 1939 and 1945, seven of which came as direct answers to National Days of Prayer called by the late King George VI, or in answer to times of *special* prayer — showing that God was indisputably *with us* in those days.

Prime Minister Winston Churchill was full of thanksgiving to God for all this when, after announcing victory in Europe to a crowded House of Commons on 8th May 1945, he turned towards the Speaker and said:- "I therefore beg, sir, with your permission, to move 'That this House do now attend at the Church of St. Margaret Westminster, to give humble and reverent thanks to Almighty God for our deliverance from the threat of German domination'."

I repeat. "God was clearly *with* us then: He was also *working* with us, and on our behalf, during all these long years of war".

Our national leaders recognised this, and many of them proclaimed at that time, "We have been saved for a purpose. God has delivered us and brought us to our present position for some great purpose and now we must seek humbly to discover what that purpose is and then to be faithful to it". I then named in Volume II who many of these leaders were. They included our then gracious Sovereign, His Majesty King George VI, and our then Prime Minister, Winston Churchill.

But I then had to lament, "Britain has forgotten all that". She has completely forgotten and even put out of her mind all these great blessings which God has so richly bestowed upon her in the past. Despite the fact that her history has been steeped in God's miracles of deliverance and acts of mercy, Britain has rejected all her rich Christian heritage. She has thrown it all overboard. And in contrast to all these experiences of divine activity on her behalf she never turns to Him now for assistance. She never at any time calls on Him in times of crisis, or of trouble. In fact she has now become a nation which has no time for God. She never mentions Him. She has shut her ears to Him, and is therefore living totally without Him. Indeed she is doing more than that. She is openly and publicly defying Him, and is deliberately and wilfully flying in His face.

Furthermore, her Parliament — the so-called Mother of Parliaments — has even gone against the nation's own Constitution as expressed in the Coronation Oath by placing on her Statute Book, laws which make legal things which the Bible expressly declares are an abomination in the sight of the Lord and which provoke Him to anger. And Parliament deliberately continues to do that. And it obtains the Royal Assent in doing so. Therefore, Britain's Parliament, by doing this, has legalised *sin*. And by deliberately changing our moral and spiritual direction as a nation it has caused the nation's spiritual and moral decline to escalate alarmingly, and has caused Britain to become a nation which has put itself on a direct collision course with God. And despite the fact that I am a very strong monarchist, I cannot see that our gracious Sovereign can be absolved from all this, since she gives her signature to the Royal Assent before these offending laws can go onto our Statute Book.

Furthermore, due to the iniquitous United Kingdom Abortion Act of 1967, which was also given the Royal Assent if you please, the nation now has the blood of no less than three and a quarter million murdered living human creatures on its hands, plus all the unrequited blood which has been shed in countless murders all over the United Kingdom since capital punishment was abolished, to say nothing of all the unrequited blood which has been shed in Northern Ireland. Britain, in consequence, has therefore become a blood-guilty nation, and God is angry. I can see very clearly from the Scriptures that God is going to require all that unrequited blood at the hands of the nation, of its leaders, and of its people. The Bible makes that very plain indeed.

I asked in desperation in Volume I of "The Trumpet Sounds for Britain", "Can't we see? Cannot any, or all of our national leaders see? Cannot our gracious Sovereign see? Cannot our Prime Minister, who was then Margaret Thatcher, see? Cannot our Church Leaders see? Cannot Parliament and all those in authority see and understand that to reverse a nation's laws and to change its moral and spiritual direction downwards as we have done, so that the country and its society becomes diametrically opposed to what God Almighty in His Word, the Bible, has commanded, is bound to put the nation on a course which is set directly against God? And that *that* means

5

that God is now *against* us, whereas before, He was *for* us, was on our side, and was working *with us* and on our behalf? But this is precisely what this nation *has* done and *is* doing, even to the extent of going directly against the written and Christian part of its Constitution which is embodied in the Coronation Oath, namely, "to uphold to the utmost of our power the Laws of God in the realm and the True Profession of the Christian Gospel".

I said all that, and asked all those questions as long ago as 1980. That was when Volume I of "The Trumpet Sounds for Britain" was first published.

But there has been no response to those questions since then. No sign that they have even been regarded. Only utter silence. Then I issued a strong warning. That was in 1980, please notice.

I said that I firmly believed that unless we, as a people, and as individuals, truly repent of having done all this and of having gone the wrong way, and take drastic steps to put it all right, and turn back to God very quickly, and embrace once again the Christian Faith which we had discarded, then a terrible crash in some form of the judgments of God is inevitable, and probably in terms of some terrible and grievous form of such judgment the like of which we had never before experienced in our long history. "For", I said, "as the Holy Spirit said through David in Psalm 119 verse 126 "It is time for thee, Lord, to work, for they have made void thy law".

Indeed, I said the nation had already been visited by a number of God's judgments at the time I then wrote (1980). For instance, I made the point at that time that in Deuteronomy Chapter 28 there are at least thirty judgments of God mentioned which can come upon a nation because God is against it, and I said, that in my opinion, Britain has already experienced twenty-seven of them, and I spelt out in detail what these were. I added that the remaining three could come upon Britain at any moment. I pointed out also that Deuteronomy 28 verse 46 says, of all these judgments: "And they shall be upon you for a sign" — for a sign that God is against you. And certainly for a sign that you are going against Him. I also identified some of the judgments proclaimed by Old Testament prophets, such as the prophet Amos, as amongst those which had already been visited upon Britain.

But in addition to all that, I was compelled to say that all the evidence shows that God has been handing us over to other forms of judgment because of our continued and obstinate national rebellion against Him. Such, for instance, as the gross forms of perversion and immorality which are mentioned in the epistle to the Romans, chapter one. Here we find it stated three times

6

over that, "because they did not like to retain God in their knowledge" — because they did not want to have anything more to do with God in other words, or even bring Him into their thinking, "God gave them up to", or "God gave them over to" such things as "uncleanness through lust", to "dishonouring their own bodies between themselves", to "vile affections", to "women changing the natural use into that which is against nature" — lesbianism in other words — to "men leaving the natural use of the woman . . . men with men working that which is unseemly burning in their lust one toward another" — homosexuality in other words — "and receiving in themselves as a result, that recompense of their error which was meet" — AIDS, for instance. And then it repeats, "And even as they did not like to retain God in their knowledge, God gave them over to a reprobate mind", to a perverted, twisted, immoral, and totally unprincipled mind, that means. I pointed this out as long ago as 1980, and we could see it happening all around us *then*. But now it has escalated all around us at an alarming rate and is being bombarded at us, and fed into everyone's mind on television and radio programmes, in newspapers and magazines, and on videos, under the demonic pretext that "this is life as it is".

But Romans Chapter One verse 18 says, All this is "the wrath of God being revealed from heaven *against* all ungodliness and unrighteousness of men". In other words, it is all part of God's judgment. He hands us over to this kind of thing as a result of our refusing to have anything to do with Him. Whenever will we learn?

But then, by the time that Volume II of "The Trumpet Sounds for Britain" was published, the situation in the country was even worse. The tragic spiritual and moral landslide which had taken place in the nation since 1945 had been escalated apace as a result of our reversing our laws and thus legalizing SIN.; I could see very clearly by then that we, as a nation, had gone as far away from God as the nation of Israel did in the later stages of her Old Testament history, if not, indeed further. I said then that we had gone as far as:-

(1)   "Committing the Sin of Jeroboam the son of Nebat — who went down in history as the king who made Israel to sin."

(2)   As far as "Committing the Sin of Solomon".

(3)   And as far as Committing the Sin of notoriously wicked Manasseh who took his nation, Judah, beyond the point of no return. So that became the burden of Volume III of "The Trumpet Sounds for Britain" published in 1985. And I spelt out

in great detail what committing the sins of these three national kings and ruling authorities meant. And it became abundantly clear that the Nation of Britain had gone exactly the way they did, and that therefore we were likely to suffer the same kind of judgment of God as they suffered.

Then came 1991. By now the Berlin Wall had been taken down. By now also Communism in the Soviet Union had collapsed. By now also in the Middle East, The State of Israel had long since come into being (1948). And in 1967 Jerusalem had come back into the hands of the Jews for the first time in nearly 2,000 years, thus fulfilling one of the most significant prophecies of Scripture in which Jesus had said, "Jerusalem shall be trodden down by the Gentiles UNTIL the times of the Gentiles had been fulfilled", Luke 21 verse 24. Then as "the dust began to settle" in the break-up of the former Soviet Union it became clear that in at least some of its former republics which began to emerge, the stage was being set for the fulfilment of the Ezekiel 38 and 39, Joel Chapter 3 and Zephaniah 3 verse 8, prophecies in which it is predicted that God will bring all nations against Jerusalem to battle. The outbreak of the Gulf War between Iraq and Ayotolla Khomeinis' Iran, to be followed by the Gulf War between Saddam Hussein and the combined United Nations Forces was a further indication that the history of the world was approaching its final culmination point when everything would come to a head in Jerusalem as the Bible had always predicted, and that therefore we were getting dramatically near to the End of this Age and to the Personal Return of The Lord Jesus Christ, who would usher in His New Age.

So a shift in emphasis of my writings was necessary. No longer must they concentrate on the National Situation only, but on the International and World Situation also. Thus "Sound the Trumpet Among The Nations" was published in November 1991 to warn the nations of the world as to where world events were fast leading us, namely to the great finale of world history.

But by then, November 1991, Britain had been smitten with a whole series of national catastrophies, tragedies and disasters in terms of the judgments of God. Isaiah 5 verse 24 says, "BECAUSE they have cast away the law of the Lord of Hosts, and despised the word of the Holy One of Israel THEREFORE is the anger of the Lord kindled against His people, and He hath stretched forth His hand against them, and hath smitten them". And when it says, "He hath stretched forth His hand against them" it means in judgment.

8

And the Bible teaches that He smites with catastrophes, calamities, national disasters and tragedies. And by November 1991 we had had a whole list of them.

We had had the King's Cross underground station inferno.

We had had the Bradford Football Stadium inferno.

We had had the Hillesborough Football Stadium disaster, the Lockerbie air crash, the Manchester air crash, after which the Queen asked in anguish, "Why another air crash?"

We had had the Clapham train disaster, followed almost immediately by another train disaster at Glasgow.

We had had the Piper Alpha oil rig disaster, another inferno which killed 167 men, which was ranked as third in world disasters.

We had had the Zeebruger Herald of Free Enterprise ferry disaster.

Then we had had the 110-mile-per-hour hurricane which hit London, and South and South-East England in October 1987, ripping up 15 million trees, bringing power lines down everywhere. The Stock Exchange, the Bank of England, and the whole of the City of London had had to close down because all the computers were put out of action, and because staff could not get in, as all London main-line railway stations had been brought to a standstill and there were no trains. Significantly enough, that morning's Bible reading said, "Shall there be evil (or calamity) in a city and *the Lord* hath not done it? Amos 3 verse 6. And a leading article in the Daily Telegraph that same morning had said:- "In John Bunyan's day, that hurricane would have been attributed to God expressing His immense displeasure at Britain".

But who had heeded?

Moslem waiters in a London hotel were saying to me in alarm at that time, "*God* is speaking, Sir. *God* is speaking."

Then a year later, the Outer Hebrides and the west coast of Scotland were hit with the same kind of fierce hurricane.

After that, we had had a major disaster in the Thames with the sudden sinking of the passenger boat, "The Marchioness", full of revellers early one Sunday morning, when a sand barge collided with it. And they still do not know how it happened.

Then between mid-December 1989 and mid-February 1990, gale after gale, and winds of storm force and hurricane force had battered and slashed these islands, wreaking havoc and destruction everywhere, from the South and West Coasts of Britain, from Hampshire to the Hebrides, in Wales and up in Scotland. The reports of them seemed to present a picture of a *rising crescendo* of hurricane-force gales. And many were saying at that time, "There is something *unusual* about all this".

This is only *part* of the list of catastrophies, tragedies, calamities, and disasters which we, as a nation, had been experiencing up to November 1991.

And the question which had been on the lips of many at that time was:- "*Why?* Why is all this battering and bruising happening to us?"

The Bible gives a very clear answer in 2 Chronicles 7 verses 21-22, which says:- [Someone will say,] "Why hath the Lord done thus unto this land ...? And it shall be answered, *Because* they forsook the Lord God of their fathers ... *therefore* hath He brought all this evil (or calamity) upon them". *That* is why. You don't need any other explanation.

But which of our National Leaders, even *now,* are prepared to admit and acknowledge this?

The national situation was so serious at that time, (even at the end of 1991), that I was having to ask myself: "Has God had to withdraw His protecting hand from these islands?" I said then, "It is a question which needs to be asked, and which urgently needs to be answered". In fact, the national situation was so serious at that time that I proclaimed, both in "Sound The Trumpet Among The Nations" and in my nation-wide Preaching:- "*Lamentations* is what is most urgently needed in Britain today. Lamentations, not celebrations".

It was at a time when, no matter what Christian Magazine or newspaper one picked up, it was celebrations, celebrations, celebrations which were constantly talked about and being advertised. It seemed to be an obsession in the Christian world — a craze. And now we have just had another one of these celebrations in St. Paul's Cathedral on Sunday, May 23rd, 1993. I said at that time also that the situation in Britain was so desperate that only *God coming down* in mighty Holy Ghost revival power will touch the situation. But I said that will not happen until there are *lamentations* about our tragic condition, *weeping, wringing of hands, howlings,* and crying out to God *in desperation* that He will have mercy on us.

I also called for *repentance*, — deep and heartfelt repentance, — of the kind that took place in the lives of the king and of the people of Nineveh under the Preaching of Jonah. And I said then that *God coming down* in Holy Ghost revival power will not happen unless and until there *is* that kind of repentance.

And I said then, "But where is it? I don't see repentance taking place anywhere". And I still don't see it taking place anywhere today!

By the winter of 1991/1992 the national moral and spiritual situation had continued to deteriorate to such an extent that in a main article which I was urgently asked to write at that time I had to raise the question, "Whither Britannia?" followed by the further question, "Doesn't it ever occur to Britannia that she is entirely off course and going the wrong way?" For instance, it was not enough that by then she had allowed legalised abortion to be passed onto her Statute Book in 1967, by Royal Assent, if you please, with the result that over three-and-a-quarter million living human beings, with souls, had been mercilessly put to death, thus exterminating life at *that* end of the human life cycle. But by *now* there was a powerful groundswell of public opinion being stirred up, which was aimed at liquidating people at the other end of that human life cycle, in terms of the legalisation of voluntary euthanasia. Which means the annihilation of the elderly, who also have souls. The subtle and underlying reason being, of course, that the elderly cost the State too much to keep! This was *really* demonic. But that powerful groundswell is still increasing, and there are forces at work behind the scenes fanning the flames.

No wonder it was necessary then to raise the question, "Britain! Wherever are you heading?"

It was not enough that in 1967 Britain allowed a Bill to be passed on to her Statute Book, which legalised homosexuality (which the Bible calls Sodomy, and which God says is wicked and *sin against the Lord exceedingly*,) from a certain age, and again with the Royal Assent if you please. But *now*, by the Winter of 1991/1992, strong pressure groups were urging that it shall be made legal in Britain's Armed Forces. And some were, and still are, even strongly advocating that it should be made legal from the age of 15 or 16. So the moral and spiritual climate in Britain was being dragged down lower and lower.

It was not enough either, that Britain had allowed easy divorce to be legalised in 1967, again with the Royal Assent, when God says "I hate divorce and putting away", Malachi 2 verse 16. But since then, Britain has allowed divorce to escalate to such an extent that the Daily Telegraph on Saturday, November 9th, 1991, had to say, "the divorce rate in Britain may be rising even faster than the unemployment figures!" And the marriages of members of the Royal Family, who should be giving Britain a lead, are now involved.

It is all making a complete mockery of marriage, and is rendering the solemn vows taken before God in Church and in Cathedral Wedding Services sheer hypocrisy. It means that those solemn vows have not meant a thing, even in Royal Weddings.

But in addition to all that, during the last few years, before the Winter of 1991/1992, Britain had seen the Houses of God all over the land profaned and desecrated in terms of her Cathedrals and Churches, and Westminster Abbey, being given over to the use of Multi-faith Services, when Hindus, Buddhists, Members of the Ba'hai Faith, Rastafarians, and Muslims, have actually been invited to take part in the services, and to pray there, in the House of God, to their own gods. And this, when God describes all such practices in the Bible as "polluting the House of God with your idols"; and as "profaning the House of God and His Sanctuary". So what, all down the long centuries of British history have been known as The House of God in terms of our Cathedrals and Churches, have now been desecrated, profaned, polluted, infiltrated, and used, by every other faith and religion of the world, and by their idols and images. And all this, with the active support of our Sovereign, our Archbishops and Bishops, not to mention the Pope.

No wonder we need to ask again, "Britain! Wherever are you heading?"

But by the Winter of 1991/1992 something horrendous and outrageous had just been introduced to our Country in the realm of medical genetics and engineering. A Report published on 8th November, 1991, said that family doctors and gynaecologists were to be allowed to give parents the opportunity to choose their babies' sex by artificially inseminating women with sexually predetermined sperm for a payment of £350. This caused an infertility expert from Hammersmith Hospital, Dr. Robert Winston, to state, "The *ultimate* example of this kind of treatment is what happened in medical practice in Nazi Germany in the 1930s, when doctors tried to breed a "master race", free from "undesirable genetic characteristics". Now we, the British, who protested in an uproar *then* at what Hitler was going all out to do, are beginning to go down the same road! How horrific!

"Britain! Wherever are you going?"

12

As one outrageous thing followed another, and then something even more outrageous and horrendous was introduced, I could not restrain myself *then* from saying, "Whyever does Almighty God withhold His Hand in Judgment?"

We were still persisting in going the wrong way and in taking the downward path; the path that leads to perdition and the abyss, and in doing so, we have been, and still are, violating every one of God's Ten Commandments. And in "Whither Britannia?" I spelt out in detail that this was so.

By now also (Winter 1991/1992), even some of our friends from overseas were lamenting our abysmal spiritual and moral condition. Dr. Kalim Siddiqui, an Islamic leader who has been living in this Country for some time, on being asked whether he thinks it is possible for the Muslim and Christian cultures to co-exist in Britain, replied, "Quite frankly, I don't think there is a Christian culture in this Country. This is a post-industrial, secular culture where prostitution, gambling, homosexuality — everything mankind has regarded as evil — have been legalised". (Sunday Telegraph, 3rd November 1991.)

What an indictment! What a clear perception too! That is how Britain was being seen, and was being analysed by our friends from overseas *then*, — in 1991.

By April 1992 a General Election was about to take place. I found myself in the embarrassing position of not being able to vote. On a Sunday early in April (1992) the "Sunday Telegraph" published on its front page that Mr Major had said he intended to back the "Gay Rights" Movement. Mr Kinnock had several times publicly declared that he was an atheist. It had also been announced that the Labour Party was in favour of bringing down the age of consent for homosexuals to 15 or 16, and the Liberal Democrats were in a similar position. Also its Leader had been found guilty of having had an "affair". Then I discovered that Mr Major had instructed Conservative Party Headquarters that moral issues were to be banned and were not allowed to be raised during the Election Campaign. So there was no way in which I could vote for any of the Parties. My conscience would not allow me to do so on moral grounds. When I informed my local Member of Parliament of this, and clearly stated my reasons, he was shaken to the foundations. But thus it had to be. I realised I was disfranchised. But so be it.

13

However, when General Election Day came, the result of the nation-wide voting took everybody by surprise. Some had said it would result in a total change of govenment. A new Government was returned, yes. But it was still the former Government led by Mr Major. By 4 a.m. on Friday, April 10th, 1992 it was clear that it was his Party which had won the General Election. Then significantly enough, I found, on buying the "Daily Telegraph" on that day, the Bible verse at the head of the Personal Column said, "The existing authorities have been put there by God". Romans Chapter 13 verse 1. That settled the argument. The result of the General Election was God's doing. And He was declaring that it was, through that verse from the Bible. I believe it was God speaking to the Nation.

That being the case, if the existing authorities had been put there by God, it carried with it a heavy responsibility. And so in my booklet entitled, "A New Government — A New Era", with the sub-title in Part I, "What is God now saying about the State of the Nation today?" I set out very clearly that "the existing authorities", namely the Prime Minister, his Cabinet, and the whole of his Government who have been put there by God, and indeed the Sovereign herself, are responsible to God as to how they behave, how they govern, and as to how they legislate. And they will have to answer to God in the long run for all that. For I pointed out that Romans Chapter 13, from which the "Daily Telegraph" had quoted, teaches that "the existing authorities", or the "state authorities", or "the powers that be", — the higher powers", are "ordained of God", and that it even refers to them as "Ministers of God"; and to each one of them individually as "*The* Minister of God". This is true whether it be the Sovereign herself, the Prime Minister, the Home Secretary, the Foreign Secretary, the Minister of Education, any Cabinet Minister, any Member of the House of Commons, or any Member of the House of Lords. It is the teaching of this chapter and of other chapters of the Bible that he is *The* Minister of God. And furthermore, that that is what he or she is, in God's eyes. And God will hold them responsible for how they govern and for how they legislate. That goes without question. So what an extremely heavy responsibility they all bear. And particularly so, as under what is known in theological terms as "God's common grace", this system of government, — of authority in a realm, — which is responsible for keeping law and order, is referred to in verse 2 of Romans Chapter 13 as "the ordinance of God", which means it is not man's system of government, but *God's* system of government. And under God's common grace it is appointed by Him to stem the flow of corruption and to hold back the spread of evil, violence and wickedness. That is its Divinely appointed function. Yet I had to point out in the booklet "A New Government — A New Era" that many Parliamentarians, Politicians, top Civil Servants, and others, say, "Oh! But you cannot legislate morals and moral standards".

To that I replied that they can legislate downwards apparently! To which I would now add in 1993, they can legislate downwards to spread the flow of sin, iniquity, wickedness and corruption!

They can legislate downwards in terms of supporting the "Gay Rights" Movement, and by bringing the age of consent down to 16 years of age or below.

They can legislate downwards by legalising easier divorce.

They can legislate downwards by legalising abortion, and thus encouraging, and even promoting, sex outside marriage.

They can legislate downwards by legalising Sunday Trading, all for extra profit and gain.

They can legislate downwards by abolishing corporal punishment when God requires it to be administered.

They can legislate downwards by bringing in a Parliamentary Bill to introduce a National Lottery and so to encourage gambling on an increasingly National Scale.

They can do all that, alright, and still more. But they can never legislate upwards! Or so they say!

When my booklet, "A New Government — A New Era" was published in July 1992 I wrote in it, "If we continue to legislate downwards in the way that we have done over the past 30 years or so, — ever since the Permissive 1960's that is, — and with the Royal Assent each time, despite the fact that the Sovereign is on Oath before Almighty God with her hand placed on an open Bible and with the whole world watching on Television — "to uphold to the utmost of our power the Laws of God in the Realm and the true Profession of the Protestant Christian Gospel" — then we are very soon going to experience a Visitation of God upon these British Isles in terms of Divine Judgment. There is no question at all about that. It is inevitable". And I said, "And none of us should be surprised were we to see that Divine judgment beginning to be visited on the Royal House of Windsor". And I said, "It is a very strong Monarchist who is saying that, a fact which is well known in Buckingham Palace".

15

But then what happened? Consternation!

Fire swept through Windsor Castle! (Friday, November 20th, 1992). This, beyond question, was singularly described as a National Calamity — a National Catastrophe. It was also a severe blow to Her Majesty, and to every member of the Royal Family, to all of whom it was their favourite home. But it is also the chief symbol of The Royal House of Windsor. Soon after that, on Tuesday, November 24th, the Daily Telegraph reported that Canon Terence Grigg, Rector of Cottingham, North Humberside, had told his parishioners, and I quote, that, "The Windsor Castle Fire may have been Divine retribution for the Synod vote for the ordination of women." He said, "No sooner has the Church of England made its decision on women priests than we have a fire at the home of its Supreme Governor". "The coincidence seems amazing", he said. But before this, only minutes after the first news of the fire at Windsor Castle had been announced on the Radio, my attention was drawn to a verse in the Book of Isaiah Chapter 29 verse 6, which says, "Thou shalt be visited of the Lord of hosts with ... the flame of devouring fire". I was immediately arrested by those words, because all the Press Reports during the next few days bore out that that was exactly what happened. Windsor Castle, the symbol of the Royal House of Windsor, had been visited with the flame of devouring fire.

It seems without doubt that the fire started in the private chapel, which, in itself, might have been of great significance. It seems too, that a spark, or a small fire, was noticed breaking out behind a curtain or tapestry, close to The Lord's Table, and that attempts were made to put it out with fire extinguishers. But then the curtain caught fire, and a witness said, "We tried to put it out, but once the drape dropped down on the carpet it was virtually like an explosion. The fire spread along the carpet and up the stairs faster than a man could run". Prince Andrew, who was there at the time, also testified to this. Then the whole place became an inferno as the fire swept along several wings.

But on the morning that the fire had first been announced I was also reminded that Amos Chapter 7 verse 4 says, "Behold the Lord God called to *contend* by fire". The *Lord God* did! That word "contend" is a strong word. It means to contend *in Judgment*. It means that God has to contend in Judgment and by fire, because there is something happening which is so serious that it has aroused His Disapproval and Divine Displeasure.

I also find that in the Book of Amos God states at least five times over in Chapter One, "I will send a fire *which shall devour the palaces thereof*". He says, too, in Amos Chapter One verse 14, "I will *kindle* a fire, and it shall devour the palaces thereof". And we need to notice that God says, "*I* will". "*I* will do it". "*I* will send a fire". There are no second causes with God.

There is still much speculation in the Press as to exactly how the fire started. One of the National Dailies says, "It may never even be known exactly how it started". There seems to be quite a mystery about it in many people's minds. But I am obliged to repeat, "There are no second causes with God". When God says, "I will send a fire and it shall devour the palaces thereof", He sends the fire, and that is the end of the matter. And when He says, "and it shall *devour* the palaces thereof", the word "devour" is an exact description of what happened in Windsor Castle, which is the chief of the Royal Palaces. It was indeed "the flame of *devouring* fire", to quote Isaiah 29 verse 6, and it *devoured* a great part of Windsor Castle, as Her Majesty saw, as she wept at the sight of it, and as all the other members of the Royal Family know only too well.

But Amos Chapter 2 verse 4 goes on to state *why* God has to do this kind of thing. He says it is *"because* they have despised the Law of The Lord and have not kept His Commandments". That is why.

It took my breath away, on the morning of the fire, to realise that as long ago as last July (1992) I had written on Page 7 of "A New Government — A New Era", "If we continue to legislate downwards in the way that we have done over the past 30 years or so, — ever since the Permissive 1960's that is, — and with the Royal Assent each time, despite the fact that the Sovereign is on Oath before Almighty God with her hand placed on an open Bible and with the whole world watching on Television — "to uphold to the utmost of our power the *Laws of God* in the Realm and the true Profession of the Protestant Christian Gospel" — then we are very soon going to experience a Visitation of God upon these British Isles in terms of Divine Judgment. There is no question about that. It is inevitable". And it startled me even more to find that I had added:- "And none of us should be surprised were we to see that Divine Judgment beginning to be visited on the Royal House of Windsor".

And now it had happened!

It took my breath away even more to realise that this is what I preached

17

in Stockport, Cheshire, on Saturday, September 12th, (1992), when I preached the entire contents of the booklet, "A New Government — A New Era" to an audience who had come from a 100 mile radius to hear this Message, and that what I said then, had been recorded on cassette tapes and was by now in wide circulation. And now it had all happened in terms of the devastating Fire at Windsor Castle, which hit the headlines all over the entire world!

But ten days before I was due to go to Stockport, common courtesy demanded that I write to the Queen, who was then at Balmoral, sending her a copy of the booklet, and advising her, in advance, that that was what I was going to preach in ten day's time. On my return from Stockport I received a most gracious reply, the wording of which indicated that Her Majesty had taken careful note of my views on all the topics I had raised. So neither she, nor her Senior Advisors could say that she had not been warned. Then after I had studied all the Newspaper Reports of the Windsor Castle Fire itself, I felt strongly constrained to write to Her Majesty again, pointed out what that verse in Isaiah Chapter 29:6, and what the verses in the Book of Amos, were saying. And I said in my letter dated Thursday, 24th November, 1992, "God is speaking·Your Majesty". And I regard it very significant indeed that soon after I had posted that letter, I began to get telephone calls and letters from people in different parts of the Country, all saying that it seemed to the writers of these letters, and to those who phoned, that Almighty God was seeking to get a Message through to the Queen. This seemed to me to be strong confirmation that I should have written to Her Majesty along the lines that I did. The Bible says, "Out of the mouth of two or three witnesses shall a thing be established". My strong contention is, that it should be placed on permanent record for all to see that these two letters have been written to the Highest in the Realm at such a tragic time of our nation's history. Indeed, I would go further. I believe that God Himself wants it to be recorded. And what God wants, must be done. Hence my reason for recording it in these lines.

But in addition to drawing Her Majesty's attention, in my letter of 24th November, 1992, to the fact that I had said in my booklet as long ago as July of that year that none of us should be surprised were we to see Divine Judgment beginning to be visited on the Royal House of Windsor if we continue to legislate downwards in the way that we have been doing with the Royal Assent each time, I also said in my letter that she would no doubt recall that in "A New Government — A New Era" I predicted that a whole series of other National catastrophies and calamities could follow in terms of the Judgments of God, as the expression of His disapproval and Divine displeasure at the wrong direction in which this Country, led by its Parliament, is deliberately and wilfully heading. I predicted in that booklet for instance a serious collapse of our National Economy as one of those visitations of the Judgment of God. We have seen that happen, ever since "Black Wednesday", when Britain suddenly had to come out of the European Monetary System, at a stroke. The pound has been in serious trouble ever since then. And every time the Chancellor of the Exchequer, or the Treasury, or the Prime Minister, announces there is a slight improvement in the National Economy, within hours sometimes, figures are produced by the C.B.I. or by other Industrial Concerns to show that the opposite has become the case. So now nobody believes the Chancellor, the Prime Minister, or the Government anymore! And on the very day that I am writing this particular page, it was confidently announced on the early morning news, that sterling had been boosted last night, prompting a confident ministerial forecast that recovery was now under way, causing the "Daily Telegraph" to carry big, black, banner headlines on its front page, announcing, "Pound rallies as hopes grow for recovery". Yet by the 1 p.m. Radio 4 News, it was stated that inflation had now begun to rise, that it was likely to increase by the end of this year, and that it is bound to rise sharply next year, (1994) when the effect of V.A.T. on domestic electricity, gas, and oil bills was making itself felt! So where are we, so far as all these Ministerial promises of Economic Recovery are concerned?

I drew Her Majesty's attention also, to the fact, that in my booklet I predicted that there would be an increase in I.R.A. activity on the mainland of Britain and in the capital, as the manifestation of the violent action of "the enemy working within our borders" and which could be interpreted as another sign of Divine chastening, or even of Judgment. I included Whitehall in that prediction. I said we have seen that happen also, with no less than 15 I.R.A. bomb explosions in London within the fortnight prior to my writing to the Queen on 24th November, 1992. I told her in my letter that it was only by the mercy of God that the whole of the Canary Wharf area was not totally devastated by a massive explosion, had not the Security guards foiled an I.R.A. van-bomb attack there on November 15th, shortly before I had written my letter. I pointed out that I had predicted in my booklet, that that I.R.A. activity on the mainland of Britain was likely to increase. And it has. For instance, on December 1st, 1992, scarcely four days after the Queen would have received my letter, a van containing a ton of homemade explosives was found and diffused in Tottenham Court Road, London. Three days later, on December 3rd, 1992, two bombs exploded in Manchester's city centre, injuring 64 people. Then a week after that, December 10th, ten people were hurt when two bombs exploded at Wood Green Shopping Centre, North London. Twelve days later, on December 22nd, bomb-blast at Hampstead tube station, North London, injured several people. Then on January 28th of *this* year, 1993, a litter-bin bomb outside Harrod's of Knightsbridge injured four people. Then up in the Midlands again, on February 26th of this year, 1993, terrorists blew up the gas-works at Warrington, Cheshire, after shooting a policeman nearby. And in connection with this, arrests were made in Nottingham. Then the very next day, February 27th, a litter-bin bomb caused devastation in Campden High Street, North London, and injured 18 shoppers. And early in March (1993) anti-terrorist squad detectives discovered 600 pounds of fertliser-based explosives, as well as Semtex and arms, together with a saloon car, in a lock-up garage in Pages Lane, Muswell Hill. The anti-terrorist police reported that this bomb-factory, believed to be the work of the I.R.A., contained explosives which, if detonated, could have caused damage on the same scale as the blast which devastated the Baltic Exchange in the City of London last year. (Quoted from "The Barnet and Whetstone Express", Friday, March 12th, and from the "Barnet Borough Times", Thursday, 11th March, 1993). Then came the second horrific I.R.A. bomb explosion in Warrington killing two boys. But since then we have had the horrific damage done in the Bishopsgate area of the City of London by I.R.A. bomb activity, and not many days later I.R.A. bombs in the Newcastle-on-Tyne area. And so it goes on.

There is no doubt therefore that I.R.A. activity on the mainland of Britain has increased, as I predicted in my booklet as long ago as July of last year (1992). It has all been happening. And it should be interpreted *spiritually*, as at least a chastisement of God, because Britain is deliberately and wilfully going the wrong way. And I believe the highest in the realm should have had this pointed out to her.

Then I also recalled to her attention, that in my booklet, I had predicted the likelihood of the Government being defeated, and thus being overthrown, because of God's displeasure at the direction it is taking. And up to the time that I wrote my letter (24th November, 1992) we had seen the Government being brought almost to the brink of being overthrown at least twice, only saving itself on one of those occasions by "strong-arm tactics" exercised by the Government Whips, — tactics which were extremely questionable, and indeed dubious, to say the least.

But then on Monday night, March 8th of this year, (1993), the Government was defeated and humiliated by a 22-vote against it, in a debate about the Maastricht treaty, despite a weekend appeal for unity by Mr Major. And it is likely that there will be more humiliating defeats of the Government during future debates on this treaty, because in no way would it appear that it has God's Blessing upon it.

So we have seen all this happening as well, as I predicted.

But then I also predicted in my booklet, that God Almighty could use His elements and atmospheric forces and weather conditions to bring about a Visitation of Divine Judgment on the Nation. And we have seen that happen, also. For on Thursday, December 3rd, 1992, only ten days after I had written to the Queen, the "Daily Telegraph" had banner headlines stating that storms had brought floods and travel chaos in the South West of England and in South Wales, causing continued disruption and long delays for travellers by road and rail in both regions, whilst homes and shops in the Rhondda, Cynom Valley, Taff Ely, and Rhymney areas were flooded. Then on January 14th, 1993, "The Daily Telegraph" again reported with banner headlines that there was chaos on the roads as 85 mile per hour gales battered the South of England, blowing over lorries, uprooting trees, swamping boats, and causing deaths. The report said chaos was also brought to London as gusts of more than 70 miles per hour blew down traffic lights, road signs, and lamp posts, and scattered debris from buildings across roads. It said Scotland also had had two days of disruption caused by some of the bitterest weather for more than a decade. Then two days later, on January 16th, 1993, the "Daily Telegraph" reported that gales and heavy rain had swept the whole of Britain the day before, that five people had died in accidents as a result — a father and his 17 year old son being killed instantly in Cumbria, a woman aged 20 had died in Shropshire as a result of a similar incident — a 43 year old butcher and his son had been crushed to death on the A596 Motorway west of Carlisle, — a man and a woman were killed outright on the outskirts of Edinburgh, crushed by a tree that fell on their car — and three people were taken to hospital in Telford, two with serious injuries. Roads were closed in many parts of Britain by crashed vehicles, floods, and by fallen trees, and especially in the North of England and in Scotland. In the Lake District two thousand power lines were brought down plunging many homes into darkness, and depriving them of heat and warmth. Cables on the main east coast railway line were also brought down, trapping passengers en route to London from Edinburgh, Newcastle, and Yorkshire. The Rivers Tay and Earn in Scotland rose rapidly, the River Nith in Dumfries, Scotland, burst its banks, and the River Forth overflowed, causing several houses in the low-lying part of Stirling to be flooded. Chaos reigned everywhere.

Two days later, on Monday, January 18th, 1993, the "Daily Telegraph" announced, again with banner headlines, that gale-force winds, torrential rain, and melting snow had brought a weekend of chaos to Scotland. The worst hit areas were Perthshire, the report said, Fife, and Central Scotland, where dozens of commuters were cut off by floods, landslips, and fallen trees. Floods had forced hundreds of people to leave their homes. The towns of Auchtermuchty, Fife, and Crieff Tayside, were virtually cut off by flooded roads, while in Perthshire more than 20 communities, including Blairgowrie, Dunkeld, and Pitlochry were cut off, according to the estimations of council officials.

The report said that the North of England and Wales also took a severe battering. Roofs were torn from houses in Co. Durham, and trees were uprooted. In Llandudno, Gwynedd, gusts of 70 miles per hour had torn through the town taking most of the roof off the Morfa Rhiannedd infant's school.

Then a week later, Monday, January 25th, 1993, the same newspaper reported that winds of 80 miles per hour had brought down power lines and damaged buildings in Shropshire; — that several cows and calves had been killed when a farm building had collapsed at Melverley on Shropshire's border with Wales; that a 76-year-old man had been drowned the day before when he and two companions were thrown into the sea at the mouth of Portland Harbour, Dorset, as their dinghy had capsized in strong waves; that five crew members of a Grimsby registered trawler, the "Loch Earn", had had to be rescued early that day by the Great Yarmouth coastguard in heavy seas off the Norfolk coast; — that at Sandown on the Isle of Wight five people, including two children, received hospital treatment after a chimney stack had crashed through the roof of a house; — that two women were cut free from their car at Chelmsford, Essex, after it had hit a fallen tree and was then crushed by a second falling trunk; — and that gales in the Firth of Forth had ripped a 34,000-ton liquid gas tanker from its berth at the Braefoot terminal in Fife.

Then a little less than a month later, on Monday, 22nd February, the worst flooding in 15 years took place in Norfolk and Suffolk and all down the east coast of England, including Essex and part of the Kent coast, due to a combination of strong north-west winds, spring tides and a near-full moon, causing an extremely dangerous North Sea "surge". 120 people had to be evacuated at Walcott in Norfolk due to the flooding caused by this "surge". At nearby Cley, on the Norfolk coast, a number of houses and a caravan site were flooded. At Hemsby in the same vicinity, five bungalows collapsed when their foundations were washed away by the "surge"; low-lying buildings in the Reedham Ferry area, Norfolk, were flooded, when the River Yare burst its banks; more than 400 people had to be evacuated from their homes in Gorleston after a flood alert in the Great Yarmouth area of Norfolk. Then further round the east-coast, in Suffolk, several beach huts and a cafe were destroyed in Southwold; homes were flooded in Aldeburgh; the wall of the River Deben at Woodbridge was partially breached; the Ferry area in Felixstowe at the mouth of the River Deben was seriously flooded; the promenade along the sea-front at Felixstowe itself was constantly battered by mountainous waves which left the actual promenade with sand, pebbles and debris at least five inches deep when once the sea had calmed; and in Essex, the sea defences were breached, and Mersea Island, Essex, was cut off for three hours. All this was brought about by exceptionally high tides and flooding caused by the North Sea "surge" — which is a large body of water brought about by atmospheric pressure, high tides, and strong north-west winds, which funnel down the East coast of England. As a result of all this serious flooding, homes had to be evacuated all along the East Coast, from Norfolk, right down to Essex and Kent.

The "Daily Telegraph" reported a week later, on March 4th, that because of some of the highest tides of this century which were expected in that coming week, when the spring equinox was due to combine with a full moon, and its close proximity to the Earth, if the weather was stormy, then the East Coast could be threatened by even more serious floods in a few days time. It was only by the mercy of God, who controls the weather, that the sea became comparatively calm during those few days; — that there were no strong north-west winds; and so even more serious floods did not take place. The threat was averted, although there were still very high spring tides.

However, all these adverse weather conditions, — all these almost hurricane-force gales, torrential rain-storms and widespread serious floodings — have been taking place as I predicted in my booklet. We have seen them all happen. So I repeat what I said in the booklet, "There is no doubt whatsoever but that God Almighty uses His very elements and atmospheric forces and conditions, at times, to bring about a Visitation of Divine Judgment on a Nation, or certainly a chastisement."

But in my letter to the Queen I drew attention too, to the fact that in my booklet I had predicted also, as long ago as last July (1992), that the Royal House of Windsor and the Monarchy would be plunged into more serious trouble. Before the booklet had been written and published, headline news in the National Press had announced that the marriage of the Duke and Duchess of York had broken up. Leading articles in such sections of the National Press as "The Times", and the "Daily Telegraph" were *then* asking, "Can the House of Windsor now survive?" And I was reminded, at that time, of a verse in the Book of the Prophet Haggai which said, "I will shake the throne of kingdoms". This was God Almighty saying that, in that Prophecy. The throne of the United Kingdom was most certainly being shaken by that news. But I later discovered that that verse actually said, "I will *overthrow* the throne of kingdoms and I will destroy their strength". This immediately caused me to ask myself, "Has the time now actually arrived for God to do this in fulfillment of that Prophecy?" Then during the next few months, since my booklet was published, we have seen the Rupert Murdoch-owned Tabloid Press launch a relentless attack on one member of the Royal Family after another, which inevitably has further shaken them. And then that scurrilous Press began to concentrate a relentless attack on the Prince and Princess of Wales' marriage. So we have seen the Royal House of Windsor and the Monarchy being plunged into more serious trouble exactly as I had predicted. But then, all too tragically, we saw Windsor Castle, the symbol of the Royal House of Windsor, and home of The Supreme Governor of The Church of England, suddenly and without warning devastated by fire. This led to the Queen saying in her Guildhall, London, speech, on the very day when I was writing my letter to her, that "1992 is not a year on which I shall look back with undiluted pleasure. . . . It has turned out to be an annus horribilis" (a horrible year).

I said in my letter to her that the question that needs to be asked is, "Why?" Why has all this been happening? We have got to go deep, and ask ourselves, "What is so wrong in the Nation and at the Head of the Nation to incur so much Divine Disapproval and Divine Displeasure?" I said I do not hesitate to answer, in the *first* place, that what is so wrong in the sight of an Holy God, is that laws can be passed on to our British Statute Book which the Scriptures plainly state are an abomination in the sight of the Lord. And I listed them all in detail. But I said "What is even more wrong in the sight of an Holy God is that such iniquitous Laws can be given the Royal Assent".

I pointed out that in my Public Addresses ever since the 1960's and early 1970's all over the United Kingdom, and in my books, booklets and other writings, I have repeatedly been saying that the Sovereign should never be expected to give the Royal Assent to what is so blatantly wrong, and especially in view of what she is on Oath before Almighty God to uphold.

I said I fully accept that a Constitutional Monarch acts on the advice of her Ministers. But I asked, "Supposing that advice is wrong? What then? Supposing it is wrong in the sight of an Holy God? What then?"

I said that my study of English History has shown me that there have been at least three occasions in our History when the Royal Assent has been withheld by the then reigning Sovereigns, and on moral and spiritual grounds so there is definitely a precedent for this.

And more recently we have had the example of the present King of the Belgiums (King Baudouin).

I said that what is also so wrong in the sight of an Holy God in the *second* place, is the way in which our British Cathedrals, Churches and Places of Worship have been and *are* being, polluted and profaned by multi-faith services, all condoned by the Archbishops and Bishops, and other Leaders of Churches, and during which, Hindus, Buddhists, Sikhs, — and Moslems who adamantly deny that Jesus is the Son of God, which is a basic tenet of the Christian Faith, — all pray publicly with the Leaders of the other faiths and religions of the world, to their various gods and deities.

And I said that what is even more wrong in God's sight, "May I say it Your Majesty", is for the Sovereign and Supreme Governor of the Established Church in the Land, who carries the title, "Defender of the Christian Faith" to condone such a thing with her presence, and even to take the heir to the throne with her on one occasion.

25

I pointed out that this is in direct violation of the First Commandment, "Thou shalt have none other gods before Me", and of the Second Commandment, "Thou shalt not bow thyself down to worship them", and which carries with it the awful pronouncement, "For I, The Lord thy God am a jealous God, and visit the iniquity of the fathers, (the parents, that means) upon the children unto the third and fourth generation of them that hate Me".

I said, that because God is a jealous God, whose glory He will not give to another, it means that to introduce other gods, or the worship of other gods into any House of God arouses His Indignation, and provokes Him to anger. And I said that that Divine Indignation is bound to express itself in the form of God's Judgments, which includes Judgment by Fire.

I said, furthermore, that these very Commandments are those which the Sovereign is on Oath before Almighty God to uphold *to the utmost of her power,* and within the Realm, and that within the Realm includes within the Cathedrals, Abbeys, and other Houses of God within the Realm, and to violate them, or any other of God's Commandments, is bound to arouse His disapproval and displeasure and to provoke Him, as an Holy God, to anger. And then we begin to experience what His Day of Visitation in Judgment is like.

I said that I could plainly see that the iniquity of the fathers (parents) of the 1960s to 1970s Permissive generation, which then abandoned God and all thoughts of God, is now being visited on the children so many generations further on, and it is being manifest in a generation gone wild, and in ever-increasing crime amongst even young children and the young. And that I couldn't help wondering whether the failure of at least three, if not four of the Royal Marriages and their break-up was not due to this.

I said I feared that what has been happening to the Royal House of Windsor, and in the Royal Family, during this past horrible year and more, is at best a chastening because of God's disapproval and Divine Displeasure at much that has been going on, — and that at worst, it is a Judgment of God. I said I did not find it easy to say this, but I must be faithful to Almighty God and to His Divine Calling and say it. I said I wish I could have put it to her in person.

Having said all that, I said the Question that now needs to be raised is, "With all this that we have done which is so wrong, What must be done to put things right, before a worse thing happens to us as a Nation?"

I said the answer is, that we must be like the people of Nineveh in the Prophet Jonah's days, whose sins and wickedness had come up before God. When Jonah, as God's Prophet, was called by God to go to the great city of Nineveh and cry against it and tell them that within forty days the city would be overthrown in Judgment because of its wickedness, the people repented in sackcloth and ashes. Then when word came to the king of Nineveh's ears, to the *then* Sovereign, as to what Jonah was preaching, he himself repented in sackcloth and ashes. Then he gathered his nobles, his Peers and his Ministers together, and issued a decree in what amounted to a Call for National Repentance from the highest to the lowest of them. And we read that when God saw their works, that they turned from their evil way: God repented of the evil (or calamity) that He had said He would do unto them, and He did not do it.

I said to Her Majesty in my letter, it is something of this nature that is needed in our Capital, and all over our Country today, in order that God's fierce anger, which has been aroused against us as a Nation, may be turned away, and nothing less than that. I said we certainly need a Call for National Repentance such as the king of Nineveh issued in terms of a decree. And I said that, as an indication that our repentance is genuine, we need to see to it that the many laws which have been placed on our Statute Book which are offensive and deeply grievous to Almighty God, and which are an abomination in His Sight, are removed forthwith, thus legislating upwards for a change! And we also need to see to it that multi-faith services and functions cease, forthwith, in all our Cathedrals, Churches and Places of Worship, and that the Pure, New Testament form of Christianity is proclaimed forthrightly, and in the Full Power of The Holy Spirit of God, in all of them without exception, and also throughout the length and breadth of our Land, with all the means at our disposal. In that way, I said, the tide could begin to be turned in our country, both morally and spiritually, and a period of God-Blessed Prosperity, perhaps as never before, could follow, to take the place of this ever increasing Recession which we are now in. For, I said, God's Blessing always rests upon a people that are right with Him. God grant that this may happen while there is still time.

Such then is the main gist of the letter which I sent to the Queen at the end of last November (1992).

And I want to place it on record, *in* writing, that this was what was written, just as the Prophet Ezekiel, as a Watchman to his Nation, placed it on record *in* writing, as to what he had said and written, and just as Isaiah, and Jeremiah, and all the prophets, placed it on record, *in writing*, as to what they had said and written, in their day, to their nation. God required them to do so. Indeed He *Commanded* them to do so, in order that it should stand as a testimony for all time, and for all generations. And I believe He requires, and indeed Commands, that the same should be done today.

Now as I come to the end of Part One of this sequel to my booklet "A New Government — A New Era", with its sub-title "What is God now saying about the state of the nation of Britain today, to Britain's Parliament, to the Royal House of Windsor, and as to the responsibility of the Nation's Church?" I need to say this:- All my books and booklets which I have mentioned in the first few lines of Page One of this sequel, have been widely circulated throughout the length and breadth of Britain. Indeed, in the case of some of them, they have been widely circulated in both Houses of Parliament, and, I understand, amongst members of the General Synod of the Church of England. So the Message contained in the books and booklets, and in other of my written materials, must, by now, be quite widely known. But it has not made the slightest bit of difference to our tragic National Situation. It certainly has made no impact whatsoever on our Nation's Leadership, either temporal or spiritual. So far as the Nation's Leadership is concerned there has been nothing but silence. Stony silence. The signals and warnings which have been repeatedly issued in all these publications of mine, have been completely ignored. They just have not been heeded. However, it is true to say that, on the other hand, there has been a truly amazing response from people all over the United Kingdom at "grass roots" level — from the men and women in the street. But not from the Leadership. And *nowhere* at all from the Leadership. It took the "Sun" Newspaper, of *all* Newspapers, to say, on its front page on Thursday, October 15th, 1992, about 3 months after "A New Government — A New Era" had been published:- "With the Country plunging ever downwards, we have four serious questions for you Mr Major.

"WHAT on earth is going on?

"WHERE the hell is this once-great country of ours heading?

"WHEN will you tell us your master plan?

"DO you even have one?"

All these questions were put to the British Prime Minister by the "Sun" Newspaper in an open, front page letter.

28

So by now, even the Tabloid Press, Fleet Street and Wapping, were getting deeply concerned. But still no answer as far as I know. Only silence. Stony silence. The National Leadership remained unmoved.

The challenging question in the Book of Job Chapter 9 verse 4 therefore, most definitely applied:- "Who hath hardened himself against God and hath prospered?" That most certainly applied to the Government which God had put in office on Friday the 10th of April 1992. It applied to our Parliamentary Leadership. But I fear it applied to much of the Nation itself.

But coupled with that, can be put what God says in Proverbs Chapter One verse 25 and following:- "*Because* ye have set at nought all My counsel, and would have none of My reproof I also will laugh at your calamities: I will mock when your fear cometh; when your fear cometh as desolation, and your destruction cometh as a whirlwind; when distress and anguish cometh upon you. *Then* shall they call upon Me, but I will not answer; they shall seek Me early, but they shall not find Me: for that they hated knowledge, and did not choose the fear of the Lord; they would have none of My counsel: they despised all My reproof. *Therefore* shall they eat of the fruit of their own way, and be filled with their own devices".

"For the turning away of the simple shall slay them, and the prosperity of fools shall destroy them".

I ask, "Is that what God is saying to Britain and to its Leadership today, in the Spring and early Summer of 1993?"

A lot of the evidence suggests that it might be. I believe that it is.

We shall see.

PART TWO

BRITAIN'S CATASTROPHIC RISE IN CRIME AND GOD'S ANSWER, FROM THE BIBLE, AS TO WHAT SHOULD BE DONE ABOUT IT.
BUT NEMESIS HAS ALREADY STRUCK IN BRITAIN.

I repeat, all these publications of mine have been widely circulated throughout the Nation and amongst the Nation's Leadership, and so have my main Addresses, which have been circulated on cassette-tapes. But they have not made the slightest bit of difference. The signals and strident warnings which have been repeatedly issued in them have been completely ignored. They just have not been heeded. In one case even, the experience of the Prophet Jeremiah has been repeated, almost exactly. In King Jehoiakim's case, as recorded in the Book of the Prophet Jeremiah Chapter 36 verse 23, when three or four pages of what Jeremiah had written in a roll of a book had been read, the king cut it with the pen-knife, and cast it into the fire that was on the hearth, until all the roll was consumed in the fire that was on the hearth. In the case that I am referring to, after three or four pages had been read, the booklet was dropped into a waste-paper basket. Then when a second copy was sent it was promptly lost! And by a Peer of the Realm.

Such has been the attitude, certainly amongst the Leadership. It has taken the horrendous murder of a toddler, allegedly by two 10-year-old boys, to SHAKE THE NATION and to HALT IT IN ITS TRACKS. A public outcry was sounded out from everywhere. People all over the Nation were saying "However could such a thing happen?" The Tabloid Press took up the cry. The "Daily Mirror's" comment was, "There is rottenness at the heart of Britain. A creeping evil of violence and fear. It has been growing like a cancer for a long time. The death of Jamie Bulger has focused the nation's attention on it". Mirror Comment, February 22nd, 1993. The "Sunday Telegraph" said on February 21st, 1993, "All Britain is talking about the tragic and horrible fate of the little boy who was abducted and probably murdered by children, on Merseyside". The "Daily Express" said on February 23rd, 1993, "It is not surprising that the murder of little James Bulger *has stopped the entire nation in its tracks*". (My italicising.) The "Daily Telegraph" said on the same day, February 23rd, "Britain can no longer ignore the evidence that, as a nation, it has somehow gone horribly wrong". And William Deedes had said in his column the day before, Monday, February 22nd, "Little James Bulger has caused rare heartsearching *about the sort of society we have become*". (My italicising.) And the "News of the World" published a huge, black, headline asking the question, "What's gone wrong with us?" Then it said, "Our society is seen to be in the grip of an exceptional moral crisis".

In their consternation, two papers went far further. The "Daily Mirror" said, "What we need to do is to 'get to grips with *the causes*' of all this". Whilst the "Daily Telegraph" had said, "We must get to *the core* of all this criminal behaviour".

So the nation had been devastatingly shocked. It had been violently shaken. And it had suddenly been brought to an abrupt halt. I was reminded that when I was listing in "A New Government — A New Era" the various forms in which a Visitation of God on a Nation could take, if it continues stubbornly and wilfully to legislate downwards, amongst the list I had said on Page Eleven, "It could take the form of some *other* and quite unexpected great National Calamity". I wondered, "Was this IT?" It was certainly a great National Calamity. And it was quite unexpected. That little boy had not been out of the sight of his mother more than two minutes.

Leaders of both the Government and of the Opposition have been asking, "Whatever must be done?" A Royal Commission on violence was demanded by M.P.s of all parties at Westminster on Friday evening, 19th February (1993).

"Hardened teenage thugs will be locked up in secure training centres under sweeping new powers", revealed the Home Secretary, Mr Kenneth Clarke, on Tuesday, March 3rd. But the "Sun" Newspaper reported next day that this crackdown will not take place until 1996!!

"Courts should be given powers to "shake young offenders to their roots", said senior judges on Wednesday, February 17th.

A Leader in the "Daily Telegraph" on Monday, February 15th, had begun with the words, "Governments come and go, *but the solution to juvenile crime remains as elusive as ever*".

When Mr Major, as Prime Minister, had stated in a speech at the end of February that Government should care more about the victims of crime and less about the perpetrators, that "society should condemn a little more and understand a little less", The Archbishop of York, Dr. John Habgood, protested on a B.B.C. programme that this was "divisive". "Crime amongst young people", he said, "was caused by a feeling of helplessness brought about partly by unemployment".

The "Evening Standard" in an article on Friday, 19th February, had reported that when Kenneth Baker, the *former* Home Secretary, had challenged Church leaders in Liverpool to give their minds to the problem of evil rather than indulging in political comments, the Bishop of Liverpool, the Right Rev. David Sheppard, said it, "was ignorant and entirely unhelpful to try to find a scapegoat for such events as the murder of James Bulger". The article said, "We are all to blame", was Bishop Sheppard's feeble comment on this Liverpool murder. "What a meaningless statement!" said the writer of the article. "Either we discard the notion of blame altogether, or we accept the fact that when a murder takes place it is the murderer who is to blame".

Mr Tony Blair, Shadow Home Secretary, in commenting on all the shocking things which News bulletins of the past week had reported, had said, on Friday evening, February 19th, "The headlines shock, but what shocks us more is our knowledge that in almost any city, town, or village, more minor versions of the same events as happened in Liverpool *are becoming an almost everyday part of our lives*". And then he came very near to the point when he said that the solution was not in legislation alone, but in a "rediscovery of a sense of direction as a country". But what he *didn't* say was "Britain is going the wrong way!"

Then the "Daily Mirror" three days later, on Monday, February 22nd, after it had said in a Leading Article, "We've got to get to grips with *the causes* of crime", said in the same article, "There is something very wrong and very sick at the heart of our society". But in all the volumes of Newsprint that has been written, or in all that has been said, over the Radio and Television Media, it is very noticeable that there has been no mention whatsoever of God, or of the Bible, or of the Christian Faith.

What has happened to our Country, of course, is the result of what we have done as a Nation ever since about 1945, when we turned away from God as a people, and overthrew the Christian Faith which we had had for centuries. What has happened, too, is the result of what we have done as a Nation ever since the Permissive 1960's and 1970's, and with the Royal Assent if you please.

We have sown the wind, and we have reaped the whirlwind. But in this case it is not only a whirlwind even, it is a hurricane, a tornado, a veritable nation-shattering earthquake, in fact.

Furthermore, we need to be reminded, all of us, that there is a God in Heaven, a God who, on the one hand, declares Himself to be a merciful, gracious, long suffering God, a God who is abundant in goodness and truth, but who on the other hand has declared that he will by no means clear the guilty; a God who visits the iniquity of the fathers upon the children, *and upon the children's children,* unto the third and fourth generation''. See Exodus chapter 34 verses 5 to 7.

And that is what has happened.

If we need to get to grips with *the causes* of the tragic condition which our country is in, and we do; if we must get to *the core* of what is really wrong, then this is one of the main causes, if not *THE* main cause. And God says it is.

But we also need to recognise that it is one of the signs of the times in which we live. The Bible says in 2 Timothy Chapter 3, verses 1 and 13:- "This know also, that *in the last days* evil men and seducers shall wax worse and worse;" and they *are* waxing worse and worse.

The Bible also speaks of evil *children.* It speaks of "children that are corrupters" and they are doing that now from a very early age, corrupting. When the disciples asked Jesus "What shall be the sign of thy coming and of the end of the world?" Matthew Chapter 24 verse 3, He gave as one of the signs, "iniquity shall abound". Matthew Chapter 24 verse 12. And iniquity certainly abounds today. It is all around us. But it is not only confined to Britain. The Leading article in the February 4th to 7th, 1993, issue of the "European" carried the banner headline, "Evil on the rampage"; and that article went on to speak of "a plague of violence and crime sweeping Europe". Another Main Article on the same page said, "Crime is growing" (in Europe). "Nothing it seems can stop the tide". It spoke of a massive increase in total crime in Switzerland; of a rise in thefts and robberies in France; of crime in Germany rising more sharply; of a massive increase in murder and rape in Italy; and of horrendous crime in Spain. Yet another Main Article said, *internation* crime grows, and both law and order are on the run. So it is by no means confined to Britain, nor is it by any means confined to the Continent of Europe. It is international. It is global. And should be seen for what it is, a sign of the times in which we are living. Evil, everywhere is waxing worse and worse as the Bible said it would. It is one of the major signs that we are living in the End Days. And that should enter into the calculations of all those who are addressing the alarming downward trend of morality and spiritual life in our society today.

But to get back to our National Situation in Britain. In mid-January of

34

this year, 1993, the "Daily Telegraph" published a Main Article which said, "Nemesis is toppling the pillars of the Establishment". "Nemesis", according to the Oxford Dictionary means inevitable retribution". The Article said, "Nemesis is punishment by the gods", which I would prefer to re-phrase — "punishmnent by God", since for centuries now Britain has not believed in a multiplicity of gods anymore. The Article went on to say, "Such Nemesis visits without warning. It leaves the victims gasping, "What have we done to deserve that?" Then to explain further what the Article is driving at, it says, "There is something much too like Nemesis *in the crisis of national institutions* that dogs the Nation day by day". Then to elaborate it said, "None of the institutions — the Monarchy, the Church, the Cabinet, the police — which find themselves tumbling from their place of traditional respect . . . none perceived that it was riding for a fall". Then later on in the Article, other British institutions which have suffered the same fate are mentioned. It says, "The National Health Service has gone into shock", "the Universities remain soured", "the schools", and "Industry" are mentioned. "Our institutions are failing us," the Article says. Then two days later, on Wednesday, January 20th, the same Newspaper published a second Article which was written in a similar vein. It said "the Establishment in the past has been found at the top of the ancient institutions: then it names what these ancient institutions are. "The Church, the Law, the universities, the armed forces, and above all, the monarchy". Then it says, "But over the past 30 years nearly all these professions *have lost some status*". (My italicising.) "Bishops, judges, and dons *have all been through major crises* of confidence", (my italicising again). "Only the military has maintained its public prestige". The Article also lists City establishments, the strongholds of decision-making such as the Treasury and the Bank of England, as being in the same category. It is very significant to me that Anthony Sampson who wrote that second Article said that it was "over the past 30 years that nearly all these professions have lost some status, because 30 years brings us back to the 1960's, when Britain brought in the iniquitous Permissive Society.

John Keegan, who wrote the first Article, in which he says, "Piece by piece society's framework seems to be failing us," says, "The reason is that we have forsaken standards and personal responsibility". But I contest that that is not the reason, because it does not go deep enough. No! The reason is that we have forsaken God. That is why the main pillars of Britain's national institutions, and the main structure of the Establishment itself, including the Monarchy, are seen to be collapsing all around us every day.

For what happens to a large, strongly constructed building, when the cement or mortar, which hold the bricks together, and when also the very foundations on which it has been built, are gradually chipped and whittled away? The answer is obvious. The entire building collapses like a pack of cards, and especially when it is hit by a strong wind, or even by just a breeze!

We urgently need to be reminded that the cement and mortar and the strong foundations on which British society, its Establishment, and all its ancient institutions were built, were the Christian Faith, belief in the Bible, and a strong Faith in God which binded and bonded our society and institutions together for so long. But now belief in God, the Christian Faith, and belief in the Bible have all been chipped and whittled away so that they are not there any more. Therefore the whole structure, the entire building has collapsed all around us. The Bible says, "If the foundations are destroyed, what can the righteous do?" And they *are* destroyed.

Or take another example. Ask any housewife what she needs to do to preserve a piece of beef if she hasn't a refrigerator or a "deep freeze". The answer she will give you is that you saturate it with salt. Because salt is the preserver. But what happens if the salt is taken out of that piece of beef? It goes bad. It begins to smell. Then it stinks. It putrifies. And then it produces maggots. Creepy, crawly maggots. And then it disintegrates altogether.

What we need urgently to be reminded of therefore is that *God* is the "Salt" — the Preserver of human society. Take away God, and all thoughts of God out of society, out of the human mind, and society is bound to go bad, to become corrupt, to begin to smell, and then to stink. Then society putrifies, then it produces maggots, creepy, crawly maggots. And we see them all around us. And what is more, the total disintegration of our British Society has set in.

And it is all because we have forsaken God as a nation, have turned our backs on Him, have entirely dismissed Him from our thoughts, from our National counsels and deliberations, have thrown the teaching of the Christian Faith and belief in the Bible overboard, and have now become a totally God*less* and *Un*godly, secular and materialistic society. And Nemesis has struck. It has struck without warning. And because it has, we see all our ancient institutions and pillars of society, including the Monarchy, collapsing all around us. And this Nemesis is now dogging the Nation and its national life day by day. And you don't have to look any further for *the root cause*, for the real *core* of why Britain is in such a tragic state today.

36

And let us never forget, the word "Nemesis" means, "Inevitable Retribution". (Oxford Dictionary). Nemesis is punishment by God, not by "the gods" as John Keegan says in his Article. And if that Nemesis leaves us, British people the victims, — all of us from the Monarchy downwards — gasping, "What have we done to deserve this?" Isaiah Chapter One verse 4 gives us the answer:- "You have forsaken the Lord, you have provoked the Holy One of Israel Unto anger". You could not have a clearer answer than that. Neither do you need one.

In view of all that I have just said, it becomes obvious that when the Prime Minister says, "We must launch a crusade against crime" that does not go anywhere deep enough. Neither does it go anywhere near to the root of the problem.

He says we must launch a crusade against crime by locking juvenile criminals away", by imposing stiffer sentences; by increasing the police force; by installing more television cameras in our main shopping centres; by building more prisons; by encouraging people to report crime; by encouraging people to lock their homes and their cars more effectively; and so on, and so on, and so on.

But you can do all that, and a lot more, but it still does not change the people themselves. You can do all these things in a crusade against crime but it leaves people exactly as they are. The people themselves are not changed in any way, even when you have introduced all these things, and a lot more. This is because the problem lies in the heart of a person, in the heart of a man: in the heart of a woman: in the heart of a boy: in the heart of a girl. The Bible says, "We do err *in our hearts*". Psalm 95 verse 10. We *go wrong* in our hearts, in other words.

Jesus said, "Out of *the heart* proceed — evil thoughts, murders, adulteries, fornications, thefts, false witness, blasphemies. These are the things which defile a man". Matthew 15 verses 18 to 20. And today, Jesus would have added:- Vandalism, filthy graffiti, rape, terrorism, brutality, muggings, children murdering children, frauds, forgery, fiddling, insider trading, break-ins, pornography, and all kinds of dishonesty.

In other words, the heart of the problem, the root cause of our national dilemma, is that man, every man, every individual that means, however young, however old, is *wrong at the centre*. All of us are *biased* to go the wrong way. All of us without exception. All of us are biased to go the wrong way, even when in fact, we try to go the right way.

37

That is what Romans Chapter 7 verse 19 teaches when it says, "The good that I would do, or want to do, I do not. But the evil which I would not, or don't want to do, that is what I do".

The truth of the matter, therefore, is, that each and every person needs to be *put right* at the centre, and until that person has been put right at the centre, he or she can never *live* right. It is impossible.

In other words, because every person *is wrong at the centre,* he or she needs to be *changed at the centre.*

And only Jesus can do that, change a person at the centre.

Mr Patten, when he was the Home Office Minister, said, "The Government will continue with its crime prevention campaign. What *else* can we do?"

My answer to that is, "A *lot* else". Crime *prevention* does not go anywhere near far enough. The answer lies in Romans Chapter 1 verses 15-16, where the Apostle Paul said, "I am ready to preach the Gospel to you that are at Rome, and elsewhere, also. For I am not ashamed of the Gospel of Christ — for *IT* is The Power of God unto salvation *to every one that believeth*".

And he would say the same today.

So Salvation is *NOT* in imposing stiffer sentences.

Salvation is *NOT* in increasing the police force.

Salvation is *NOT* in building more prisons.

Salvation is *NOT* in locking young criminals away.

Salvation is *NOT* in spending millions of pounds of taxpayer's money on projects and schemes to make our cities, our houses, our railways, our Underground systems more safe.

Salvation is *NOT* in installing more television cameras in town and city shopping centres, or in equipping the police with more modern and sophisticated equipment, such as computers, control systems, and modern technology.

Salvation is *NOT* in encouraging the police to make more arrests.

Salvation is *NOT* in reintroducing some form of national service for 16 to 18 year olds.

Because all these things are *preventative* measures.

They don't *change* people. None of them do. When any, or all of them, are introduced, they leave people *exactly as they are.* Salvation is in this Gospel which Paul the Apostle is talking about.

The answer to the alarming and appalling rise in the Crime Rate, and to Britain's tragic and moral spiritual decline, is to Preach the Gospel! It is as simple as that! And the sooner that that is realised, and the sooner the Country, its Industry and The Government is prepared to spend millions of pounds to ensure that *this* Gospel is Proclaimed in The Full Power of The Holy Spirit to the 56 million people who inhabit these islands, by means of Television, Radio, and all *other* means of communication which are at the Country's disposal, with no restrictions or regulations placed upon those who are qualified to Preach it, the sooner we shall be GETTING SOMEWHERE. It would result in LIVES BEING CHANGED all over the Country. And CHANGED LIVES all over the place, and all over the Country, could TURN THE TIDE IN OUR COUNTRY — *GODWARDS* in next to no time!

Look what happened, for instance, at the time of the Welsh Revival. Public Houses, Gambling Dens, Cinemas and Theatres were all empty, because the former occupants were all now crowding into the Churches. And it could happen again, all over the British Isles!

Not only is there no reason whatsoever why the widespread Preaching of The Gospel in the Full Power of The Holy Spirit by every modern means at our disposal could not be done, but we are committed by our Constitution, on Oath before Almighty God, in the Coronation Oath, to do it. And the result of doing it would be, that the Crime Rate would drop most significantly, because lives of would-be offenders would be changed in considerable numbers under The Power of The Preaching of *This* Gospel. And so would the lives of many other people.

Furthermore, Britain's tragic moral and spiritual decline would be reversed. So WHAT ARE WE WAITING FOR?

If, however we are to wage a crusade against crime as the Prime Minister says we should, and which I have already made plain is merely a *preventative* measure, then on the *positive* side we must also launch a stern, forthright, and robust teaching and preaching crusade in parallel with it. And that teaching and preaching crusade should be undertaken by those who are spiritually qualified to do it, and only by those. And by that I mean, by those who are wholeheartedly, and unashamedly Bible-believing Christians, and who have truly been Born-Again by the Holy Spirit of God. It should not be done by anybody else. And the *first* thing that we must do in that teaching and preaching crusade, is to instil in the hearts and minds of people everywhere, young children, teenagers, and older people alike, a healthy *fear of God*. Because as a result of our forsaking God as a Nation, of our jettisoning our formerly-held Christian faith, and of becoming a totally God*less* and *un*godly people, there is now *no fear of God* whatsoever before any of our people's eyes. And certainly not before the eyes of our infants, young children and teenagers, whereas fifty years or so ago there used to be.

And that is yet *another* cause of the alarming rise in criminality and misbehaviour.

Yet the Bible says, "The fear of the Lord is the beginning of wisdom and knowledge of the Most High is understanding". Proverbs 9 verse 10.

So that is where we need to start.

That is where true education needs to start.

And we need to start instilling that healthy fear of God in our homes, in our schools, — infant and nursery schools included, — in our universities and polytechnics, in Industry, in the Banking and Financial World, in the City, and dare I say it, in Parliament, and amongst the Highest in the Land, and in every strata and at every level of our society.

We need to begin by instilling in all these areas, I say, a healthy fear of God in the hearts and minds of people of all ages.

That means that we must boldly, courageously, and unflinchingly proclaim the full truth as to the true nature of Almighty God. Because for all too long now, all we have been hearing, ad nauseum, is a sloppy, sentimentalised presentation of God being a God of love, and only a God of love, and a very sentimental one at that. And when I say "ad nauseum" that means we hear it to the point when it makes us sick and squirm. And that is all that we have been hearing.

But all through the pages of the Bible I read of God saying, "They have provoked Me *to anger*". "They have filled Me with *wrathful indignation*. I will pour out My *fury* upon them". The Bible talks about God being a Consuming Fire.

In fact the *Anger of The Lord* is mentioned at least 150 times in the Bible.

The *Wrath of The Lord* is mentioned at least 130 times.

The *Great Indignation of The Lord* is mention over 30 times.

Provoking God to Anger is spoken of at least 58 times.

God Himself referring to *My Fury* occurs over 60 times.

God's *vengeance* is spoken of at least 40 times.

God's *revenging* or *avenging*, is referred to over 30 times.

The Bible also speaks of *His Fierce Wrath*, and of *The Fierceness of His Great Wrath*. It speaks of God *punishing*, and of His *punishment* at least 60 times.

Then it speaks of The *Day* of His Wrath; of The Day of The Lord's *vengeance*; of The Coming Day of His *Great Indignation*.

But we never hear anything about any of that. Nothing whatsoever. And at no time whatsoever.

So we have an entirely distorted view of what is the real Nature of the God of the Universe, and of what are all of His Divine Attributes. It is a totally jaundiced view, in fact.

Therefore we need urgently to get back to the true Biblical presentation and proclamation of the Nature of God. And when we do that, we need to state, first and foremost, that God is *LIGHT*. Dazzling, white, blinding light, — far more dazzling than any flash of lightning. That is the very essence of His Nature.

We put it all the wrong way round, and in the wrong order. The emphasis that *we* make is, that God is Love. We start with *that* emphasis. But that is not where *the Bible* starts. It is not even where Jesus Himself started when He began to proclaim what is the Nature of God. When we look at The First Epistle of John Chapter One verse 5 for instance, what do we find?

We find that John the Beloved says, "This is the message which we have heard from Him, (from Jesus, that means), that God is *LIGHT*".

That tells us where Jesus started when He proclaimed what is the True Nature of God. And that is the message that He talked with His *first* disciples, Peter, and James and John etc, about. So John the Beloved started from there in his First Epistle, "That God is *LIGHT*".. And it is not until he gets to Chapter 4 verse 8 in his First Epistle that the Apostle John makes the statement, "For God is Love". So we have got the emphasis entirely the wrong way round. I repeat, the very essence of God's Nature is LIGHT, dazzling, white, blinding *LIGHT*.

The Apostle John makes the same emphasis in John's Gospel Chapter One. Referring to John the Baptist being the messenger whom God had sent to prepare the way before Jesus, His Beloved Son, John the Baptist, said:- "The same came for a witness, to bear witness of the *LIGHT*, that all men, through Him, might believe. He was not that *LIGHT*, but was sent to bear witness of that LIGHT. That was the true *LIGHT*, which lighteth every man that cometh into the world". John I verses 6 to 9.

It is not until we come to John's Gospel Chapter 3 verse 16 that we have the statement:- "For God so loved the world etc." We need therefore to get things in the right balance. We need to start where *The Bible* starts, and where Jesus Himself started, namely, "That God is *LIGHT,* and in Him is no darkness at all". I John I verse 5. That means He is *PURE* Light. Purer than any dazzling flash of lightning.

As Paul the Apostle says in I Timothy 6:16:- "Who only hath immortality; dwelling *IN LIGHT* which **no man can approach unto**". We need to pause and consider what that means.

And it goes on to say, "whom no man hath seen or can see".

A Christian Hymn sets out the awesomeness of this when it says:-

"Eternal *Light!* Eternal *Light!* How pure the soul must be, when placed within Thy searching sight, it shrinks not, but with calm delight can live, and look on Thee.

"The Spirits that surround Thy throne, may bear the burning bliss. But that is surely theirs alone, since they have never, never known a fallen world like this.

"O how shall I, whose native sphere is *dark,* whose mind is dim, before The Ineffable appear, and on my naked spirit bear *the uncreated beam?*"

We have long since lost that awesome emphasis, and we need to recapture it, and get back to it.

Or take what happened to Saul of Tarsus on the Damascus Road as he was on his way to arrest the true believers who were in Damascus and throw them into prison. It was midday, where, in the Middle East, the midday sun dazzles one by its brilliance. So in his testimony about what happened, he said, "At midday I saw in the way *A LIGHT* — from Heaven, *above the brightness of the sun* shining round about me and them that journeyed with me". *Acts 26:13.*

This *LIGHT,* therefore, that shone in the way, was so *DAZZLINGLY BRIGHT* that it made the midday sun in the Middle East seem dark in comparison, when that sun normally is so brilliant that you have to shade your eyes from it. But the LIGHT that appeared to Saul of Tarsus in the way far outshone the sun. And Saul and his companions were struck down to the ground by it. Indeed, Saul himself was blinded by it. And he remained blind for three days.

The Lord Jesus, therefore, when He appeared to Saul of Tarsus appeared as *LIGHT*. He was, in fact, clothed with *LIGHT,* — DAZZLING, WHITE, PURE, BLINDING LIGHT. And it is interesting that nowhere in any of the accounts given by the Apostle Paul about what happened does the word LOVE appear. He does not even say anywhere that he was surrounded by an overwhelming sense of LOVE!

God, in Jesus, when He appeared to Saul on the Damascus Road, appeared as *LIGHT.* His very *essence* is LIGHT.

Or consider the description that is given of the Holy City, New Jerusalem, in the Book of the Revelation Chapter 21 verse 23. It says:- "And the city had no need of the sun, neither of the moon to shine in it: for *THE GLORY OF GOD* did lighten it; and the Lamb (meaning The Lord Jesus) is the *LIGHT* thereof".

Therefore we see that God, in all His Glory, *LIGHTS* that city, because He is *LIGHT.* His very *Essence* is LIGHT. And The Lamb, the Lord Jesus, LIGHTS that city, because Jesus, who is God, is *LIGHT*.

I hope we are getting the message!

I need to tell you this:- God Almighty is such DAZZLING, BRILLIANT, WHITE, PURE, BLINDING LIGHT that were we ourselves to be exposed to Him right now, we would shrivel up, and burn up, *in an instant,* and at the flick of an eye-lid. We would be entirely and utterly consumed. We would *PERISH,* immediately and instantaneously.

Like the examples given several times in the Old Testament appearances of God amongst His people of Israel when they had grossly sinned against Him, we would be smitten by a plague with something akin to radio-activity, something far worse than the fall-out which results from any nuclear explosion, such, for instance as happened when atom bombs were exploded high over Japan during the Second World War. A graphic description of what would happen is given in the Book of the Prophet Zechariah Chapter 14. Read it for yourselves to see what I mean. It speaks, at least three times over, as "the plague", — as "the plague wherewith *the Lord* will smite all the people that have fought against Jerusalem", "and the plague wherewith *the Lord* will smite the heathen that come not up to keep the feast of tabernacles". So it is a plague that comes *from the Lord,* something very much like powerful Radio-Activity, or the result of nuclear fall-out, which emanates from the God who is LIGHT. PURE, WHITE, DAZZLING, UNAPPROACHABLE LIGHT, which is the very *ESSENCE* of His Nature.

43

And *because* this is the very *ESSENCE* of His Nature, that is why Almighty God, the Creator of the Universe, The *LIVING* God, has always had to *cover Himself* whenever He has appeared to, or revealed Himself to people. This is why we read in Exodus 13 verse 21, "And The LORD went before them by day *IN A PILLAR OF CLOUD,* to lead them by the way, and by night *IN A PILLAR OF FIRE,* to give them light".

It says, "The Lord went before them". It was *The LORD* alright! But He covered Himself in a Pillar of Cloud, and in a Pillar of Fire. He *had* to. Because He could not expose His actual self, — the very *Essence* of His Nature — to them and they still survive. *"FOR NO MAN CAN SEE GOD AND LIVE!"* says Scripture many times over.

Then take that *Awesome* Event which took place on Mount Sinai — right in front of about 600,000 of the children of Israel soon after they had been delivered out of Egypt by God's Almighty Hand.

It says in Exodus Chapter 19, at least three times over:-

"The *LORD* came down upon Mount Sinai".

The *LORD* did, in the sight of no less than these 600,000 people of Israel.

But the question is:- *"How* did The Lord come down?"

Well, The Lord Himself gives the answer in Exodus 19:9 which says:-

"And The Lord said unto Moses, 'Lo I come unto thee *in a thick cloud*". He covered Himself, in other words, in a thick cloud. So we read:- 'And so it came to pass on the third morning, that there were *thunders* and *lightnings* and *a thick cloud* on the Mount". "And Mount Sinai was altogether *on a smoke"*. It says in The Epistle to the Hebrews Chapter 12 verse 18, "the mountain burned *with fire"*.

WHY?

Because The Lord had descended upon it *IN FIRE.* We need to note that.

And it says, "And the smoke of that *FIRE* ascended as the smoke of a *FURNACE"*. That means that God coming down had set fire to the mountain!

And then we read, "the whole Mountain quaked, and shook, and reverberated".

WHY? Because The Lord had come down upon Mount Sinai, on the top of the Mountain. The God who is *LIGHT* had. *That* is the God I am talking about, and whose *Attributes* I am talking about.

And He had to cover Himself with a thick cloud, with smoke, because

He came IN FIRE, — as it were in the midst of a burning, fiery, furnace, and therefore could not expose Himself, lay Himself bare to these 600,000 people and they still survive.

And we read several times over in Scripture that He spake WITH A GREAT VOICE — "so that the people MAY HEAR when I speak unto thee, Moses".

And then immediately He had, indeed, come down, He said to Moses, "Charge the people, lest they break through unto the LORD and gaze, and many of them PERISH".

"Keep them back!" He said. "Keep them back! Keep them back! LEST the LORD break forth upon them and consume them". It was the same Principle being stated, therefore. "No man can look upon God, and be exposed to God, AND LIVE".

And why not?

Well the account of this MOST AWESOME event which took place on Mount Sinai as related in the Epistle to the Hebrews Chapter 12 verses 18 to 29 gives us the answer when it says, "For our God is a Consuming Fire". Hebrews 12 verse 29.

So the very Essence of His Nature is not only DAZZLING, WHITE, BRILLIANT, BLINDING LIGHT, even. The very Essence of His Nature is also CONSUMING FIRE, and we can never be exposed to it without being consumed. No person can.

That is The God I am talking about, and whose Attributes I am talking about. The God who is LIGHT, who is FIRE, who is a CONSUMING FIRE, and who therefore has always to cover Himself if He has to appear to people, or to reveal Himself to people. He is The Holy God, The ALMIGHTY God, the EVERLASTING, ETERNAL God. He is God The Creator of Heaven and Earth, the LIVING God, The God who cannot by any means look upon Sin. He is the God who can be PROVOKED TO ANGER by that Sin. He is the God who is LOVE, yes. But He is also a God of Wrath, and a God of Judgment, the God who is A CONSUMING FIRE. This is The GOD OF THE BIBLE, even if this is not the God who is being Preached in many of our modern pulpits, in our present day Churches, in our Cathedrals, by Archbishops and Bishops, and by Radio and Television today. But He still remains The One True, and Only God, The Living God. And it is vitally important that all these Attributes of His Divine Nature, without exception, should be boldly and forthrightly stressed today in the proclamation of any

45

true, Christian Message. And because He is a God of Judgment, and a God who is a Consuming Fire, as well as a God of Love, we need to stress also that we should regard Him with reverence and with a godly fear. And when such a healthy fear of Almighty God has been instilled in the hearts of people everywhere, people of all ages, young and old alike, that in itself will serve as a *major* deterrent against wrong-doing, and against crime. And especially when, as a result of such strong and forthright Biblical teaching and preaching, everyone will once again realise that each and every person, including the very youngest, will be answerable to that Almighty God in the long run, and on the Day of Judgment, for the way that they behave.

Then in this teaching Crusade, in addition to that, there needs to be a clear presentation of the basic facts of The Gospel of Salvation, and of The Way of Salvation, and of how a person enters into that salvation.

There is an urgent need, for instance, to teach and preach, all over again, what The Lord Jesus Christ, The Head of The One True Church on Earth, and the *ONLY* Head of The One True Church on Earth, said about what The Gospel of Salvation, namely the Christian Message, is all about.

He said in the *first* place, when He was here on Earth, "The Son of Man is come to seek and to save that which was lost". Luke 19 verse 10.

He said in the *second* place, "I came not to call the righteous but sinners to repentance". Luke 5 verse 22.

And before He was born, the Angel of The Lord said to Joseph: "Thou shalt call His Name JESUS: for He shall save His people from their sins". Matthew 1 verse 21.

So the True Christian Message is all about the saving of souls.

The True Christian Message is all about the saving of sinners.

The True Christian Message is all about the saving of the lost.

The True Christian Message, therefore, is unquestionably all about *salvation,* about *eternal* salvation. That is why it is called in Scripture "The Gospel of Salvation", and "The Way of Salvation".

So salvation from *SIN*, and from the dire consequences of *SIN* — banishment for ever in a place which Jesus Himself called Hell and the place of Eternal Torment, is what the Message of the True Christian Gospel is all about.

The Apostle Paul stated it in this way:- "Christ Jesus came into the world *to save sinners,* of whom I am chief". I Timothy 1 verse 5.

The *purpose* of the True Christian Message therefore, is to point

46

people to The Lord Jesus Christ as their *means* of salvation. It is, in fact, to *bring* people to The Lord Jesus Christ, and to bring them to a personal knowledge of Him, so that they come to trust Him as the One who can save them eternally, and as the *Only* one who can save them eternally. It is, in fact, to bring them to the point where they are able to say, as the words of a Hymn says, "Jesus I will trust Thee. Trust Thee *with my soul.* Guilty, lost, and helpless, Thou canst make me whole".

Then it needs to be stated very clearly that the heart of the Christian Gospel Message, its very core, is The Death of The Lord Jesus Christ on The Cross, and the shedding of His Blood. That is absolutely basic. When proclaiming the very basics of the Christian Message, this is the *chief* of the basics. And yet in Church Service after Church Service that I attend, or listen to, today, it is very noticeable that this is what is being by-passed.

But the reason why The Death of The Lord Jesus Christ and the Shedding of His Blood is the chief amongst the basics of The True Christian Message is because of what He achieved there, as the only way of accomplishing any individual's salvation. Because another vitally important basic of the True Christian Message is that because of every individual's *SIN,* without exception, every individual who is not yet Born-Again from Above and by The Holy Spirit of God, without exception, has become estranged from God, and cut off from God. Therefore there is a barrier between every such individual and God. There is a separation between them. They are separated from one another, in other words. And that which separates them is SIN. SIN is what has caused the separation. The Bible puts this quite plainly when it says, "Your iniquities have separated between you and your God, and your sins have hid His face from you, that he will not hear." Isaiah Chapter 59 verse 2.

But The Lord Jesus Christ came into the world to take away that SIN, and thus to take away that barrier. That is why the True Christian Message is called "THE GOOD NEWS".

And The Lord Jesus Christ has actually done it. He has taken away the barrier on every person's behalf. He has removed it.

He did it nearly 2,000 years ago.

He did it when He went to The Cross on the First Good Friday.

There, on the Cross, He put away SIN by the Sacrifice of Himself, which has never at any time to be repeated. Nor need it to be repeated. That is what The Bible teaches in Hebrews 9 verse 26.

So the barrier is not there any more.

The great divide is not there any more. It just does not exist.

There is no more separation between God and man.

So God and the individual can be joined together again *as one.* Whereas they had become estranged from one another, they can now be brought together.

And that is what the Bible describes as God and man being *reconciled* to one another. How? The Bible says, "We are reconciled to God *by the death of His Son"*. Romans 5 verse 10. That is How.

That is why, therefore, the Death of The Lord Jesus Christ is the very heart, the core, of the True Christian Gospel. It is *central* to it. Without His Death on the Cross there could be no eternal salvation for anybody, — only an eternity spent in Hell.

That is the essential truth of the matter.

What He did when He died on the Cross, and what He did when He shed His Blood, goes to the very root of The Truth. For God has laid it down that without the shedding of blood there is no remission, no cancelling out, of sin. No way of wiping them out, that means. Hebrews 9 verse 22. But now there *IS* a way, because Jesus has shed His Blood.

That also is basic.

He did it nearly 2,000 years ago.

So God can now wipe out our sins. He can blot them out *on that basis.* In fact He has already done so. He *HAS* removed them. And He has removed them to an immeasurable distance. He says, "As far as the east is from the west, *so far* has He removed our sins from us". He did not say, "As far as the North is from the South", because you can measure the distance between the North Pole and the South Pole. But as far as the east is from the west is an immeasurable distance. And it is The Lord Jesus Christ who has removed them. That is why John the Baptist said, when he saw The Lord Jesus approaching him, "Behold, The Lamb of God that *taketh away* the sin of the world". John 1 verse 29. And He has done it. He took the sin of the world away when He went to The Cross, and when He shed His blood nearly 2,000 years ago.

And therefore the Bible says, that up there, on The Cross, God was, in Christ, reconciling the world unto Himself, not imputing their trespasses unto them". 11 Corinthians 5 verse 19. And in verse 18 of the same chapter it says:- "He *hath* reconciled us to Himself *by Jesus Christ*". He *has* done it, it says. He brought about the reconciliation, the bringing together again, nearly 2,000 years ago — when The Lord Jesus Christ, God's Son went to the Cross, and when God made Him to be SIN, for us, Him who knew no sin, in order that we might be made the righteousness of God in Him". 11 Corinthians 5 verse 21.

So it is a finished work of reconciliation. It has been done. It was done nearly 2,000 years ago. And nothing whatsoever needs to be done to add to it. Nothing *can* be done to add to it. It is therefore a fully accomplished work.

All *we* have to do is to receive it.

All *we* have to do is to accept it, and Praise and Thank God for it.

All *we* have to do is to humbly take it from a Merciful God as a Gift — as a *Free* Gift from Him, on account of what His Son has done for us. There is nothing whatsoever that we can do, or *need* to do, to earn our eternal salvation. Nothing. "It is not of works lest any man should boast", says The Bible in Ephesians 2 verse 9. "For *by grace* are ye saved through faith; and that not of yourselves. It is the gift of God". Ephesians 2 verse 8.

"For the wages of sin is death: but the gift of God is eternal life *through Jesus Christ Our Lord*". Romans 6 verse 23.

And there are only two things you can do with a gift. One is to totally reject it, and have nothing whatsoever to do with it. By doing that, you reject, for all time, the eternal benefits which would have been yours on receiving it. The other thing you can do with the gift when you are being offered it, and in *this* case being offered it by God Himself, is to take it, — is to receive it, and then thank The Most Generous and Merciful Giver for it.

These then are some of the main basics of the True Christian Message, — the main basic facts of The Gospel of Salvation, and of The Way of Salvation, in other words.

But when did we last hear them being clearly proclaimed and presented by our Archbishops, by each and every Diocesan Bishop, to the whole of his Diocese? When did we last hear them being forthrightly and boldly proclaimed in each and every one of our Cathedrals, in each and every Church in the Land, and on Radio and on Television? When did we last hear them being clearly and fearlessly proclaimed and presented, or even written about, in any aspect of the present "Decade of Evangelism"? If they have been, I haven't heard anything about it. Neither have I read any reports of any such clear preaching and proclamation, in any of our Church Newspapers and Magazines.

I say, therefore, that in any teaching and preaching Crusade that is launched in parallel with The Prime Minister's, and the Government's crusade against crime, there needs, in addition to a clear and fearless declaration as to The True Nature of Almighty God, to be a clear and forthright presentation and declaration of The Gospel of Salvation, and of The Way of Salvation and of how a person enters into that salvation.

But I would stress very strongly that in addition to that, the preaching and teaching of that Gospel of Salvation and of The Way of Salvation, most urgently needs to be done against the background of the teaching of the Ten Commandments, with each and every one of them being spelt out in detail, with a clear explanation of what each word in every one of them means.

The Home Secretary has been saying, we need to teach children the difference between right and wrong. And so have others. But we *first* need a clear definition of what is right and what is wrong. How we measure it, for instance. Yet no-one in the debate has even mentioned the Ten Commandments, not even the Archbishops and Bishops so far as I know.

The only way anyone can accurately measure what is right and what is wrong, and the difference between them, is to measure them between what is right and what is wrong *in the sight of The Lord,* not by what is right or wrong according to public opinion, or according to humanistic, materialistic, atheistic or liberal standards. And what is right and what is wrong *in The Sight of The Lord* has been set out *for all time* by God Almighty in the Ten Commandments. And they are Commandments. *God's* Commandments. And when God gave them to Moses on Mount Sinai, He did not say, "Now take them down to your 600,000 people and get them to put them to the vote!" In other words, God did not submit them to public opinion. They are Commandments. *His* Commandments. And God's Commandments are to be obeyed. And there is a penalty to be paid for not doing so. But not only do they need to be taught. They need to be memorised. They need to be presented everywhere by clear, forthright teaching, and by a national crusade, whose aim is to put them up on the inside walls of every school classroom, on the inside walls of each and every

50

church, of every Christian place of worship, of every Cathedral, for all to see and read. The crusade needs to aim at putting them all up on the hoardings everywhere, in our towns, in our villages, in our cities, on the outside and inside of all buses, on trains, on all Underground Platforms, and on each and every Underground train itself. And they should have a bold and clear caption saying, "This is the way God requires each one of us, of whatever age, to live".

And it should be financed by the Government, by Industry, and by Large Business Consortiums, such as our Big Chain Stores. And why not? They should be prepared to do this if they really cared about arresting the present alarming moral and spiritual decline. If such a bold venture was launched, that would indeed be one major step in the right direction. I say, if we are to engage in a crusade, let us engage in a crusade, and let it be completely Nationwide, and let us show that we mean business about it.

"Oh", but someone will say, "If you do all that with the Ten Commandments you are going to instil a sense of guilt in everyone, because they will know that they are not living up to them, nor can they live up to them".

Exactly. That is why I said the clear presentation of the Gospel of Salvation and of the Way of Salvation needs to be made — against the background of the teaching of these Ten Commandments.

Furthermore, if you are making that kind of objection, all you are telling me is, that you don't know the *purpose* for which God gave them.

He gave them, in the *first* place, in order that people should not live law*less* lives. He recognised that if people everywhere were not to be utterly law*less,* then they needed to be living under law, and living under law until the time came when He could show them He had a better way by which they could live. I will be returning to that last point a little later.

He gave them, in the *second* place, in order to provide them with His Own Divinely- Appointed framework of behaviour within which they could live. And that Divinely-Appointed framework of behaviour is divided into two sections, namely, into what should be our behaviour towards God, and what should be our behaviour towards everybody else. Church catechisms state it this way:- Our duty towards God; and our duty towards our neighbour.

But God gave the Ten Commandments in the *third* place, in order that everyone might see what is wrong in the light of what they teach, when

51

these Ten Commandments are clearly taught and preached. To use the language of the Bible, God's intention was to use them to bring about *the knowledge of SIN*. The Apostle Paul says, in Romans Chapter 7 verse 7, "I would not have known *SIN*, but by the law". He even said, in verse 13 of Romans Chapter 7, that it is by the Commandment that God has given, that *SIN* becomes exceedingly SINFUL". In other words, it is in the light of the teaching of the Ten Commandments that SIN is seen for what it is — exceedingly SINFUL, LOATHSOME, and OBNOXIOUS.

Then the Apostle Paul stated it even more specifically in Romans Chapter 7 verse 7 when he said, "I would not have known *SIN* but by the law, (or apart from the law) for I would not have known *lust* (for what it is, he means) except, or unless, the law had said, "Thou shalt not covet".

Now all this ought to make sense in this modern age, when we see young children, and young teenagers, stealing from shops and other places, committing rape, engaging in all kinds of promiscuity, beating people up, crashing other people's cars, 10 year-olds even committing murder now, and a host of other things, *and not seeing anything wrong with it*. How should they, when they have been given no framework of behaviour to live by, in their homes, in their schools, in universities, or anywhere else?

But immediately they are told very clearly what God's Ten Commandments are, in the light of what they hear taught from them, they are likely to see their present behaviour for what it is. *SIN*. And in many cases as something exceedingly *SINFUL*, LOATHSOME, OBNOXIOUS, and EXCEEDINGLY WICKED.

I can quote a case in point. Just before I began to write this section of this booklet I went into an Indian Restaurant for a meal. There was a 15 year old Moslem waiter there. At a moment when he had no customers to serve, he came over to my table and said, "What are The Ten Commandments?" As a young Moslem he had no idea what these were. So I began telling him. I said, "The first one is, 'You shall have no other gods beside Me".

"Oh", he said, "I agree with that alright". He would do, being a Moslem. They quite rightly say there is only One God.

I said, "The second one is, 'You shall not make to yourself any graven image . . . you shall not bow yourself down and worship them".

"I believe that alright", he said, very enthusiastically. "The Hindus do that, and it is very wrong. They have hundreds of gods".

I said, "The third Comandment is, 'You shall not take the Name of The Lord thy God in vain'."

He broke in and said, "What does that mean?" I said, "Put simply it means you shall not use the Name of God, or of The Lord Jesus Christ as a swear word".

"Oh, I agree with that", he said, again very enthusiastically.

I said the Fourth Commandment is, "Remember the sabbath day to keep it holy. Six days shall you labour and do all that you have to do, but the seventh day is the Sabbath of the Lord your God".

He broke in again and said, "What does the word sabbath mean?" I said, "Put simply, it means a day of rest. God created the world in six days, and He rested on the seventh. And He says we should have one day's rest in seven. For the Jews it is a Saturday, for the Moslems, as you know, it is a Friday, and for the Christians, because the Lord Jesus Christ rose from the dead on the first day of the week, it is a Sunday, the first day of the week".

"I agree with that", he said.

Then I said, "The fifth commandment is, 'You shall honour your father and your mother'."

"Oh yes, I agree with that", he said with great emphasis.

I said, "The sixth Commandment is, 'You shall not steal'."

"Yes, I agree with that", he said.

I said, "The seventh Commandment is 'you shall not kill', which means you shall not commit murder".

He said, "I agree with that".

Then I said, "The next Commandment is 'You shall not commit adultery'."

"What does that mean?" he said.

I said, "In the first place it means, 'You shall not have sexual intercourse with somebody else's wife', and it also means, 'You shall not have sexual intercourse outside the marriage relationship'."

He said immediately, "But everybody does it, everybody does it. Christians do it too. Christians do it", he repeated with great emphasis.

And because everybody does it, it appeared to him to be normal. It must be alright if everybody does it. That was the rule he appeared to be measuring by. But there, in the Restaurant, for the first time, he began to see it as wrong, and he was beginning to see it as wrong because he had

53

been shown what that particular Commandment meant.

He would not have realised otherwise, because of the climate of opinion today. (He goes to a school where there are several hundred children of both sexes).

In other words, to quote Romans Chapter 7 verse 7 again, "he would not have known *SIN* (for what it is) but *by the law*, — but by the Commandment. And now he was beginning to see.

My prayer is, that his eyes may continue to be opened, so that by the Commandment *SIN* might become exceedingly sinful, to quote Romans Chapter 7 verse 13 again. It could eventually lead to his eternal salvation.

I hope this last major point has been taken. This 15 year-old Asian Moslem had seen, from having that particular Commandment explained to him, in detail, how that the sexual immorality and sexual misbehaviour which he had witnessed going on around him, and amongst his school chums, was, in the sight of Almighty God, *wrong*, that it was *sin*, and sin *in The Sight of the Lord*. He had begun to see that for the first time.

Imagine what could be the result, if all of these Ten Commandments were taught and explained, in detail, to people of all ages, old, very young, and teenagers alike, all over the United Kingdom. What a vast difference it would begin to make!

But God gave the Ten Commandments in the *fourth* place, to convince individuals of sin, or to use the theological term, to convict them of their sin.

Speaking of the Ten Commandments, Romans Chapter 3 verse 19 says, "Now we know that what things soever the law saith, it saith to them who are under the law: that every mouth may be stopped, and all the world may become guilty before God".

Then the Epistle to the Galatians describes all unregenerate people everywhere as those who are *under the law*. Galatians 4 verse 5, for instance. So the same description is given of them in both these Epistles.

Then Romans Chapter 2 verse 12, and the second part of the verse, says, "as many as have sinned in the law shall be judged *by the law*."

Therefore the law, — The Ten Commandments, are the "measuring stick" by which God judges human beings and their behaviour. It is the *measure* by which God judges people in other words.

And Romans Chapter 3 verse 9 says, that by that measure, "all are under sin". It says, "we have before proved both Jews and Gentiles, that they are all under sin". That is, *all*, without exception. Again Romans Chapter 3 verses 22 and 23 says, "For there is no difference: for *all* have sinned, and come short of the glory of God". They have missed the mark, in other words. Furthermore Romans Chapter 2 verse 23 says that through breaking the law we dishonour God".

This means that by God's measuring stick, the Law, the Ten Commandments, all are found guilty. To repeat Romans Chapter 3 verse 19, "Now we know that what things soever the law saith, it saith to them who are under the law: that every mouth may be stopped, and all the world may become guilty before God".

So there is nothing we can say in our defence. We are left speechless.

It can be described as being in the dock, in a High Court Room, with God Himself there, on the Bench, as the High Court Judge.

So I need to repeat that, the *fourth* purpose God had in mind in giving The Ten Commandments, was to convince, or convict, every individual, of his or her sin, and to show each one of them that they are guilty. Guilty before Almighty God, the Judge of all the Earth, that means. Therefore, I need to stress very strongly that there should be a Preaching of The Law whenever, and wherever, there is a Preaching of The Gospel. The Gospel of Eternal Salvation, in other words, should be preached against the background of The Law of God and the Ten Commandments, otherwise the Gospel of Salvation doesn't even begin to make sense. And it always used to be preached in that way until about 50 years ago, from which time the Gospel Message has been so whittled down, and so simplified, that it has lost most of its power and meaning. But recently, there had been a book published in America, the emphasis of which is, there is an urgent need to get back to the Preaching of The Law and The Ten Commandments as the essential, and truly Biblical background, to the Preaching of The Gospel of Salvation.

This brings me to the *fifth,* and glorious purpose which God had in mind when He gave The Ten Commandments. And that was to show us, and every individual sinner, on being convinced or convicted of their sin, that they need to flee to The Lord Jesus Christ to be eternally saved. That is, to be eternally saved from God's condemnation of their sin, from His pronouncing, as Judge, His sentence on the guilt of their sin, and from the eternal consequences of that pronounced sentence, which would mean banishment from the Presence of God, as guilty sinners, for ever and ever, in a place which Jesus Himself called Hell and the Lake of Fire. (I am merely quoting the Scriptures, and what The Lord Jesus Christ Himself taught.)

Concerning this *fifth* and glorious purpose of God giving the Ten Commandments, the Epistle to the Galatians Chapter 3 verse 24 puts it this way, "Wherefore the law was our schoolmaster to bring us unto Christ". Or again, in Galatians Chapter 4 verses 4 and 5, it says, "When the fulness of the time was come, God sent forth his Son, made of a woman, made under the law, to redeem them that were *under the law,* that we might receive the adoption of sons". To "redeem" means "to buy back". It means "to reclaim". It means "to save from the consequences of sin", (Oxford Dictionary) which I have already said is judgment and hell.

Or, as The Epistle to the Romans Chapter 8 verses I to 4 puts it:- "There is therefore now no condemnation to them which are in Christ Jesus, who walk, not after the flesh, but after the Spirit. For the-law-of-the-Spirit-of-life in Christ Jesus hath made me free from the law of sin and death.

"For what the law could not do, in that it was weak through the flesh, God sending his own Son in the likeness of sinful flesh, and for sin, *condemned* sin in the flesh", that, — (in order that) — the righteousness of the law might be fulfilled in us, who walk not after the flesh, but after the Spirit".

Now what these Scriptures stress, is, that God sent His Son, Jesus Christ, into the world, to achieve, or bring about, our eternal salvation. That means there was no way of achieving it ourselves.

"For God so loved the world, that he gave his only begotten Son, that whosoever believeth in Him should not perish, but have everlasting life. For God sent not his Son into the world to condemn the world: but that the world through Him might be saved. He that believeth on Him is not condemned: but he that believeth not is condemned already, because he hath not believed in the name of the only begotten Son of God". John's Gospel Chapter 3 verses 16 to 18.

But what really did God's Son, The Lord Jesus Christ, come into the world to do?

The answer, *firstly* is, that he came into the world to fulfil the Law *on our behalf.* That is what he meant when he said, "I did not come to destroy the law, but to fulfil it." Matthew 5 verse 17. Try as we might, *we* could not keep, or fulfil, all the Ten Commandments all of our lives. The Epistle of James Chapter 2 verse 10 even says:- "For who soever shall keep the whole law, and yet offend in one point, he is guilty of all". That means that, if we so much as break one of them, we are guilty of breaking them all.

But when Jesus came into the world he fulfilled them all on our behalf. And He did it for thirty three years, without ever breaking any one of them, once. So that is the *first* thing that he did. He honoured the Law, *on our behalf,* for a life-time. That is a major part of the Good News of the Gospel. He did it *for us.* He *kept* it for us.

But for us to break any one, or all of the Commandments, God says is SIN.

And God has said he must punish SIN. He said he would punish it, so He must punish it. But He has laid it down for all time, even before the time when Adam first sinned in the Garden of Eden, that the punishment of sin is death, and banishment from the face and presence of God for ever.

He said to Adam concerning the fruit of the tree of knowledge of good and evil, "Thou shalt not eat of it: for in the day that thou eatest thereof thou shalt surely die". Genesis 2 verse 17.

Ezekiel Chapter 18 verse 20 says, "The soul that sinneth it shall die." Romans Chapter 6 verse 23 says, "The wages of sin is death".

But each and every one of us is a sinner. The Bible says, "There is no man that sinneth not".

Romans Chapter 3 verse 23 says, "There is no difference, for *ALL* have sinned and come short of the glory of God". And that means, all without exception. Or as we have already seen in Romans 3:19, "Now we know that what things soever the law saith, it saith to them who are under the law: that every mouth may be stopped, and all the world may become guilty before God". So not only is each and every one of us a sinner, each and every one of us is found guilty in God's Holy Sight. This must be so, if all the world has become guilty before God.

So each and every one of us, without exception, deserves God's penalty for sin to be passed on us. And the penalty for sin is to die. So each and every one of us should die. We deserve to have God take our lives from us, as we stand before Him in the Dock as our Judge, because that is the penalty that God has laid down. And He would be absolutely just if He did so. And we would have nothing whatsoever to plead. All that we could do would be to ask for mercy.

But what do we discover at this crucial moment?

We discover that God has provided a substitute. Someone to stand in our place and take our punishment for us.

57

So the *second* thing that Jesus did when He came into the world, was to take our place, as our Substitute, — as our *God-Provided* Substitute. It was all part of God's Plan to save people from their sin, and from the consequences of their sin. And to do it *eternally*. So what Jesus did, when he went to The Cross on the First Good Friday, was to put Himself in our place. He was "numbered with the transgressors" as our Substitute. And as our Substitute, God made Jesus responsible for our sins. He placed them upon Him, and God dealt with them there, and punished them there, *on Him*. *We* should have died for them. But He died for them, for us. He died *instead* of us, in other words. To put it more plainly *I* should have been there on The Cross, because I am the guilty one. It should have been *me*. YOU should have been there, whoever is reading this. It should have been YOU. But Jesus suffered the penalty of death to the full, instead of us, as guilty death-deserving sinners, having to have our lives taken from us by God. His life was forfeit, when our lives should have been forfeit. As the Apostle Peter puts it: "Christ also hath suffered *for sins,* the just one for the unjust ones that He might bring us to God". I Peter Chapter 3 verse 18. That means, to bring us to God in terms of our being brought into a right relationship with God while we are here on earth, because on the basis of what Jesus has done on The Cross for us, God can now justly forgive us of our every sin. The barrier between God and ourselves which was caused by our sins has now been removed, so reconciliation between ourselves and God has now become gloriously possible. But what the Apostle Peter also means, is, and then to bring us to God *ultimately* in Heaven.

But when God raised Our Lord and Saviour Jesus Christ from the dead again, *that* whas the proof positive that God had accepted what His Son had done for us, and on our behalf, as our Substitute. And it is on that basis, and on that basis alone, that God can not only now forgive us our every sin, but accept us as His forever. It is all summed up in the words of Romans Chapter 4 verses 24 and 25, where it talks about, "Him that raised up Jesus our Lord from the dead, who was delivered *for our offences,* and was raised again for our justification" — the word "justification" meaning, the act of our being put right with God, or made right with God, and of being made just in the sight of God. It can also mean "being made just as if we have never sinned at all, in God's sight".

Now the Bible makes it plain that all this is offered to us by God as a gift. It is spoken of in Romans Chapter 5 verse 15 as "the *free* gift", and in the same verse, as "the gift by grace"; and in verse 17 of the same chapter as, "the gift of righteousness". Verse 19 of the same chapter says, "so by the obedience of One, — (Jesus Christ) shall many be *made* righteous". God, as Judge, can now say to the person in the dock, "Acquitted".

It cannot therefore be overstressed that what you do with a gift, with a *free* gift, is to receive it. And that is how the True Christian life essentially begins. It begins when a person receives what God offers as a gift, on the basis of what His Son, The Lord Jesus Christ, achieved on our behalf, as our Substitute, on The Cross. This is quite contrary to the impression which is given in so many of the Broadcast Church Services today.

The impression given in Services broadcast on the B.B.C. is that the Christian life begins with Baptism, and by that is implied, Infant Baptism. But it doesn't.

The Christian life begins with *TRUSTING*. It begins with TRUSTING IN THE LORD JESUS CHRIST. That is what the Apostle Paul says in Ephesians Chapter 1 verse 12, where he numbers himself with those "who *first* trusted in Christ". Then he goes on to refer to the Ephesian Christians in verse 13 of that chapter by saying, "in whom ye *also* Trusted".

But then he says *HOW* they trusted, in verses 13 to 14. "In whom ye *also* trusted AFTER that ye heard the word of truth, the gospel of your salvation". Then he elaborates still further by saying, "In whom *AFTER* that ye *believed*, ye were sealed with that holy Spirit of promise which is the earnest (guarantee) of our inheritance until the redemption of the purchased possession".

So the Divine Order of becoming a Christian is:

(1) To hear the word of truth. What is that? It is the gospel of your salvation, which must be *preached* in order that a person may hear it.

(2) It is to TRUST IN JESUS *after* that person hears that word of truth — the Gospel.

   In other words, it is to *believe* verse 13. And it is to believe *in Jesus.*

And no babe-in-arms can do all that. He or she does not know or understand what is going on at a Service of "Infant Baptism". Then:

(3) It is to be sealed with the Holy Spirit. When? Answer: *After* that ye believe.

So Baptist should be *after* individuals believe. That is why it is called in some Christian circles, "Believers' Baptism".

The Christian life, therefore, begins when a person is sealed with the Holy Spirit; when that person is Born Again of the Holy Spirit of God; when that person is Born from above. And that happens as a result of that person hearing the Word of Truth preached, and then as a result of that, TRUSTING IN JESUS. So the Christian's life begins with something which is done to him, or her, by God, and with something which is done to him or her immediately he or she believes. The Apostle John, in his First Epistle, refers to such believers many times over as, "he that is born of God". He does the same in the first chapter of his Gospel, in verses 12 and 13, where he says, "But as many as receive Him — (Jesus, the True Light that came into the world) — to them gave He power to become the sons of God, even to them that *believe on His Name*; which were born, *NOT* of blood, *NOR* of the will of the flesh, *NOR* of the will of man, but *of God*". John Chapter 1 verses 12 to 13. I repeat. It says they are born *of God.* The New Testament's description of all True Christians everywhere, therefore, is "those who are born of God". Jesus Himself, when He was talking to Nicodemus about the absolute necessity for a person to be born again, referred to them in John Chapter 3 verse 8 as "everyone that is born of the Spirit". And *that* happens when a person hears the Word of Truth preached, I say, and then as a result of *that*, — TRUSTS IN JESUS.

It is *then* that that person receives the free gift of eternal salvation, the free gift of justification, — (of being made, in God's Sight, just as if they had never sinned at all) — the free gift of righteousness, the free gift of eternal life.

The Apostle Paul therefore, referred to all those Ephesian believers who had *trusted in Christ* before he had even met them, as those about whom he had, "heard of *their faith in the Lord Jesus*". Ephesians Chapter 1 verse 15.

So another true New Testament description of all genuine Christians everywhere is, "those who have faith in the Lord Jesus". And yet another New Testament description of them is, "Those who have obtained *MERCY*". For becoming a Christian is all about obtaining *MERCY.* That was the Apostle Paul's description of himself. As Saul of Tarsus he had made havoc of the church, entering into every house, and hailing men and women committing them to prison. See Acts Chapter 18 verse 3. He even breathed out threatenings and slaughter against the disciples of the Lord, and went unto the high priest and desired of him letters to Damascus to the synagogues, that if he found any of this way, whether they were men or women, he might bring them bound to Jerusalem. See Acts Chapter 9 verses 1 and 2.

But then the Lord Jesus met him in dazzling, blinding Light on the road to Damascus, and later, as The Apostle Paul he said, "I was before a blasphemer, and a persecutor, and injurious: but I obtained MERCY". I Timothy I verse 13. He did not say, "I made my decision for Christ". Neither did he say, "I committed my life to Christ". And he did not say, "I made my commitment". There is nothing in the New Testament about "making a decision for Christ" or "committing one's life to Christ" or "making a commitment".

This is modern phraseology. It only came in about 50 years ago. It was never used before then. And it is not Biblical. If I say "I made my decision for Christ", or, "I committed my life to Christ", or "I made my commitment" I am saying that I have contributed towards my personal salvation, which is impossible. There is nothing I myself can do to achieve my personal salvation, and nothing I can do to earn it.

The Apostle Paul said, rather, "I obtained *MERCY*". I repeat, Becoming a Christian is all about obtaining *MERCY*. When God Almighty, the Judge of all the Earth, says to the one in the dock who has been found guilty, "You are acquitted as a result of your believing that My Son, The Lord Jesus, paid the full penalty of your sins, as the Substitute I have provided for you, and you can now go out free clothed with My Own Righteousness which I have now given you as a free gift", that person goes out free because he has obtained *MERCY*.

For God has not only said He has concluded all under sin, and that the whole world is guilty before God. He has also said "For God hath concluded them all in unbelief, that He might have *MERCY* upon all". Romans Chapter 11 verse 32.

So I say, yet another New Testament description of all True Christians everywhere is, "those who have obtained *MERCY*".

All this, therefore, needs to be included in the Teaching and Preaching Crusade which needs to run parallel with the Prime Minister's and the Government's Crusade against Crime. And as a result of it, many criminals and would-be criminals, as well as many other people all over the United Kingdom, could be numbered amongst those who have obtained *MERCY* from Almighty God, and who have the same faith in the Lord Jesus as the early believers in Ephesus did.

But running in parallel with the Prime Minister's and the Government's Crusade against Crime, and in parallel with this Christian Teaching and

Preaching Crusade, there should also be a Crusade to instil a strong form of discipline amongst very young children, and then at every age level, as they are growing up. They should not be allowed to run wild and loose all over the place, completely untamed. The Bible says, "Train up the child in the way he should go: and when he is old he will not greatly depart from it". Proverbs 22 verse 6. And we need, as a people, to get back to that principle.

In the Horticultural world, for instance, no gardener worth his salt, would plant a row of sweet peas in his garden and then, when they come up, allow them to grow and run along the ground all over the place. No. He puts in a row of canes along where he has planted his sweet pea seeds, and when the young plants come up, he trains them up to those upright canes, and if necessary, ties their stems to the canes so that the plants grow up them, and become upright. So it needs to be with children from the moment they are born. They need to be trained to behave. And training involves discipline, strong discipline sometimes. And discipline involves correction. And correction sometimes requires a good slap on the bottom, or on the hand, if a child won't behave. And God Almighty has laid it down that this should happen. He even says He does it with believing people who are His children, because He says, in Hebrews Chapter 12 verses 6 to 11, "Whom the Lord loveth He chasteneth, and scourgeth every son whom He receiveth. If ye endure chastening, God dealeth with you as with sons: for what son is he whom the father chasteneth not?" And furthermore, God makes it plain that He thoroughly approves of the parent correcting his child when necessary by giving him or her a good slap, by saying in the same passage of Scripture, "Furthermore we have had fathers after our flesh (human fathers, that means) which corrected us, and we gave them reverence: Shall we not much rather be in subjection unto the Father of spirits and live? For they verily for a few days chastened us after their own pleasure: but He for our profit, that we might be partakers of His holiness". Then it says, "Now no chastening for the present seemeth to be joyous, but grievous: nevertheless afterward it yieldeth the peacable fruit of righteousness unto them which are exercised thereby".

It is abundantly plain from all this, therefore, that God Almighty has not only laid it down that correction by chastening should happen, and that He does it Himself, but that He also expects it to be done. It is part of His Divine Ordinance for children and young people as they are growing up.

Furthermore, He expects those children and young people, when they themselves become parents, to discipline their children in the same way. Now this is tragically what we have lost in this modern age today. And this is why we see so many of our children and young people running wild in our streets, and totally out of control.

Take, for instance, the example of the pathetic mother which was reported in the "Sun" Newspaper on Wednesday, March 3rd of this year (1993). She was sobbing in desperation because her 14 year-old son, having committed no less than 200 shop burglaries, had walked out of court for the 33rd time, quite free, because there was nowhere to lock him up. He had admitted to stealing almost £58,000 cash and goods in his latest spree of 31 break-ins, and it had taken the clerk of the court 12 minutes to read out the list of offences which he had committed. The mother sobbed in desperation, saying, "He'll be at it again before the week's out". But my question is, "Why did she not thresh him after the very first offence?" I repeat, thresh him. And when he had committed the second offence, why did she not thresh him after that? I guarantee that a good threshing would have prevented him from committing no less than 200 shop burglaries!

Or again, take the example of the pathetic mother which was reported in the "Sun" Newspaper the day before, Tuesday, March 2nd of this year (1993). She said her son started committing crimes when he was 12, and she said she got so desperate that she put her house on the market and took a £20,000 loss to get him away. "Now," she said, "we live 20 miles from his tearaway friends, and I pray he'll sort himself out". But why did she not belt him after he had committed his first crime? I repeat, belt him.

Or take another example which was reported in the "Sun" Newspaper on the same day. An ex-policeman had reported that his car was stolen by a boy of 14. Police caught him, and he admitted that he had broken into more than 50 cars, but had walked away from court scot-free because of his age. I ask again, "But why did not his parents thresh him after he had broken into the first car?" I repeat, thresh him.

To quote yet another example quoted by the same Newspaper on the same day. A flower-shop owner told, the day before, how boys as young as nine had raided her shop at least six times. The police caught the gang, but told her there is little that they can do, because the boys are so young. So she said, "When they walk past my shop they smirk and keep sneering at me".

But why were they not belted by their parents? I repeat, belted.

As I say that, I am reminded of how I walked into a Newsagents a week or so ago, which is run by an Asian Moslem and his wife. On this particular day, their three-year-old son was in the shop, and he was "playing up" like mad. His Asian mother spoke to him sharply, but he took no notice whatsoever, and continued "playing up". So she picked him up in front of all the customers, and with the palm of her hand, walloped him three times on the bottom, and twice on his hand. Then she said, "I am taking you straight home, and I will put you straight to bed". This was at 4.30 in the afternoon. So she walked out of the shop with him in her arms, got straight into her car, and drove off with him. No nonsense! Her Asian Moslem husband was serving behind the counter. So when I went to pay for the Newspaper I had bought, I said to him in the hearing of a number of English school-children who were in the shop, "That is the way to bring up children". He said to me immediately, "He is not behaving, so he must be smacked. That is the only way he will learn". I said, again in the hearing of all these English school-children, "I only wish all our English children were brought up like that".

Not many days later, the "Daily Express" carried front page news that a new controversy had broken out the evening before, Friday, March 19th (1993), over parents' rights to punish their children, after magistrates cleared a father who had punished his two young sons with a belt. This case was also reported, in full, in "The Daily Telegraph" on Saturday, March 20th. I studied both reports very closely. The father had said, "I believe parents have the right to chastise their own children without ending up in front of a court". He said, "If more parents were stricter with their children we might not have 10-year-olds killing toddlers, and mugging grannies". His own boys were aged eight and five, and he had strapped them for being naughty, for, in fact, carving a dining-room chair with a knife. He had shouted at them to stop, but when they didn't, "I gave them three of the best with my belt," he said.

When the case was heard, I was overjoyed to read that the defending magistrate had said, "There is no law in this country preventing parents from punishing their children". When I read that, I breathed a Hallelujah. The magistrates' retired for ten minutes to consider the case. Then when they returned, the chairman of the bench told the father, "The case against you is dismissed. You are free to go".

Of course it should have been dismissed. God Himself is on the side of that father. He requires that parents chastise their children when they misbehave. In fact, He says in His Word, "He that spareth his son hateth his son: but he that loveth him, chasteneth him betimes". Proverbs 13 verse 24.

And again, "Withhold not correction from the child: for if thou beatest him with the rod he shall not die. Thou shalt beat him with the rod, and shalt deliver his soul from hell". Proverbs 23 verses 13 to 14. Then again, God, in the Bible, talks several times about "using the rod of correction". He says, for instance, in Proverbs 29 verse 15, "The rod and reproof give wisdom: but a child left to himself bringeth his mother to shame". Or yet again, in Proverbs 19 verse 18, "Chasten thy son while there is hope, and let not thy soul spare for his crying".

So Almighty God Himself is well and truly on the side of that father who used his belt on his two young sons who wouldn't listen to him, and He is totally against The National Society for the Prevention of Cruelty to Children when they say, as they did just after that court case, "We don't approve of the physical chastisement of children". As a Society which began with Christian origins, they ought to know better. And God Almighty is most certainly totally against Valerie Howarth of Childline when she said after that case had been dismissed, "I think to beat two small children with a belt is abuse". It is not. It is part of the Divinely Ordained Ordinance in the upbringing of children provided it is done in the way that that father did it. Furthermore, it is the way of nipping crime, unruliness, and misbehaviour in the bud.

As Mr Justice Judge, a High Court Judge, told the House of Commons Select Committee on Home Affairs on Wednesday, February 17th, of this year, "If juveniles could be deterred from forming the criminal habit at the outset, many would perhaps avoid the steady climb up the seriousness ladder and constant offending". Daily Telegraph Report, Thursday, February 18th, 1993.

He had already said to that Select Committee on that day, that Courts should be given powers to "shake young offenders to their roots". But he went on to lament that "there is no short sentences available to shake the young offender to his roots before he has formed the habit".

But it is not short sentences which are needed. They need clumping. Walloping. A good Threshing. That would shake young offenders to their roots more than anything. As Andrew Grimson in his "Sunday Telegraph" Column "At The Bar of World Opinion" said on Sunday, March 7th, of this year (1993). "A Glasgow lad beat up another lad *in the Isle of Man.* He was birched". "If these first offenders were given the birch, most of them would not come back for more". . . . . "The birch," he said, "is a fantastic deterrent, if you get them at an impressionable age".

That is more to the point than short sentences.

And it is certainly more to the point than constantly letting young criminals off with cautions or putting them on probation.

As Judge Felix Waley, chairman of the criminal sub-committee of the Council of Circuit Judges said on February 17th of this year (1993), "the excessive reliance on letting teenage thugs off with cautions is breeding contempt for justice. Far too much is being shuffled away by way of cautions," he said. "The danger is always that by the time they reach any sort of deterrence they regard the system with derision and you have hardened criminals".

But my point is, that if they had the deterrent of a good threshing or belting by their parents in their own homes, or a good hard wallop on the bottom when they begin to go wrong, it would nip misbehaviour and criminal tendencies in the bud anyway, and they might never even become the teenage thugs that he is talking about. And God shows us abundantly clearly in His Word, as I have shown, that this is the way of going about it. Yet in all the reports that I have read, all kinds of suggestions have been made as to what should be done with these young tearaways and young offenders. "Parents should be made to pay for the things which some of them have taken," says one Report. "We must pray that they will sort themselves out," says another. "More policemen should be put on the streets," says another. "Young criminals should be sent to work in places like children's homes," says yet another. "They should be put into care to stop them breaking the law," says even yet another. "They should be locked up." "The courts should put young people away," says two others. "Parents should be made to pay compensation for their victims," says even yet another.

But nowhere does anyone say, in any one of these Reports, that they should be punished and disciplined by their parents in their own homes.

The Government itself has proposed the setting up of new secure units which will enable 12- to 15-year-old persistent offenders to be detained for up to two years, and may even be considering extending this to cover all those who have attained the age of criminal responsibility, which is now from at least ten years of age onwards. This would be at the cost of literally millions of pounds of tax-payer's money. And I understand that none of these new secure units could be available until at least 1996. So what would be done in the meantime?

My contention is, that if a Crusade were to be launched to instil a strong form of discipline amongst the very young children, and then at every age-level as they are growing up, to run parallel with The Prime Minister's and the Government's Crusade against crime, and to run parallel, at the same time, with a Christian Teaching and Preaching Crusade, many of these problems amongst children and young people gone wild, that I have been talking about, could be resolved, and these new secure units which the Government and Home Office have been talking about, might not even be necessary.

But is it all going to be done, I wonder?

Is the Prime Minister's and The Government's Crusade against crime even going to be done? Whenever such ideal Plans or Proposals have been envisaged in the past, they have "fizzled out", one by one, for one reason or another. For instance, a month or so after the war in Europe had been brought to a conclusion in 1945, the Plan "Towards the Conversion of England" was published. But despite the fact that it aroused such interest, and caused such excitement in Christian circles that, within four months, it has been reprinted four times, it all came to nothing. Rather than put the plan into operation, it was "shunted into a siding" where it has remained ever since, and reunion with Rome was put "on the main line," rather than the proclamation of the Gospel all over the United Kingdom.

Then came Dr. Coggan's "Call to the Nation" soon after he became Archbishop of Canterbury. But for some unknown reason, that never really "got off the launching pad".

Then two years ago the "Decade of Evangelism" was much publicised and discussed. Certain appointments were made in order to "get it off the ground". But until very recently, that also seemed to have become dormant. In fact, Canon Michael Green admitted in an Article published on Friday, February 26th of this year (1993), in "The Church of England Newspaper", that since "Springboard", the Church of England's instrument for bringing about "The Decade of Evangelism" in Church of England Dioceses was launched with considerable splash (his words) in St. Paul's Cathedral back in September last, (1992), "there has been a deafening silence" about it. But now he heads his Article, "Springboard gets into gear". He does not say, however, into *what* gear! And it seems significant to me that he does not say, "into *top* gear".

He says the four of them who were appointed to spearhead the Church of England side of the "Decade of Evangelism" "have been going round the country, seeing the situation on the ground".

He says they have had "10 consultations with representative Anglican and other leaders from all the dioceses in the country".

He says they have "run a conference on apologetics", and even says that he and one other, "are writing a book on apologetics in the Decade of Evangelism" — as if we have to apologise for the Christian Faith!

I don't find any of the Apostles ever doing that, after being anointed with The Holy Spirit on the Day of Pentecost! Rather they spoke boldly to make known the mystery of the Gospel. They never apologised for it.

He says at the time he wrote his article that as a result of doing all that, "we now know at least an outline of the situation in England". But nowhere in his Article does he so much as mention what the Message of the "Decade of Evangelism" is going to be. And he most certainly does not give a clear and authoritative scriptural definition of what evangelism really is, and what it is all about, which is what I myself have urgently been calling for, ever since my Article entitled, "The Decade of Evangelism. The Extreme Urgency of it" was first published in the Summer 1991 issue of the "News Bulletin for the National Council for Christian Standards in Society", and which I understand by them was mailed to every member of The Church of England General Synod.

In fact, when one looks at the list of names which he gives in his Article of the instructors who will be helping "to equip Christians in evangelism", one gets very dubious indeed about what the Message is going to be. At best, it seems, it will be a mixed Message, a compromised Gospel no doubt.

I doubt very much if it will be the forthright, bold, clear-cut, uncompromising Preaching of The New Testament Gospel of Salvation in all its glorious fulness. Indeed, he gives a clue as to what its Message is going to be, when he says in his Article "But evangelism could degenerate into proselytism!" Whatever is he talking about? My Concise Oxford Dictionary tells me that to proselytise is to convert from one opinion, creed, or party, to another. It is to convert. It says a convert is "one who has come". And by that it means, "one who has come to an entirely different opinion or outlook". In spiritual terms it means "one who has come to a faith". And

68

surely that is what real evangelism is all about. It does not degenerate to that. Why! that is its object. That is its aim. That is its whole purpose. Take what happened in the New Testament days under the preaching of the early Apostles. The world at that time was full of the other faiths, cults, cultures and religions of the world. The Greeks had their gods, the Romans had their gods, the Asians had their gods, and the Celts had their gods. I have listed them all in great detail in my booklet, "A New Government — A New Era" with its sub-title "So what is God now saying (a) About the state of the nation of Britain today? (b) As to the responsibility of its Church?

But then, as the result of the Preaching of the Gospel in the full power of the Holy Spirit by the Apostle Paul, for instance, the Church at Corinth came into being, the Church at Ephesus came into being, the Church of Galatia came into being, and the seven churches which are in Asia, mentioned in the opening chapters of the Book of The Revelation, came into being. And each and every one of them were comprised of proselyts who had been converted by that Preaching of the Christian Faith, from the worship of all these other gods. This was true also of the Christians who were at Rome to whom The Apostle Paul wrote the Epistle to the Romans. And look what happened in Jerusalem on the Day of Pentecost where there were Jews gathered together for that Jewish feast out of every nation under heaven. Acts Chapter 2 verse 5.

The Holy Spirit came down on the 120 disciples who were all with one accord in one place, then the Apostle Peter preached in the streets in the hearing of all these Jews, and as a result about three thousand of them were swept into the early Christian Church in Jerusalem, then a few days later about five thousand were added to them, and still later on a great number of the Jewish priests believed. So the early Church in Jerusalem under the Preaching of The Apostle Peter and of the other eleven disciples consisted of proselyts. They had been converted to Faith in the Lord Jesus Christ from the Hebrew Religion, from the Jewish faith. And do we read anywhere in the New Testament that this was evangelism degenerating into proselytism? Of course we don't. They are both one and the self-same thing. The Oxford Dictionary, and other Dictionaries are right, therefore, when they say to proselytise is to convert from one opinion, belief, creed, outlook, or party to another. And that is what true Evangelism is all about. It is all about converting people.

But when Canon Michael Green says in his Article, "But evangelism could degenerate into proselytism" I fear he is fighting shy of fulfilling, relentlessly the Lord's Command and Commission "Go ye into all the world and preach the Gospel to *every creature*". For every creature includes all those of other faiths, cults, religions and beliefs, which also includes the Jews". And that statement of his seems to imply that the "Decade of Evangelism" is not only going to fight shy of doing that, but has no intention of doing that.

In fact there is a considerable amount of wooliness and unclarity, vagueness, running through the whole of his Article which makes one wonder what the Message of the "Decade of Evangelism" is going to be. The four who have been appointed to spearhead this "Springboard" aspect of it just have not declared themselves with regard to this, or come out into the open about it.

But that wooliness, that vagueness, that unclarity is not only confined to this Article or to these four, or to all who have been involved in discussions and Conferences about the "Decade of Evangelism". At the time that I am writing this section of this booklet it has just been announced that the Archbishop of Canterbury has written in a House of Commons Magazine against the Disestablishment of The Church of England. According to the announcement, he has written to say we need to maintain the Established Church "in order to preserve the idea of kingship, and in order to ensure that people still realise that they have their Churches and Cathedrals to go to when they want to get married and when they want to bury their dead". He did not say one word, apparently, about when they want to go into the Churches and Cathedrals in order to hear the Gospel of Salvation and as a result to be eternally saved. That does not enter into it any more. So it is not only wooliness, vagueness and unclarity, that abounds. The very reason for the Church's existence, namely the salvation of souls, now seems to have become entirely lost.

It is true that Canon Michael Green says at the end of his Article that "a notable start to "The Decade of Evangelism" will be the "Prayer Mission" which Bishop Marshall is leading around all the Cathedrals of this land in the fortnight after Easter (1993) (three a day, morning, noon and evening). He says, "It will be a major opportunity for Christians of all stripes (his words) to come to the Cathedral and pray for the conversion of England". But we need to ask in this ecumenical, multi-faith age, especially when the phrase "Christians of all stripes" is being used, what does he mean by "the conversion of England?" The conversion of England to what? Because when certain

Anglo-Catholic clergymen began to talk about leaving the Church of England and going over to the Church of Rome when the General Synod vote went in favour of the ordination of women to the priesthood, Cardinal Basil Hume said he believes he could be witnessing "the conversion of England, for which we have prayed all these years". But he did not, by any means, mean the conversion of England to the New Testament Faith in Christ and to New Testament based Christianity. That is not that for which they have prayed all these years.

What he meant was, "the conversion of England to Roman Catholicism, which The Popes, the Vatican, and the Roman Catholic Church have been praying for, and have been trying to bring about, ever since the Glorious Reformation. Nay, ever since Gregory The Great sent Augustine to these islands in 597 A.D. to bring the already existing, virile, Celtic, New Testament and Truly Bible-Based Church into submission to Rome. That was the Church which had existed and thrived in these islands well over 500 years before the arrival of Augustine with his Roman Catholic version of Christianity, and which was independent and free.

The question urgently needs to be asked therefore, "What is the *Aim* and *Object* of this 'Decade of Evangelism?' as well as urgently to ask, "What is going to be its Message?"

It may not "fizzle out", or turn out to be "a damp squib" or "come to nothing" like the other two "Plans" or "Proposals" which I have mentioned. But it may be taking an entirely different direction to what the undiscerning and the gullible are envisaging. The "wooliness", the "vagueness", the "unclarity" and the unwillingness to come right out into the open with a clear, Biblical definition of what real evangelism is, and what is its Message, may all turn out to be deliberate. To quote the title of an Article by William Oddie published in "The Sunday Telegraph" on March 7th of this year (1993), it may all well be "Romeward bound".

All Truly Born-Again Believers need therefore to be *WARNED*.

THE MONARCHY AND THE CONSTITUTION
Should the Constitution be changed?

But meanwhile what has been happening with respect to the Monarchy and in respect of the National Church, the so-called "Established Church"?

71

The Archbishop of York, Dr. Habgood, stated during a Television interview on the B.B.C. programme, "Heart of the Matter" on Sunday, 24th January of this year (1993), that because society had changed so dramatically since the last Coronation in 1953, the Coronation Oath would have to be revised to take account of these dramatic changes in the nation's religious outlook. He said, "If the Coronation Service is going to unify the nation, as it must do, then it must recognise that we live in an Ecumenical and multi-faith society".

This gives rise to real cause for *ALARM*. I repeat, ALARM!

In the *first* place, it might be true that there has been a massive change in religion, and in the religious outlook in this Country, but the fact remains that God does not change.

The nature of man does not change.

The Gospel of Salvation does not change.

The Lord Jesus Christ, the One and Only Saviour of the World, does not change.

Whatever else may happen by way of change, all these remain the same, and not one of them, or all of them put together, can in any way be changed by the prevailing climate or outlook of the day.

Furthermore, God's Ten Commandments have not changed, either. They remain the same, and always will remain the same. They are Absolute, and never can be altered. And God has specifically declared, "Thou shalt have no other gods before Me". Exodus Chapter 20 verse 3. He also says, "I the Lord thy God am a jealous God". Exodus Chapter 20 verse 5. That means He can brook no other. He can tolerate no other, or no others.

So that rules out immediately multi-faith worship, or any *form* of multi-faith worship. So there is no basis whatsoever for "unifying the nation" by recognising that "we live in a multi-faith society" as Dr. Habgood says we must do.

I say that that statement of his gives rise to real cause for ALARM, because a study of the whole of the Old Testament reveals that for a Nation which has been under God for centuries, as this Nation has been, to go in that direction, — the direction of *unifying* with other faiths and religions — spells the end of that Nation, as a Nation.

For instance, when the Northern Kingdom of Israel went in that direction from the reign of King Rehoboam onwards, it aroused the indignation and wrath of Almighty God to such an extent that He said He would have to act in Judgment and they would cease to be a Nation. And they *did* cease to be a Nation. You cannot play around, or fool around, with an Holy and Almighty God.

Or again, when the Southern Kingdom of Judah went in that direction under King Solomon, despite all his wisdom, we read, "Wherefore the Lord said unto Solomon, 'Forasmuch as this is done of thee . . . I will surely rend the Kingdom from thee . . . notwithstanding in thy days I will not do it . . . but I will rend it out of the hand of thy son'." I Kings Chapter 11 verses 10 to 12. And then again, in the same chapter, and in verse 31, God says, "Behold I will rend the kingdom out of the hand of Solomon".

And it happened. You cannot fool around with God.

I say again, to go in that direction spells the end of a Nation, as a Nation, so far as Almighty God is concerned. And as I proceed to quote a number of Scriptures it will be clearly seen that I have an unarguable case. For when confronted with such a statement as that which has been made by the Archbishop of York, the first thing to do is to ask, "But what saith the Scriptures?" for the Scriptures are our one and only Authority in deciding matters of Faith and Conduct. And I myself have re-read the whole of the Old Testament, from Genesis to Malachi, since the Archbishop of York made his alarming statement at the end of January (1993), and all the relevant New Testament Scriptures as well, so I think I can claim to know what I am talking about.

For instance, Israel in the Old Testament was a Nation under God. That is, under The True, The Living God, the Creator of the Heavens and the Earth, the Only God that there is. And the Prophet Samuel said to them in *his* day, "If ye do return unto the Lord with all your hearts, then *put away* the strange gods and Ashtaroth from among you, and prepare your hearts unto the Lord, and serve Him *ONLY*". I Samuel Chapter 7 verse 3.

This is the direct opposite to what the Archbishop of York says we should do, when he says we must "unify the nation by recognising that we live in a multi-faith society". The Prophet Samuel did not say to the Nation of Israel in his day, "You must unify the Nation by recognising the strange gods and Ashtaroth which are among you". He said "Put them away. Put them away". "Separate yourselves from them. Sever every connection with them. And serve The Lord *ONLY*". That is a far cry from what the Archbishop of York is telling us we should do. The answer is to, "Put them away", not unite with them.

Then in the Book of Exodus, Chapter 22 verse 20, God says, "He that sacrifieth unto any god, save unto the Lord ONLY, he shall utterly be destroyed". It therefore carried the Death Penalty in those days.

So how can anyone say, let alone an Archbishop, "There is room now, or even the need now, for the amalgamation of all the faiths and religions of the world", or "that the Nation of Britain needs now to be *unified* with a multi-faith society"? He is speaking directly contrary to God.

Then Exodus 23 verse 13 even says, "Make no mention of the name of other gods, neither let it be heard out of thy mouth". Which means that we should not even mention them, let alone be *unified* with them.

How then can anyone say, let alone an Archbishop, "God wants us all to merge together as one, because they all believe in the same God"?

Then Exodus 23 verse 24 also says, "Thou shalt not bow down to their gods, nor serve them, nor do after their works — (their customs, their culture) —; but thou shalt utterly overthrow them, and quite break down their images". This is the exact opposite to inviting them to take part in Christian Services in our Cathdrals, Churches and Places of Worship, and in Christian worship.

Furthermore, Exodus 23 verse 32 says of the other nations with which Israel was involved at that time, "Thou shalt make no covenant with them, *nor* with their gods, . . . for if thou serve their gods, it will surely be a snare unto thee".

But this is exactly what the Archbishop of York and others are doing. They are making a covenant with these other faiths and religions if they say we need to *unify* an ecumenical and multi-faith society, and unify the nation by recognising that we now live in an ecumenical and multi-faith society. We are making a covenant with them by so doing, I say.

The teaching of The Bible makes it abundantly plain that we are NOT to do that. And to do it, is to go directly against the expressed Will of God who says we are NOT to do that.

When Almighty God gave that Commandment to Israel, through Moses, at the foot of Mount Sinai, there were six hundred thousand of the people of Israel there, at that time. They did not say, "Oh but we must recognise all these other religions and faiths and their various gods, and we must be *unified* with them". They said rather, and with one voice, "All the words which the Lord hath said will we do, and be obedient". All six hundred thousand of them did. In other words, they said they would do the exact opposite to what the Archbishop of York now says the nation of Britain must do. See Exodus 24 verses 3 and 7.

Then turning to the Book of Deuteronomy, God specifically says, in Deuteronomy Chapter 6 verse 14, "Ye shall not go after other gods, of the gods of the people which are round about you", which is exactly what the Archbishop is saying we *should* do, when he is saying we should *unify* with them in order to *unify* our nation and our society. In fact, he says, the nation of Britain *must* do that in order to *unify* the Nation; it must recognise that we live in an Ecumenical and multi-faith society. And the Coronation Oath, and the Coronation Service will have to be revised if we are going to *unify* the Nation in that way. That is what he is saying. So he is saying we should go after them.

But after God Almighty had said in Deuteronomy Chapter 6 verse 14 'Ye shall not go after other gods, of the gods of the people which are round about you". He went on to say, "For the Lord thy God is a jealous God among you, lest the anger of the Lord thy God be kindled against thee, and *destroy thee from off the face of the earth*". And when God said "destroy thee from off the face of the earth" He *meant* destroy thee from off the face of the earth". Which is why I said the Archbishop of York's statement gives rise to cause for ALARM. Because if we go in the direction in which he is saying we should go, that is what could happen to Britain, make no mistake about it. You cannot fool around, or play about, with God. We could be destroyed as a Nation, or cease to be a Nation.

For God says again in Deuteronomy Chapter 30 verses 17 to 18, "If thine heart turn away ... and be drawn away, and worship other gods and serve them; (be *unified* with them, in other words;) I denounce unto you this day, that ye shall surely perish". And when God says, "Ye shall surely perish", He means "perish". Because this is to go in direct disobedience against what He has specifically commanded, and to go in direct disobedience against Almighty God *HIMSELF*.

Or again in Deuteronomy Chapter 20 verses 17 to 18, we find that the instructions which God gave to Israel against the Hittites, the Amorites, the Canaanites, and the other nations with whom they were to be surrounded, and against their gods and forms of worship, were so severe that He said, "Thou shalt utterly destroy them in order that they teach you not to do after all their abominations which they have done unto their gods: so should you sin against the Lord your God".

75

This is very strong language. And it is a far cry from being *unified* with these other gods. It is directly opposite to doing that, and it is a strong warning against ever doing it.

But this is only a *beginning* of what the Scriptures say against such unification with the other faiths and religions of other nations and peoples.

I go on to quote a few Old Testament examples, bearing in mind that the New Testament teaching about Old Testament events is, that they should serve as examples to us, to the intent that we should not lust after the same things or go in the same direction. (See for instance 1 Corinthians Chapter 10 verse 6). 1 Corinthians Chapter 10 verse 11 also says, "Now all these things happened unto them (Old Testament Israel) for ensamples: and they are written for our admonition, upon whom the ends of the world are come". That is US!

The first Old Testament example I want to quote, is in the Book of Judges Chapter 3. But before quoting it, let me remind you of what the Archbishop of York said. He said that because of the dramatic changes which have taken place in our nation's religious make-up during the last few years "if the Coronation Service is going to unify the nation *as it must do* (my italicising) then it must recognise that we live in an Ecumenical and multi-faith society".

Now the example which we are given in the Book of Judges Chapter 3 should serve as an extremely strong warning against doing that kind of thing. It is a Key Chapter so far as *not* unifying with other gods and religions (multi-faith societies) are concerned.

The background to that chapter is this:- After Joshua had led God's people, the children of Israel, into the promised land, and under his leadership were in full occupation within their promised borders, Joshua died. But in the process of occupation, God had left certain of the nations of Canaan in the land. These nations included the Canaanites, the Hittites, the Amorites, the Perizzites, the Hivites and the Jebusites. And each of these nations had their own gods, their own form of religion, and their own various cults. So the children of Israel, the worshippers of The One, True, Living God, the *Only* God, found themselves living in a multi-faith, multi-religious, multi-cultural society. For verse 5 of this chapter says that the children of Israel dwelt among all these. But verses 1 and 4 of this chapter specifically says that The Lord had left these nations there *to prove Israel* by them, to know whether they would hearken unto the commandments of the Lord, which He commanded their fathers by the hand of Moses.

This immediately makes one wonder whether Almighty God has now caused us, the people of Britain, to be living in a multi-faith, multi-religious, multi-cultural society for the same reason. It is a question we need to ask in the light of such Scriptures as this. Has God caused them to be there in order *to prove* Britain by them?

But what happened so far as the Nation of Israel was concerned? Judges Chapter 3 verse 6 tells you. "They took their daughters to be their wives, and gave their daughters to their sons, *and served their gods*". (My italicising.) In other words, they *unified* themselves and their nation with these other nations and with their gods by so doing.

And what was Almighty God's attitude to that, may I ask? Verse 7 tells us, "It was *evil* in the sight of the Lord." It says, "And the children of Israel did *evil* in the sight of the Lord, and forgot the Lord their God, and served Baalim and the groves". Furthermore Judges Chapter 2 verse 19 tells us that, "in following other gods to serve them", a nation which is under God such as Israel was, and such as Britain is, (or *has* been), has corrupted itself. And Judges Chapter 2 verse 17 tells us that "to go after other gods is to be guilty of whoredom — spiritual whoredom. It says "they went a whoring after other gods", and the Oxford Dictionary says that means spiritual prostitution.

And verse 8 of Judges Chapter 3 tells us that when the Nation of Israel unified themselves and their nation with these other nations, and with their gods — with this multi-faith, multi-religious, multi-cultural society, it brought the Judgment of God down upon them. It says, "Therefore the anger of the Lord was hot against Israel, and He sold them into the hand of the king of Mesopotamia for eight years. Mesopotamia is present day Iraq. So it was the equivalent of being sold into the hands of Saddam Hussein for eight years!

Britain! You need to be WARNED!

For the Nation of Israel, in fact, did, at that time, what the Archbishop of York says *we* should now do, "unify the nation, as we must do", he says, "by recognising that we live in an Ecumenical and multi-faith society".

And look what happened to Israel!

But it happened to Israel repeatedly, all through the time of the Judges, because they would persist in going in the same direction. And therefore they repeatedly came under God's Judgments.

I take by way of contrast, a second Scriptural Example. This time, the example of good king Asa, as recorded in The First Book of Kings Chapter 15 verses 11 to 23, and in The Second Book of Chronicles Chapter 14.

By the time he came to reign, the land of Judah and of Benjamin was full of the idols and images of strange religions. Altars to strange gods existed all over the place. Their abominable idols and images were in every town and city. They were everywhere.

In other words, this one Godly man, as king, inherited a multi-faith, multi-religious, multi-cult society. Furthermore, homosexuality was rife all over the land. Sodomites, in other words, abounded. They always do, in apostasy. So what did he do? Well the first thing that we read about him is, that *"he did that which was right in the eyes of the Lord"*. I Kings 15 verse 11. And as such he proceeded to remove all these abominable images and idols from wherever they existed. He ruthlessly broke down all the altars to strange gods that had been erected everywhere. He made a clean sweep of them all. His mother had made an idol in a grove near Jerusalem, and he went to it, and smashed it, cut it down, stamped upon it, and burned it in the brook Kidron. And he removed his mother from being queen, because she had made it and had set it up to worship before it. He took away and removed all the idols that his forebears had made. And he took away the sodomites out of the land and banished them. Thus he cleansed the land from all these offensive things, because he knew they were offensive to God and provoked Him to anger.

Now this was not to unify the nation and its religion with the various religions and faiths of these other gods with which he found himself surrounded! It was not to recognise the multi-faith, multi-religious, multi-cult society which he had inherited. Far from it. It was quite the opposite. And as the ONE Godly man, who as King, did that which was right in the sight of the Lord, he stands as an example for all those who follow.

"These things were our examples". I Corinthians 10 verse 6.

"All these things happened unto them for ensamples: and they are written for our admonition, upon whom the ends of the world have come". I Corinthians 10:11.

It should be seen by now that the Archbishop of York is not only completely out of line with Scripture by what he says; but that he is going completely against it, and against God.

Then take the Example of Elijah, in The First Book of Kings Chapter 18.

Under the evil and wicked King Ahab, and under Jezebel his wife, the land of Israel had become a land of Baal-worshippers. So much so, that we read that the prophets of Baal numbered no less than four hundred and fifty, and the prophets of the groves, four hundred, whilst Elijah, the prophet of God, said unto the people "I, even I only, remain a prophet of The Lord". I Kings 18 verses 19 to 22. Furthermore, the wicked woman Jezebel had suppressed the worship of the One True God by cutting off the prophets of The Lord". I Kings 18 verse 4. So Elijah was under the impression that he was the only prophet left. Added to which, all the altars of The Lord had been thrown down by Ahab and Jezebel as they were killing all the prophets of The Lord with the sword. So if ever a Man of God lived in a multi-faith, multi-religious society this man did!

But Elijah did not say, "The nation's religious make-up has now changed so dramatically that we must revise its Constitution so that it unifies the nation, as it must do, by recognising that we now live in a multi-faith, Baal-worshipping society".

Of course he didn't!

He did quite the opposite.

He gathered all the false prophets, and prophets of false religions together on the top of Mount Carmel in the presence of King Ahab, and he said in effect, "We will now prove who is The True and Only God".

"You call on the name of your gods, and I will call on the name of my God, and the God that answereth by fire, let him be God".

So they called on the name of Baal, their false god, from morning unto noon. They even cut themselves with knives and with lancets, until the blood gushed out upon them, crying out, "O Baal, hear us. O Baal, hear us". But there was no answer. No voice. They even leaped upon the altar which they had made. But it made no difference.

Then Elijah came near, and said, "Lord God of Abraham, Isaac, and of Israel, let it be known this day that thou art God in Israel, and that I am thy servant, and that I have done all these things at thy word. Hear me, O Lord, hear me, that this people may know that thou art the Lord God, and that thou hast turned their heart back again".

Then the fire of The Lord fell, and consumed the burnt sacrifice, and the wood, and the stones, and the dust, and licked up the water that was in the trench. And when all the people saw it, they fell on their faces: and they said, The Lord, He is the God: the Lord, He is the God''. I Kings 18 verses 24 to 39 (abbreviated).

Oh that we had a modern Elijah in Britain today to issue such a challenge to all these people of other faiths and religions that are around us, and to their leaders! And oh that we could see the same result happening! And why not? God is the same God who answers by Fire. Oh that in answer to a modern Elijah's cry we could see the Fire of God fall and turn our peoples' hearts back again from following a multi-faith, multi-cultural, and even New Age religion, to following The One, True, Only God! And why not? It happened to Israel *then*. Why cannot it happen to us? But I fear it would not be the Archbishop of York who turned out to be the modern Elijah who issued the challenge! It is reported that he has said he doesn't believe in a God who can listen to, and answer thousands of prayers that are coming to Him from all over the world at once''. He says, "God has not got that kind of computerised system in Heaven"! I don't see any of our Bishops doing it either! But it is high time *someone* was bold and courageous and fearless enough to issue such a direct challenge to all the other religions, cults and faiths that there are now in this Country, and indeed that are all over the world. I wonder who that somebody will be?

Then I take as a *fourth* Example, that of good King Hezekiah, as recording in the Book of the Prophet Isaiah Chapters 36 and 37. In his days the Assyrian Empire was expanding rapidly, and it had already taken the Northern Kingdom of Israel captive so that they ceased to be a nation on account of their going after other gods, and Assyria was beginning to encroach on Hezekiah's Southern Kingdom of Judah. Sennacherib, King of Assyria, himself named the various gods of this expanding Empire. They included the gods of Hamath; the gods of Arphad; the gods of Sepharvaim; the gods of Gozan; the gods of Haran; the gods of Rezeph; the gods of the children of Eden; the gods of Hena; the gods of Ivah; all of which countries Sennacherib had overrun and taken with his armies. Then there was Sennacherib's own god Nisroch. So King Hezekiah lived in a multi-faith world, and this fast-expanding Assyrian Empire was multi-faith, multi-religious and multi-cultural in every respect. And under its influence the religious make up of all these nations, including the Northern Kingdom of Israel and now the Southern Kingdom of Judah was changing dramatically.

But King Hezekiah did not say that because of this he had to take account of these changes and unify the nation by recognising that they now lived in a multi-faith, multi-religious and multi-cultural society and submit to Rabshakeh's, the King of Assyria's spokesman's pressure.

Rather, he made his bold and courageous stand. He prayed unto The Lord, saying, "O Lord of hosts, God of Israel, that dwellest between the cherubims, thou art the God, even thou *alone,* of all the kings of the earth; thou hast made heaven and earth. Incline thine ear, O Lord, and hear; open thine eyes, O Lord and see: and hear all the words of Sennacherib, which hath sent to reproach the living God . . . Now therefore, O Lord our God, save us from his hand, that all the kingdoms of the earth may know that thou art the Lord, even thou *ONLY!''* Isaiah Chapter 37 verses 15 to 20 (abbreviated).

King Hezekiah's stance, therefore, was completely opposite to that of the present Archbishop of York. It was God and God *ONLY* for him, not a unification with all these other faiths and religions. Furthermore, when he said in his prayer, "thou art the God of all the kingdoms of the earth, even thou *alone''*, he meant the God of all those nations which Sennacherib and his armies had overrun and taken, including all the other kingdoms of the earth. The present day advocates of multi-faith societies and nations would never dare to say that today!

It would be considered offensive to the various other faiths and religions to do that. But Hezekiah did it. He did it fearlessly and boldly and unequivocably. And God vindicated him and his prayer. Because that night God caused the angel of the Lord to go forth. *One* angel! And phut! One hundred and eighty-five thousand, — (the whole of the Assyrian army) — perished, because that one angel smote them all. And when Hezekiah's people arose early in the morning, behold, they were all dead corpses. Isaiah Chapter 37 verse 36.

Oh that we had such fearless, bold, courageous, totally uncompromising Monarchs, Archbishops, Bishops, Leaders of Churches, Leaders of the Nation, and Leaders of men, today!

But of all these examples that I have quoted, the Supreme Example is that of good King Josiah, the young King of Judah.

To understand the significance of his outstanding example it is necessary to know the background against which he acted.

His great-grandfather, the good King Hezekiah, had brought about a remarkable religious reformation. We read in The Second Book of Kings Chapter 18 verse 3 that Hezekiah did that which was right in the sight of The Lord; and in verse 5 of that chapter, that he trusted in the Lord God of Israel; so that after him was none like him among all the kings of Judah, nor any that were before him. For he clave to the Lord, and departed not from following Him, but kept his commandments, which the Lord commanded Moses". And so verse 7 of that chapter says, "And the Lord was with him; and he prospered whithersoever he went forth". And no wonder!

But in the process of bringing about this outstanding spiritual and religious reformation Hezekiah had taken drastic action to remove all the other faiths and religions out of the land. We read in The Second Book of Chronicles Chapter 31 verse 1 that under his dynamic spiritual leadership all Israel went out to the cities of Judah and broke the images of all the other religions and faiths in pieces, threw down all the altars which had been erected to all the foreign faiths and religions, and cut down the groves, and threw down the high places where they were worshipped until they had utterly destroyed them all. In other words, King Hezekiah purged his land completely of all other gods, religions and faiths. He made a clean sweep of them all. He did not say, by any means, "We must unify our nation with this multi-faith society which has come into being". Quite the opposite. He thrust all these other faiths and religions, with all their false gods, away from him, and utterly destroyed them all.

But his son Manasseh, King Josiah's grandfather, brought them all back again. We read in The Second Book of Kings Chapter 21 that he built again the high places which Hezekiah his father had destroyed. He reared up altars to the foreign god Baal. He even built altars to foreign religions and faiths in the House of The Lord, The Temple, at Jerusalem, and thus desecrated and defiled the Temple. And we have been doing something comparable, by introducing multi-faith and multi-religious services in the House of God at Westminster Abbey, and in our Cathedrals and Churches all over the land. For to hold multi-faith and multi-religious services in Westminster Abbey, in our Cathedrals, and in our Churches, is to do something very similar to what King Manasseh did. And furthermore, it is to desecrate and pollute The House of God, and The Houses of God in the land.

82

We read that Manasseh built altars for all the host of heaven also, in the two courts of the House of The Lord. This was further desecration. He also set a graven image that he had made in the House of The Lord, which is the equivalent of putting an image of Buddha or of a Hindu god there, and is desecrating the House of The Lord even further, thus provoking the Lord to anger. We read that he dealt with familiar spirits, which is to indulge in spiritism and seances which The Lord, in Scripture, strongly forbids. He also used enchantments and wizardry.

And concerning all this, the Scripture says that Manasseh did that which was *evil* in the sight of The Lord, like unto the abominations of the heathen, — (the worshippers of other gods, faiths, and religions) — whom the Lord had cast out before the children of Israel. In other words, he unified his nation and his people with them, and with all their gods and religions.

In fact, it says in 2 Kings Chapter 21 that Manasseh seduced his people to do *more evil* than did the nations whom the Lord destroyed before the children of Israel. And there was a terrible consequence to all this. God said Nemesis would strike, because under Manasseh's evil and wicked leadership his nation had passed the point of no return. So we read, The Lord spake by His servants the prophets saying:-

"*BECAUSE* Manasseh King of Judah hath done these abominations, and hath done wickedly above all that the Amorites did, which were before him, and hath made Judah *also* to sin with his idols: *THEREFORE* thus saith the Lord God of Israel, "Behold, I am bringing such evil — (such calamity) — upon Jerusalem and Judah, that whosoever heareth of it, both his ears shall tingle ... I will wipe Jerusalem as with a dish — wiping it, and turning it upside down. And I will forsake the remnant of mine inheritance, and deliver them into the hand of their enemies ... *BECAUSE* they have done that which is *evil* in My sight, and have provoked me to anger".

So The Judgment of God had now been pronounced on the Southern Kingdom of Judah and nothing could now turn it back. It was irrevocable.

All that, therefore, is the background to the Supreme Example which I now quote of good King Josiah.

The *first* thing that we read about him is, that at the age of 16, (when he was still a teenager) — while he was yet young, he began to seek after the God of David his fore-father.

The *next* thing we read is, that "he did that which was right in the sight of the Lord". II Kings 22 verse 2. And he did that, despite the fact that he came into a generation which was the most wicked since the Flood, because Manasseh, his grandfather, had been the most wicked king in the whole history of Israel.

Then the *next* thing that we read is, that the Book of The Law was found in the House of the Lord by Hilkiah the high priest. And when this was read before the king, by Shaphan the scribe, it revealed the perilous position which his nation was in. For when young King Josiah heard the words of the Book of The Law, he was filled with consternation, he was terrified, he trembled, he rent his clothes, he was terror-stricken. He said, in effect, "If what you are reading from that Book is true, we are already under Judgment, for great is the wrath of the Lord that is kindled against us, *BECAUSE* our fathers have not hearkened and done according unto the words of this Book which is written concerning us". And in utter desperation he wrung his hands, and said to Shaphan and Hilkiah, "It is too late! Judgment is already on the way. It has already been pronounced. What shall we do?" Then he said, "Go quickly to Huldah the prophetess, and ask her if there is any message from The Lord. Ask her if it is too late".

And the message that came back was, "Judgment is at the door. Judgment is coming. Judgment is on the way. Thus saith the Lord God of Israel, Thus said The Lord, "Behold, I will bring evil — (calamity) — upon this place, and upon the inhabitants thereof, even all the words of this Book which the King of Judah hath read *BECAUSE* they have forsaken me, and have burned incense unto *other gods,* that they might provoke me to anger with all the works of their hands. *THEREFORE* my wrath shall be kindled against this place, and shall not be quenched . . . They shall become a desolation and a curse".

So God's Divine Judgment was therefore being clearly repeated. Nemesis was soon to strike.

But what kind of National Situation was it that King Josiah found himself involved in, and surrounded with, at this time? Well Manasseh his grandfather had erected altars to other gods, deities and religions all over the place. So all these were there. The temple to Chemos was still there. The Ashtoroth temple was there. The Milcom Centre was there. The Zidonite temple was there. Manasseh had brought altars for other religions and faiths right into the courts of the House of the Lord, the Temple, which is the equivalent to desecrating Westminster Abbey and our Cathedrals with multi-faith services. And these altars to other faiths, religions and their deities were still there. They were even right inside the Holy of Holies in the Temple, in the Holy Place, and in the Outer Court. Everywhere, Manasseh had set up false deities, and they were still there. He had set up a god in the valley of Hinnom, and had incinerated his own son at its false altar. And that god was still there.

Then the sodomites, the homosexuals and lesbians, had taken over the Country, and were flaunting their sins everywhere. They had homosexual temples, homosexual churches, there were homosexual prostitutes up and down the streets. In fact, male and female prostitution was rampant all over the land. And every nation on earth had their false deity temples, shrines and places of worship up and down the streets of Jerusalem and in all other towns and cities. There were shrines and temples to every god. And they were all still there.

So the nation's religious make-up had not only changed dramatically during the fifty seven years of Manasseh's reign, and during that of his wicked son Amon. It had changed exceedingly dramatically. So what was young King Josiah's reaction? After all, he was only 20 by now.

Well he did *not* say, as the Archbishop of York has said, "Because the religious make-up of the nation has changed so dramatically during this last fifty-seven years we must recognise that we now live in a multi-faith society, take account of all these changes, and unify the country, as we must do, on that basis".

Far from it.

He did quite the opposite.

Suddenly there is this man, a monarch, a sovereign, only 20 years old, in what was the equivalent of Buckingham Palace, who has a heart for God. Hearing what the Book of The Law said he gathered his priests, his elders, his nobles, his ministers and his people together, and he delivered to them the Word of God as he had heard it. In other words, he laid the Word of God down, saying "Thus saith The Lord". That was the first thing that he did. And that is the first thing that has to happen today. And it has to be done fearlessly, and totally uncompromisingly, and "straight down the line".

Young King Josiah knew that once God had pronounced that He intended to visit his Nation with Judgment, God would not change the Judgment.

He, next, as Monarch and Sovereign, sent for Hilkiah the high priest, his equivalent of the Archbishop of Canterbury, and commanded him to bring forth out of The Temple of the Lord, (the House of God,) everything that related to, or had anything to do with, foreign gods, other faiths and religions. And he commanded them to be burned outside Jerusalem, and the ashes of them to be carried to the North of the Country, even to Bethel, and there to scatter them.

This was a far cry from "recognising the religious changes that had taken place, and that they now lived in an ecumenical and multi-religious society". It was a far cry also from saying that, "because the religious make-up of the country had changed so dramatically they needed now to unify the nation by recognising these other faiths and religions, with their gods and different forms of worship".

No. The House of God in the Capital, The Temple, the equivalent of Westminster Abbey, was seen by the sovereign, the young King Josiah, to have been defiled, polluted, and desecrated by them, so he commanded his High Priest, the equivalent of his Archbishop, to sweep them all away. In other words, the monarch cleansed the Temple. And he did it drastically.

We read, in the Second Book of Kings Chapter 23 verse 4, that "the king commanded Hilkiah the high priest, and the priests of the second order (the equivalent of the Bishops) and the keepers of the door, (the equivalent of the vergers) to bring forth out of the Temple of The Lord, all the vessels that were made for Baal (the foreign god), and for the grove, and for all the host of heaven. And he burned them without Jerusalem (outside of Jerusalem) in the fields of Kidron, and carried the ashes of them unto Bethel". Notice it was the Monarch, the Sovereign, who did this!

Then we read in verses 5 and 6, "And he put down the idolatrous priests, whom the kings of Judah had ordained to burn incense in the high places (to other gods) in the cities of Judah, and in the places round about Jerusalem". He sacked them, in other words! "them also that burned incense to Baal, to the sun, and to the moon, and to the planets, and to all the host of heaven. And he brought out the grove from the House of The Lord, without Jerusalem (outside of Jerusalem) into the brook Kidron, and burned it at the brook Kidron, and stamped it to small powder, and cast the powder thereof upon the graves of the children of the people".

Such was the zeal for The Lord of this young Sovereign that he made a clean sweep of them all, right out of The Temple. He knew full well that they should not be there. It seems that the Cleansing of The Temple by the Lord Jesus, at a later stage, was nothing compared with what this godly and God-fearing young Monarch did! And I say that with absolute reverence.

Then in the *third* place he turned his attention to the Country itself, with temples and places of worship to false gods and religions all over the place. And he said in effect, "O God. Judgment may be coming. But these temples are not going to be standing there when Judgment comes".

The Temples to Chemosh, to Ashtoreth, to Milcom and to many others were all there with all their idols and images, all over the nation. So young King Josiah gathered his wrecking crews, with their mattocks together, and he went out in his chariot with them, and he pointed to the Temple of Chemosh and he commanded, "Hack it down". And they hacked it to pieces with their mattocks. Then he drove with them to where the Ashtoreth Temple stood, and he commanded saying, "Tear it down". And they tore it down. Then he drove on, in his chariot, to where the Temple of Milcom stood, and he commanded them saying, "Bring it down. Stone by stone, brick by brick, bring it down". And they razed it to the ground with their mattocks. And so he did to all the foreign temples and places of worship to false faiths and religions, everywhere. He swept the land of them. Then he sent out troops all through the land to tear down the idols and images that stood everywhere to false gods. And he said, "Grind them to powder". And they ground them to powder. For we read in the Second Book of Chronicles Chapter 34 from verse 3 onwards, "And in the twelfth year (of his reign) he began to purge Judah and Jerusalem from the high places, and the groves, and the carved images, and the molten images. And they broke down the altars of Baalim in his presence; and the images, that were on high above them, he cut down; and the groves, and the carved images, and the molten images, he broke in pieces, and made dust of them, (pulverised them, that is), and strewed the dust upon the graves of them that had sacrificed unto them. . . . And so he did in the cities of Manasseh, and Ephraim, and Simeon, even unto Napthali, with their mattocks round about. And when he had broken down the altars and groves, and had beaten the graven images into powder, and cut down all the idols throughout the land of Israel, he returned to Jerusalem.

Then he said in effect, "This homosexual thing, this lesbian thing, all this sodomy, has gone on enough". So he went through the land imprisoning all of them who would not repent, those who would not turn from this evil and wicked way. He destroyed the houses of prostitution that had been set up for both male and female, (gay and heterosexual). He destroyed the equivalent of all the gay bars and the brothels. He destroyed all of them. He wiped it all out. You can read all the details in 2 Kings Chapter 23, and 2 Chronicles Chapter 34.

Then he put away all the witches, the wizards, the workers with familiar spirits — (meaning the spiritists), the mediums, those who engaged in seances, all who were involved with the occult, the satanists and Satan-worshippers, — the fortune-tellers, the purveyors of horoscopes. He sent out spies to find them.

All these, this Godly King Josiah put away. He made a clean sweep of them all. And he put them all away, swept the land completely of them, for two reasons. *First* because he said, "Great is the wrath of The Lord that is poured out upon us, *BECAUSE* our fathers have not kept the WORD OF THE LORD, to do after all that is written in the Book which we have found". And *secondly,* "BECAUSE Huldah the prophetess had said, "Thus saith The Lord God. "Behold I will bring evil (calamity) upon this place, and upon the inhabitants thereof, even all the curses that are written in the Book which they have read before the King of Judah. *BECAUSE* they have forsaken Me, and have burned incense unto *other gods,* that they might provoke Me to anger with all the works of their hands: *THEREFORE* My Wrath shall be poured out upon this place, *and shall not be quenched*". II Chronicles Chapter 34 verses 23 to 25.

King Josiah drastically put all these offensive and wicked things away therefore. He swept the land of them, because he knew that all of them had made The Most High God exceedingly angry, and that He had already pronounced Nemesis on his Nation, and that that Nemesis was already on the way.

He knew this, also, because, when that newly discovered Book of The Law had been read out loud to him by Shaphan the scribe, he had heard that God had said in that Book, "Take heed unto yourselves lest ye forget the covenant of the Lord your God, which He made with you, and make you a graven image, or the likeness of any thing, which the Lord thy God hath forbidden thee. For the Lord thy God *is a consuming fire*, even a *jealous* God. When thou shalt beget children, and children's children, (which means several generations of children), and ye shall have remained long in the land (which would have meant even up to the time of King Josiah, in King Josiah's case) — and shall corrupt yourselves, and make a graven image or the likeness of anything, and shall do evil in the sight of the Lord thy God, to provoke Him to anger, (which they had, indeed, done by now), I call heaven and earth to witness against you this day, that *ye shall soon utterly perish* from off the land . . . ye shall not prolong your days upon it, but *shall utterly be destroyed''*. Deuteronomy Chapter 4 verses 23 to 26.

King Josiah had heard that God had pronounced Nemesis against this kind of thing, therefore.

He had also heard from that Book of The Law which had been read out loud to him, "Ye shall not go after *other* gods, *of the gods of the people which are round about you*" (which is exactly what the Archbishop of York has been saying that we, in Britain, *should* do, when he says we should unify with them in order to unify our nation and its society). "For the Lord thy God is a jealous God among you, lest the anger of The Lord thy God be kindled against thee, and *destroy thee from off the face of the earth*". Deuteronomy Chapter 6 verses 14 to 15.

So he had heard Nemesis being pronounced against that kind of thing a *second* time.

But then he had heard it read out loud to him yet again from the Book of The Law, that God has said, concerning the peoples of the other nations and their other religions and faiths with which they would find themselves surrounded, "Thou shalt make no covenant with them . . . for they will turn you away from following Me, that they may serve *other* gods; so will the anger of the Lord be kindled against you, *and destroy you suddenly*". Deuteronomy Chapter 7 verses 2 to 4 (abbreviated).

So he had heard God pronounce the warning of Nemesis against affiliation with other faiths and religions yet a *third* time.

But then, even yet again, he had heard it read out loud to him from that self-same Book of The Law, that God had said, "And it shall be, if thou do at all forget the Lord thy God, and walk after *other* gods — (other faiths and religions that means) — and serve them, and worship them — (in terms of being associated with them in multi-faith forms of worship), I testify against you this day *that ye shall surely perish*. As the nations which the Lord destroyed before your face, *so shall you perish: BECAUSE* ye would not be obedient unto the voice of the Lord your God". Deuteronomy Chapter 8 verses 19 to 20.

So a *fourth* time he had heard God Almighty pronouncing a very stern warning, that His Nemesis was bound to fall upon them, as a Nation, if they thus identified themselves with the other faiths, religions and gods which were around them.

But then even a *fifth* time he had heard it read out aloud to him from

89

that Book of the Law, that God had said, "Take heed to yourselves, that your heart be not deceived, and ye turn aside, and serve *other* gods, and worship them; and then the Lord's wrath be kindled against you . . . and *lest ye perish quickly* from off the good land which the Lord giveth you". Deuteronomy Chapter 11 verses 16 to 17 (abbreviated).

So for a *fifth* time he had heard God warn of this Nemesis which He was pronouncing.

But there was at least a *sixth* time that he heard it read out to him from that Book of The Law, that God had said, "If thine heart turn away, so that thou wilt not hear, but shall be drawn away, and worship other gods, and serve them — (be unified with them that is) I denounce unto you this day, *that ye shall surely perish* and that ye shall not prolong your days upon the land . . .". Deuteronomy Chapter 30 verses 17 to 18.

So for at least the *sixth* time he had heard the Voice of God pronouncing and proclaiming that there would be inevitable Nemesis. But not only that, he had heard God state very clearly exactly what that Nemesis would be. It would be that they would surely perish; *that they would cease to be a Nation*. And that filled him with consternation. He was terrified. He was petrified. He trembled! He rent his clothes. He wrung his hands in anguish. And because he saw the inevitable fate which was coming upon his Nation, in terms of the Judgment of God which God had already pronounced upon his land, he swept it clean of all that was offensive, abhorrent, and wicked in the sight of that Holy and Almighty God. And at the end of the account of that clean sweep that he had made, we read, "There was no one like this king, no king before him who had turned to the Lord with all his heart, with all his soul, and with all his might, neither after him arose any king like him". (See The Second Book of Kings Chapter 23 verse 25.)

Oh that we had monarchs, Archbishops, Bishops, Prime Ministers, Cabinets, Peers of the Realm, Members of Parliament, Leaders of Churches, and Leaders everywhere in the Nation whose hearts were as much on fire for God as his was, today! What would it be like in our Nation if our Government became so set on fire for God that they made laws to sweep everything which is offensive and wicked in the sight of Almighty God completely away, as young King Josiah did. Such laws, without question, could certainly be given the Royal Assent, and by our gracious Sovereign personally! God raised up good and Godly King Josiah *then*. God could raise up a similar National Leader today. The Bible and history have shown that God always raises up such men, and such voices, in a Land before Judgment comes.

But it is a very solemn and sobering thought to remember, that despite all that good King Josiah had done, despite the clean sweep which he had made, the Judgment which God had already pronounced upon his Nation in wicked King Manasseh's day, was still on the way. King Josiah was able to delay that Judgment for a number of years, yes. But he wasn't able to change the Judgment. Because at the end of the full, Scriptural Record of the courageous, bold, and most fearless stand that he had made for God in his land we read the awful word, "NOTWITHSTANDING".

"NOTWITHSTANDING", — (IN SPITE OF ALL THIS, that means), the Lord turned not from the fierceness of His great wrath, wherewith his anger was kindled against Judah, because of all the provocations that Manasseh had provoked him withal. And The Lord said, "I will remove Judah also out of My sight, as I have removed Israel (the Northern Kingdom) out of My sight, and will cast off this city Jerusalem which I have chosen, and the house (The Temple) of which I said, "My Name shall be there". II Kings Chapter 23 verses 26 and 27.

That meant the Southern Kingdom of Judah would cease to be a Nation, as the Northern Kingdom of Israel had ceased to be a Nation.

And it happened. It happened exactly as God had said it would.

Because as soon as King Josiah died, wickedness broke out like a flame once again. His son Jehoiakim came to the throne. He had grown up in the Spiritual Reformation and Time of National Cleansing that his fearless father had brought about. "He was twenty-five years old when he began to reign". II Kings 23 verse 36. So he had seen it all. Yet we read, "He did that which was *evil* in the sight of The Lord". II Kings 23 verse 37. And as soon as his father had died, as soon as his voice of thunder had gone, he and his people turned back to their sins. It was even he, King Jehoiakim, who, if you please, cut up the Prophet Jeremiah's Scroll of Prophecies which warned of the inevitable Judgment which was coming, and threw them all, piece by piece, into the fire. Today they just throw such writings into the waste-paper basket! A Peer of the Realm does!

And then the Judgment fell.

The Bible says, "The Lord sent against him and against his nation Judah, armies to destroy it". See II Kings 24 verses 1 and 2. It says He did this, "according to the Word of The Lord, which he spake by His servants the prophets".

Then it says in II Kings 24 verses 3 to 4:-

"Surely *at the Commandment of the Lord* came this upon Judah, *to remove them out of His sight,* for the sins of Manasseh, according to all that he did; and *also for the innocent blood that he shed: for he filled Jerusalem with innocent blood: which the Lord would not pardon". I repeat, "which the Lord would not pardon".*

So Nemesis had now struck.

And they ceased to be a Nation, as God had said they would.

And let us never forget that the Word of God says, "Now all these things happened unto *them* for ensamples: and they are written for our admonition, upon whom the ends of the world are come". I Corinthians 10 verse 11. Which goes on to say, in verse 12, "Wherefore let him that thinketh he standeth take heed lest he fall".

So what is that admonition saying to us today?

It is, that the Judgment of God is irretrievable.

It is irreversible for a people who persistently, wilfully, and deliberately go after other gods and religions and faiths, and identify themselves with them in worship, as first, the Northern Kingdom of Israel did, and then as secondly, the Southern Kingdom of Judah did a few years later on.

For we need to realise what the enormity of doing such a thing really is.

I have already pointed out from the Scriptures on a previous page, that to depart from the Lord, the One and Only True and Living God, is to corrupt ourselves. But now let us turn to the Books of the Prophets — where we find it is also to commit great whoredoms, — spiritual whoredoms. Hosea Chapter 1 verse 2 says, for instance, "the land hath committed great whoredoms in departing from the Lord". And Hosea Chapter 4 verse 12 says, "for the *spirit* of whoredoms hath caused them to err, and they have gone a whoring from under their God". So it is a *spirit* at work, an *evil* spirit, luring and drawing people away from The One True God. Hosea Chapter 5, verses 3 and 4 says something similar:- "O Ephraim — (the name for the Northern Kingdom of Israel) — thou committest whoredom, and Israel is defiled. They will not frame their doings to turn unto their God: for the *spirit* of whoredoms is in the midst of them, and they have not known the Lord" (my italicising). Again it says it is a *spirit* at work, an *evil* and alluring spirit, drawing the nation away from The True God, in favour of an amalgamation with other faiths and religions.

Then II Chronicles Chapter 21 verses 10 and 11 make it plain that to forsake The Lord and to go after *other* gods, faiths, and religions, is to commit spiritual fornication. It says of Jehoram, King of Judah, "He had forsaken the Lord God of his fathers. Moreover he had made high places in the mountains of Judah, and caused the inhabitants of Jerusalem *to commit fornication,* and *compelled* Judah thereto". (My italicising.)

Jeremiah Chapter 2 verse 20 says it is to play the harlot. It quotes the land of Israel as saying "for of old time I have broken thy yoke, and burst thy bands: and thou saidst, "I will not transgress; when upon every high hill and under every green tree thou wanderest, playing the harlot". Playing the harlot *spiritually* that means, with other gods and faiths.

Jeremiah Chapter 3 verse 2 says that to do such a thing is to pollute the land. It says, "thou hast polluted the land with thy whoredoms and with thy wickedness".

Ezekiel Chapter 36 verses 17 to 18 says, it is to defile the land. It says, "Son of man, when the house of Israel dwelt in their own land, they *defiled* it (my italicising) by their own way and by their doings: their way was before Me as the uncleanness of a removed woman. Wherefore I poured my fury upon them for the blood that they had shed upon the Land, *and for their idols* wherewith they had polluted it". (My italicising.)

Jeremiah Chapter 3 verse 8 says that to do such a thing is to commit spiritual adultery. God is saying in that verse, and in the verses immediately following it, "And I saw, when for all the causes whereby backsliding Israel *committed adultery* (my italicising) I had put her away, and given her a bill of divorcement; yet her treacherous sister Judah feared not, but went and played the harlot also. And it came to pass through the lightness of her whoredom, that she defiled the Land, and *committed adultery* (my italicising) with stones and stocks". Meaning with altars raised to false gods. Jeremiah 3 verses 8 to 9.

So according to verse 8 of this chapter, to go after other gods, faiths, and religions, is to be treacherous to God also, as well as to be guilty of committing spiritual adultery., Jeremiah Chapter 32 verse 34 says, that to bring anything to do with other gods and religions into the House of The Lord is to set abominations there. God says in that verse, concerning the children of Israel and the children of Judah, "They set their abominations in the House, which is called by My Name, to defile it".

Ezekiel Chapter 11 verse 18 refers to such things as, "detestable things" and as, "abominations". And Ezekiel Chapter 20 says, several times over, that for people who are under God, as the people of Israel were, to identify themselves with, and go after the idols of other gods and faiths is to defile *themselves* and to pollute *themselves*. It is not only to defile the Land in which they live, and to pollute that Land.

Ezekiel Chapter 20 says, several times over also, that for such a people who have known God to go after the idols and religions of other nations is to rebel against God Almighty. It is open rebellion. God says, for instance, concerning Israel to whom He had made Himself known in the land of Egypt. "Then said I unto them, Cast ye away every man the abominations of his eyes, and defile not yourselves with the idols of Egypt: I am the Lord your God."

"But they *rebelled* against Me, (my italicising) and would not hearken unto Me; they did not every man cast away the abominations of their eyes, neither did they forsake the idols of Egypt: then I said, I will pour out My fury upon them . . . ." Ezekiel Chapter 20 verses 7 and 8.

God even says in the same Chapter, that to go after these other gods is to *blaspheme* God. He says in verses 27 and 28, "Therefore, son of man, speak unto the house of Israel, and say unto them, 'Thus saith the Lord God: Yet in this your fathers have *blasphemed Me,* (my italicising) in that they have committed a trespass against Me. For when I had brought them unto the Land, for which I lifted up Mine hand to give it to them, then they saw every high hill, and all the thick trees, and they offered there their sacrifices, and there they presented the provocation of their offering; there also they made their sweet savour, and poured out there their drink offerings".

And to make it clear what this involved, He goes on to say, in verse 31, "Ye pollute yourselves with all your idols, even unto this day". And in verse 32, "Ye say, "We will be as the heathen". That means , "we will be identified with them, as the families of the countries, to serve wood and stone".

Then in verse 9 of Ezekiel Chapter 20, God says that to do such a thing is to pollute His Name. He says in that verse, "But I wrought for My Name's sake, that it should not be polluted among the heathen, among whom they were, in whose sight I made Myself known unto them, in bringing them forth out of the Land of Egypt".

And in Ezekiel Chapter 22 verse 8 it says, it is to despise God's Holy Things. It says, "Thou hast despised Mine Holy Things" which meant, according to verses 3 and 4, having idols to other gods and faiths where the worship of The One True God Only should have been taking place. And to despise God's Holy Things today would include His Holy Word, The Bible; His Ten Commandments which forbid the worship of other gods; the Pure Gospel of Salvation by Faith in The Lord Jesus Christ alone; and His Body of Born-Again, Bible-Believing People, which is His Church.

And to cause people to go after other faiths and religions and to become identified with them, and to be unified with them, is most certainly to commit the Sin of Jeroboam the son of Nebat, and thus cause the Nation's people to sin.

All this shows the Enormity of the gross sin and wickedness in doing such things. Furthermore the opening verses of Ezekiel Chapter 22 show that a city, a Capital, as well as a Nation and an individual, can defile itself in this way. Speaking of Jerusalem at that time, the Lord God said to Ezekiel, "The city . . . maketh idols against herself to *defile* herself", verse 3. And again in verse 4:- "Thou . . . hast *defiled* thyself in thine idols which thou hast made".

Then in Ezekiel Chapter 6, God's terrible Judgment is pronounced on all the idols and images of the other religions and faiths which Israel, which was a nation committed to the worship of the One True God, had persistently gone after. It says from verse 3 onwards, "Thus saith the Lord God . . . 'Behold I, even I, will bring a sword upon you, and I will destroy your high places — (which were devoted to other religions and faiths). And your altars shall be desolate, and your images shall be broken: and I will cast down your slain men before your idols. And I will lay the dead carcases of the children of Israel before their idols: and I will scatter your bones round about your altars. In all your dwelling places the cities shall be laid waste, and the high places shall be desolate: that your altars may be laid waste and made desolate, and your idols may be broken and cease, and your images may be cut down, and your works shall be abolished. And the slain shall fall in the midst of you, and ye shall know that I am the Lord". Ezekiel Chapter 6 verses 3 to 7.

This is the language of God, bringing in an invading enemy army into the Land and using it as His Instrument to utterly destroy and make a clean sweep of all these images, and idols, and places of worship, which Israel had erected all over its land to these other faiths and religions. All this, too, that God said to Ezekiel, was about to come to pass, was clearly to be a manifestation of the fury, the wrath, the anger, of an Almighty and jealous God being visited upon all those other gods and their altars, high places and images.

So how can an Archbishop possibly say that because the religious make-up of our Country has changed so dramatically, the time has come when we need to be unified with all the other faiths and religions of the world? The religious make-up of the Nation of Israel had changed exceedingly dramatically by the Prophet Ezekiel's day, and this was God's attitude to that dramatic change *then*. Is His attitude likely to be any different today? Verse 9 of Ezekiel Chapter 6 tells us clearly, exactly why this dramatic change had taken place in his Nation at that time. It says it was because the people's whorish hearts had departed from God, and because their eyes had gone a whoring after these other nations' faiths and religions, and as a result, they had committed all kinds of abominations with them. So God had pronounced this devastating Judgment upon them and upon all the foreign gods and idols which they were now going after.

We need to take heed lest a similar devastating Judgment of God fall upon us.

God said to the Nation of Israel in the Prophet Ezekiel's day, "Thus saith the Lord God: *"REPENT,* and turn yourselves from your idols; and turn away your faces from all your abominations". Ezekiel Chapter 14 verse 6.

So unification is not the way ahead. Not according to the whole body of the teaching of Scripture. Turning away from all foreign religions and faiths is! Repenting of going after them, is! It is an unanswerable case according to the whole weight of Scriptural teaching.

Then concerning an individual who goes after other gods, and influences others to go in the same direction, who therefore is a false prophet, God says this in Ezekiel Chapter 14:-

"Therefore speak unto them, and say unto them, Thus saith The Lord God; Every man of the house of Israel that setteth up his idols in his heart, and putteth the stumblingblock of his iniquity before his face, and cometh to the prophet: I the Lord will answer him that cometh according to the multitude of his idols; that I may take the house of Israel in their own heart,

96

because they are all estranged from Me through their idols: — (which is the effect of going after other faiths and religions. It estrangeth them from The One True God). — "For every one of the house of Israel, ... which *separateth himself from Me* (my italicising) and setteth up his idols in his heart and putteth the stumblingblock of his iniquity before his face, and cometh to a prophet to inquire of him concerning me, I the Lord will answer him by Myself. *And I will set My face against that man,* and will make him a sign and a proverb, and I will cut him off from the midst of My people and ye shall know that I am the Lord". Ezekiel 14 verses 4 to 8.

So that tells us quite clearly how God Himself regards going after idols, and after that which represents other religions and faiths. He sets His face against any man who perpetrates it. And that is what He does with an Archbishop who says we should go down the road of unification with the other religions and faiths. God says I will set My face against that man. I would not be in the Archbishop's shoes for anything!

And God even says, "And if the prophet be deceived when he hath spoken a thing, *I the Lord have deceived that prophet*". (My italicising.) We need to take careful note of what God says here. *Then* He says, "And I will stretch out My Hand upon him, and will destroy him from the midst of My people Israel". Ezekiel 14 verse 9.

And He goes on to say, "And they, (My people Israel) shall bear the punishment of their iniquity: the punishment of the prophet (false prophet) shall be even as the punishment of him that seeketh unto him: that the house of Israel may go no more astray from Me, neither be polluted any more with all their transgressions: but that they may be My people, and I may be their God, saith the Lord God". Ezekiel 14 verses 10 and 11.

In any case, concerning all the other faiths, religions, and cults, with their gods and objects of worship, God Himself says in Jeremiah Chapter 10 verses 10 and 11: "The Lord is the true God, He is the living God ... Thus shall ye say unto them, 'The gods that have not made the heavens and the earth, even they shall perish from the earth, and from under these heavens". That means they will be no more. Not so much as one of them! They will all be done away. So much, therefore, for the statement being made by so many today that all roads lead to Heaven, and that all the faiths and religions of the world lead to the same God.

That is not what God says.

He says the exact opposite. He says in the end there will be none of them left.

He says they all will be done away, without exception, leaving only one Faith remaining. And that one Faith remaining will be that which worships the True God, the Living God, and Jesus Christ Our Lord. Concerning all the others God Himself says, in Jeremiah 10 verse 15, "they are vanity, and the work of errors: in the time of their visitation they shall perish". And by "visitation" it means visitation in Judgment. This has happened all down the history of the human race. God judged the gods of ancient Egypt at the time of Moses when He brought Israel out of Egypt by terrible judgments, and those gods of Egypt were destroyed. So were the Assyrian gods similarly destroyed; so were the gods of Ancient Greece, so were the gods of Ancient Rome and its Empire. And so will the various gods of today likewise perish. God Himself says they will. "They shall perish from the earth, and from under these heavens". So however can anyone, let alone an Archbishop, want to be unified with them?

That therefore is the Old Testament case against any such practice. And it is utterly irrefutable.

But when we come to the New Testament case, and to the history of The True Christian Church ever after then, the same is seen to be true. Take the case of Paul the Apostle on Mars Hill in Acts Chapter 17 for instance. We read in verse 16 that while he was waiting for Silas and Timothy at Athens, his spirit was stirred within him, when he saw the city *wholly given to idolatry*. (My italicising). In other words, they were wholly given in their devotions to the worship of other gods, faiths and religions. Athens was a Greek city, and at that time, in Greece, a multitude of gods were worshipped. There was Poseidon, there was Hermes, and deities such as Pan. There was Demeter the earth goddess of harvest and corn. There was Ares the god of war, Hestia the goddess of the hearth, Dionysus the god of wine, Appollo the sun god, Zeus and Hera the guardians of marriage, Aphrodite the goddess of love, and Asciepius the god of medicine. The Greeks also worshipped Athene the goddess of wisdom. And they all had magnificent temples and sanctuaries dedicated to them, all over Ancient Greece. There were so many of these gods and goddesses that when the Apostle Paul arrived in Athens and saw all their various heathen altars, temples and shrines, he was deeply disturbed in his spirit because the city was completely and wholly given over to this idolatry. And the Scriptures called it idolatry. They did not describe it as "other ways to heaven and to God!" Now when the Apostle Paul saw all this, did he say, "The way forward is to unify my Christian Message with all these other faiths, gods, and religions?" Of course he didn't. He kept it distinct from them, and preserved its uniqueness. Furthermore, he said in effect, "The God whom I worship is The One, True, Living God, the One who you call "The Unknown God". He is the One that made the World and everything in it. He is the One, too, who has made of one blood all nations of men for to dwell on the face of the earth and has determined the times before appointed, and the bounds of their habitation in order that they should seek after *Him*, the Lord, if haply they might feel after Him, and find Him".

Then looking at all these altars and shrines to the other faiths and religions which existed at that time, all of which represented sheer idolatry, he said in effect, "God has winked at all this idolatry which you ignorantly engage in, up till now. But no longer. No longer does He wink at it now, or pass it over. But now rather, God commands all men everywhere to repent of it. That means to turn from it. To put it away. Because He has appointed a day in which He will judge the World in righteousness by that man whom He hath ordained: — (meaning by His Son, The Lord Jesus Christ) — whereof He has given assurance unto all men, in that He has raised Him from the dead".

So, far from being a Message of Unification with these other faiths and religions, it was a call to repent and be separated from them, and to become worshippers of this One True Living God and of His Son, Jesus Christ Our Lord. Today, he would have been accused of proselytising, of targeting other faiths!

Then moving on from the pages of New Testament history, into the history of the later Christian Church to the time of the Emperor Constantine. Now whatever may be said of Constantine, head of a Roman Empire that was full of such practices as the worshipping of the sky god Jupiter, of Venus the goddess of love, of Mars the god of war, of Mithras the bull-slayer, and of Cybele the Asiatic mother goddess, — when, in A.D. 330, he brought the world's first Christian Empire into being, and declared that Christianity and the Christian Faith was to be the religion of that Empire, he did not say, or rule, that the Christian Faith should be unified with all these other gods, faiths and religions which existed all over the Roman Empire at that time so that they all should become one. In fact, under the power of the Christian Gospel they all submitted to that Gospel, and eventually ceased to exist, except as Museum pieces in the British Museum, and in other Museums of the World, along with the gods of Ancient Egypt, Assyria, Babylon and Greece! And none of these Roman gods are worshipped in the present day.

Then let us now come to the history of the early arrival of New Testament Christianity in these British Isles of ours. That New Testament form of Christianity was firmly planted here, well over 500 years before the arrival of Augustine in 596 A.D. I have pointed out in detail in Volume I of "The Trumpet Sounds for Britain" how it must have arrived here either directly after Pentecost, or not long after Pentecost, if not direct from Pentecost. In any case, it was in the year A.D. 43 that the Roman legions landed in Kent. From A.D. 43 therefore, Britannia became one of the forty-five provinces of the Roman Empire, and remained so, for four hundred years, until 407. That is a fact of history. The historians say of this period, "The Roman occupation of Britain *gave time for the Christian faith to be planted*". (My italicising.) They also add that, "It was within that period that there arose a British Christian Church which sent its Bishops to the early church councils". Early Christianity would have had to be quite strongly established to be in a position to do that. G. M. Trevelyan, one of our most noted historians, places it on record that "when the last of the Roman legions left these shores, and the Romans passed out of the story of Britain, they left behind them just three things of value, and the first of these was Welsh Christianity.

But wait a minute! What more do we know about this early arrival of the New Testament form of Christianity to these islands which is relevant to my theme? Well, the evidence which is furnished for us by the historian Eusebius (A.D. 260-340) states that "The apostles passed beyond the ocean to the isles called the Britannic Isles". The apostles did! Other early church historians state who these apostles were. They included the Apostle Paul and the Apostle Peter. Now if this was so, what kind of Britannic isles did they come to? The answer is that long before the days of Julius Caesar (55 B.C.), the British Isles had been the chief centre of ancient Druid worship. People from many a far-off land had come to receive instruction about this cult, and to learn its heathen practices, where sacrifices were offered on heathen altars. The Druids had various other gods as well, often in the form of sculptured stone images, bronze statuettes, carvings of wood, and other effigies. In fact, there were at least 400 of these gods, some of whose stone images and bronze statuettes still exist as relics in some of our museums today. This was the kind of Britain, therefore, that the Apostles Paul and Peter would have found when they arrived here. So what did they do? Did they say, "There are all these other faiths and religions and cults in these islands, we must unify our Christian Faith with all of these, until they are merged into one. We must take account of them all as we proceed to move amongst them?" Far from it. They proceeded to Preach the Gospel in the full Power of The Holy Spirit, totally uncompromisingly, as did others who followed after them, until eventually, the early Celtic Churches came into being. History tells us that the very earliest Scottish Church was Celtic, so was the very earliest Irish Church. And by a very early stage of our English history it was Celtic Churches which had been established all over Cornwall. And each and every one of them had been formed from converts as a result of the Preaching of The Gospel and The Way of Salvation. In fact, the New Testament form of Christianity was taking root and spreading during the period of the Roman occupation of Britain (A.D. 43 to A.D. 407) to such an extent, that Churchill, in his "History of the English Speaking Peoples", thrilled with excitement, and caught up with the spirit of its onward march, proclaims with great exuberance, "The new creed was winning victories everywhere". Furthermore, as Winston Churchill continues the thrilling story of Christianity's early advance in these islands he says, of the period which was a good two hundred years before King Alfred, that God brought us to the point when:- "There was no kingdom in the realm in which heathen religions and practices prevailed. The whole island had become Christian".

So, far from unifying with the other faiths and religions which then existed, the exact opposite was the case. All these other faiths and religions had submitted to The Preaching of The Saving Gospel of The Lord Jesus Christ so that they were no more. They no longer existed. So the answer to the other faiths, religions and cults, is to Preach The Gospel in the Full Power of The Holy Spirit. It is as clear as crystal.

Furthermore, the island, where, later, temples to Mithras had been erected during the Roman occupation, and where still later, after the invasion of the Vikings, the ancient gods of Thor and Woden held considerable sway, had so rallied to the Christian Faith, that the Venerable Bede was able to give this description of it: "A Christian England . . . divided into seven kingdoms of varying strengths, *all professing the Gospel of Christ*". (My italicising).

So other faiths and religions in these islands at that time were no more.

101

And then we have the example given to us by King Alfred. The Viking invasions of these islands took place at this time, and a large part of the British Isles was eventually over-run by them. The Vikings were of another religion and faith entirely, and were worshippers of Thor and Woden, and of other false deities. So did King Alfred say that the religious make-up of the Country has changed so dramatically that we now have to revise our entire outlook about it, and that the "Heart of the Matter" is now that we must unify the nation and take account of all these changes by recognising that we now "live in a multi-faith and in an Ecumenical society?" Never! King Alfred's reaction was the direct opposite of doing that. King Alfred was a Christian. He also sought above all else, to bring about the conversion of the Vikings to the Christian Faith, not by force of arms, but by a Christ-like example. And he was not fearful of targetting them with the Christian Gospel either! So when he had eventually defeated Guthram, the king of the entire Viking invading army, and when he had surrounded them all on the downs outside Chippenham in Wiltshire, and had them at his mercy, instead of annihilating them all, as he could have done, he invited Guthram and thirty of his prominent chieftains into his camp, where he entertained them for twelve days. King Alfred treated them as brothers. He showed them Christian love. He must also have talked to Guthram and his thirty chieftains during those twelve days about trust in The One and Only Living God, the Creator of the Heavens and the Earth, and about faith in The Lord Jesus Christ as the Only Way of Eternal Salvation. Because after the twelve days were over, Guthram emerged from King Alfred's camp a baptised Christian! Furthermore, according to the historians, Alfred now looked on Guthram as a son, which is full of significance if "son in the Lord" is what it meant.

The great miracle therefore had happened. A whole series of Viking conversions followed, and they continued until they became quite widespread. Hundreds, indeed thousands of them, were converted to faith in Christ, of their own violition. Nobody forced them into it. As a result, they abandoned the worship of Thor and Woden for the worship of Jesus Christ, which is a far cry from unifying their former religion with the Christian Faith. And they began to settle down in the land as Christian families.

It had always been King Alfred's long-term spiritual aim to bring about the conversion to Christ of these savage foes, certainly not to unify with them and with their religion. And now it had happened. But history shows that that was what God Almighty Himself had intended to do. So King Alfred's attitude, of all attitudes, was the right attitude. He was absolutely in line with the Will of God in what he did, which is more than can be said of our Archbishops and Bishops if they are talking about unification!

Winston Churchill was so impressed by the outcome of all this, that he said in his "History of the English Speaking Peoples", "We must still wonder how the hearts of these hard-bitten swordsmen and pirates could be changed in a single day." But of course The Power of the Gospel when it is faithfully, fully, and uncompromisingly preached can do that. Then Winston Churchill reflected, "The workings of the spirit are mysterious".

Furthermore, he had said earlier in his history of King Alfred's times, "It remained only for the conversion to Christianity to mingle these races inextricably in the soul and body of the nation". But now it had happened! But it would never have happened if King Alfred had said, "We must unify our faith with this other faith and religion of the Vikings". It would never have happened either, if King Alfred had not "targetted" the Vikings with the Message of the Saving Gospel of The Lord Jesus Christ. (See "The Trumpet Sounds for Britain", Volume One and Two, "The Life and Times of King Alfred").

My strong argument is, therefore, that the whole weight of both the Old Testament and New Testament teaching, and of the early and later history of the Christian Church in this Country, is totally and completely against the Archbishop of York's statement that the Coronation Oath will have to be revised to take account of the dramatic changes that have taken place in the last few years in the nation's religious make-up, and that "if the Coronation Service is going to unify the nation as it must do, then it must recognise that we live in an Ecumenical and multi-faith society". Quite the reverse is seen to be true. Furthermore, the whole weight of the Old Testament and New Testament Teaching, plus the history of the early Christian Church in this Country, and its later history, show very clearly, that the Archbishop is entirely out of step. He is out of step with the entire teaching of Scripture, both Old and New Testament, he is out of step with the history of the development of the early and later New Testament Christian Church in this Country, and he is entirely out of step with the revealed Will of God, as can clearly be seen by so many of the Scriptures themselves. And so he is out of step with God Himself.

Furthermore, this whole obnoxious idea and concept, that because the religious make-up of the nation has changed so dramatically during the last few years that we must take these changes into account, and recognise that we now live in a multi-faith society, and so must unify the nation on that basis, is completely contrary to what God has laid down in the Epistle to the Philippians Chapter 2 verses 5 to 11, and in its counter-part in Isaiah Chapter 45 verse 23.

Philippians Chapter 2 verses 5 to 11 says:- "Let this mind be in you, which was also in Christ Jesus: who, being in the form of God, thought it not robbery to be equal with God: but made Himself of no reputation, and took upon Himself the form of a servant, and was made in the likeness of men; And being found in fashion as a man, He humbled Himself, and became obedient unto death, even the death of the cross. Wherefore God also hath highly exalted Him, and given Him a name which is above every name; that *at the name of Jesus every knee should bow,* of things in heaven and things in earth, and things under the earth, *and that every tongue should confess that Jesus Christ is Lord, to the glory of God the Father"*. (My italicising).

And its counterpart says in Isaiah Chapter 45 verse 23, "I have sworn by Myself, the word is gone out of My mouth in righteousness, and shall not return; that unto Me every knee shall bow, and every tongue shall swear". For when Philippians Chapter 2 verse 10 says "that at the Name of Jesus every knee shall bow", it means every Moslem knee, every Hindu knee, every Buddhist knee, every Sikh knee, every Rastafarian knee, and every other knee of any other religion that exists in the world today. And when it says, "and that every tongue shall confess that Jesus Christ is Lord to the glory of God the Father" in verse 11, it means likewise, every Moslem tongue, every Hindu tongue, every Buddhist tongue, every Sikh tongue, every Rastafarian tongue, and every other tongue of any other religion that exists in the world today. For let it be clearly and uncompromisingly stated, that the Christian Faith, and the Christian Gospel is the Only Way of Eternal Salvation, and that The Lord Jesus Christ is the One and Only Saviour of the World, and of the Individual, (of whatever other faith and religion), who puts his trust in Him to save him eternally. Therefore not only is the Christian Faith the Superior Faith and Religion of the World, it is unique. It stands by itself. It is the Only Way of Salvation. So all other faiths and religions must give way to it, and must submit to it. No other religion, faith, or cult in the world can offer salvation to the individual from sin and from the eternal consequences of sin. So on that ground also, the Christian Faith is Supreme.

It is no good therefore for any leader of any other faith or religion in our multi-faith society, whether he be a Moslem leader, a Buddhist leader, a Hindu leader or whatever, complaining, as some have, that the Christian religion in this Country must not predominate, or take precedence over, all the other religions and faiths. The fact remains that it does, and that it should. And for the simple reason that at the Name of Jesus every knee shall bow and every tongue shall confess that Jesus Christ is Lord, no matter what other religion, faith, or cult, he or she may be following at this present time.

I tell you, therefore, that if Dr. Habgood has his way, and the Coronation Oath is revised to take account of the dramatic changes which have taken place in recent years in this nation's religious make-up so as to unify the nation by recognising that we now live in an Ecumenical and multi-faith society, as he says it must do, then that would spell the end of the United Kingdom. There is no question whatsoever about it. When the Northern Kingdom of Israel went in that direction, and then when the Southern Kingdom of Judah later went in that direction, God said, "You shall surely perish". And they did. Both of them in turn ceased to be a Nation. And so shall we, if we allow this change to take place.

For "all these things happened unto *them* for examples: and they are written for *our* admonition, upon whom the ends of the world are come". I Corinthians Chapter 10 verse 11. (My italicising).

That is what God is saying to the Nation of Britain today. "If you go down that road you are finished. You will surely perish. You will cease to be a Nation". Separation and complete severance, therefore, from all the other faiths and religions of the world is what God requires, and always has required of all His truly believing people, not unification with them. The whole weight of the Bible's Teaching bears that out.

Every decadent society ultimately comes to an end. And Britain today is unquestionably a decadent society. But then that decadent society is replaced by a more robust and strong society. The question arises, where is there a society which will replace the now decadent United Kingdom society?

The answer may well be revealed in the concluding pages of this book.

THE MONARCHY. ITS ESSENTIAL ROLE.

But before coming to that, what of the Monarchy itself, as distinct from what the Archbishop of York has said about the so-called need to revise the Coronation Oath and the Coronation Service? And what of The Sovereign herself? Well Her Majesty should be strongly advised that to take such a step, in favour of the other faiths and religions, would unquestionably mean the end of Britain as a Nation. There is no question about it. And she should be so advised by a strong, Bible-Believing Adviser, and one who knows his Scriptures thoroughly. And then having been so advised, she should make an extremely firm stand against taking such a step. It was stated on the "Daily Mail's" front page on Saturday, January 30th of this year (1993) that there is growing pressure inside the Labour Party to downgrade the monarch's constitutional position. But rather than downgrade it, it is my firm conviction that it should be upgraded and greatly strengthened. My strong conviction is that our Sovereign's constitutional position should be restored, at least, to that which was enjoyed by her late father, His Majesty King George VI, who many times took the initiative in calling this Nation to God in prayer, and whose Prime Minister, the late Sir Winston Churchill, was only too pleased to agree with him, and come into line with him. But my conviction is that Her Majesty's constitutional position needs to be strengthened to enable her to make a firm stand, because in this issue which has been raised by Dr. Habgood, the future of True Christianity in this Country is at stake. And this is at a time when over the Easter Period, and even before then, "The Times" Newspaper, in Leaders and Articles, has been saying that "the church is directionless" and entirely without strong leadership. But the Sovereign, as the Supreme Governor, under God, of the Church of England, by making such a firm stand, could begin to give the True Christian Faith in this Country the strong leadership which it requires. And no doubt other True Christians in a position of leadership would very quickly come into line. Such strong leadership, once given, would also, no doubt, halt the present landslide which is at present taking place from the Church of England.

The Sovereign's constitutional position needs also to be strengthened in view of the position which she holds in the eyes of Almighty God. He has declared in His Word, "It is by Me, that kings (sovereigns) reign". *Proverbs 8:15.* and that fact was fully recognised by the words of the Prayer for the Queen in The Service of The Lord's Supper which say, "Duly considering Whose authority she hath". And it was recognised in the words of that prayer until that Form of Service was foolishly discarded. But that recognition, that it is by God that Sovereigns reign, needs urgently to be restored, together with the respect that is due to a Sovereign who, in the eyes of God, holds such a position.

At the time of writing it has just been announced that "The Times" Newspaper is sponsoring a conference organised by Charter 88 on, "The monarchy, the constitution, and the people", at the Queen Elizabeth Conference Centre in London on Saturday, May 22nd of this year (1993). My earnest prayer is that these suggestions might be put at that Conference.

And in any case, it is imperative that something is done to strengthen the Sovereign's constitutional position, because, as Norris McWhirter, the Chairman of The Freedom Association, pointed out in a letter which he sent to the Speaker of the House of Commons, and which was published in the February 1993 issue of "Freedom Today", "The Ratification of the Maastricht Treaty would put Her Majesty The Queen in breach of her solemn Coronation Oath and thereby be in breach of the Coronation Act, 1953, the terms of which bind her not for part of her reign but for her entire reign".

Furthermore, Article 8 of The Treaty (a copy of which I have) reduces the Sovereign to becoming a compulsory European citizen who becomes unconstitutionally open to arraignment (indictment before a tribunal) under the civil and criminal law of the European Community.

And since in Britain, at the moment, Parliament comprises the Sovereign, the Commons, and the House of Lords, all that, would be set aside, or abolished. Because if the Treaty were ratified, it would mean that, for the first time since the constitutional landmark of the Bill of Rights of 1689, a power other than the "Queen in Parliament" can make or amend our laws.

There is no doubt that it could be said, of course, that all this, were it to happen, would be the outworking of God's Judgment on the Royal House of Windsor and of the Nation itself. It could be said, for instance, that a warning signal of judgment to come for the Royal House of Windsor came first, about 5 years ago, when in the middle of February 1988, Windsor Castle suffered serious structural damage following a shift in part of its ancient foundations. The Round Tower, built by King Edward III and part of the heraldic badge and symbol of the Royal House of Windsor itself, moved, bringing down plaster and causing cracks to appear in the stonework. This was interpreted by some, as an omen. And it was a sign to the Monarch of a more powerful warning to come.

Then on 20th November 1992, the day of the Queen's 45th Wedding Anniversary, came the terrible fire at Windsor Castle, starting in the Queen's

Private Chapel above The Lord's Table, shortly after 11.30 a.m., and about which I have already commented in earlier pages.

Then on 9th December 1992, the whole Nation was shaken when the Prime Minister, John Major, made the announcement in the House of Commons that the Prince of Wales, heir to the throne, and the Princess of Wales, were to separate.

So in all this, there was no question but that The Royal House of Windsor was being severely shaken. And I myself had already pointed out in a letter which I had sent to the Queen on Tuesday, November 24th, three days after the Windsor Fire, that that Fire was God speaking, and that He was voicing His Displeasure and Disapproval at much that had been going on in the Royal House, and of the Sovereign herself condoning, with her presence, multi-faith services in Westminster Abbey and in our Cathedrals.

So it could be argued that, were the Maastricht Treaty to be ratified, and, as a result, the Sovereign were to be reduced to becoming a compulsory European citizen, and a power other than the "Queen in Parliament" were to be making or amending our laws, it could be argued, I say, that this was all an outworking of God's Hand in Judgment on our Royal House, and on our Nation.

Indeed, an Article in the "London Evening Standard" on Wednesday, 19th May (1993), which was serialising A. N. Wilson's book, "The Rise and Fall of The House of Windsor", whilst discussing certain things that may need to be changed, said, "It looks perilously as if the monarchy is going to be one of those things which is allowed to go because no one can think of a good word to save it". But I myself can most certainly think of a good word to save it.

I say very strongly, that if the Royal House of Windsor, and the Sovereign, have indeed been undergoing a period of Judgment, then the Sovereign's position in that Judgment could be redeemed, were she, right now, to take a strong stand on behalf of the True Christian Faith in this Country, and give it the strident leadership which it so urgently needs. It could also result in turning God's Judgment away, not only from the Royal House of Windsor, but from the Nation itself. And to back that up, I would state the following:-

In all that has, for months now, been printed and published about the Royal Family, journalists have been casting about asking what is the role of the monarchy? They have been suggesting a number of different things, such as "to be an example of family life", or "to uphold certain moral standards", etc. But they seem to be at a loss. So the journalists have been busy trying to invent a role, when that role is there all the time if they would only acknowledge it. It is in the constitution. The very reason for the monarchy's existence is to uphold the Protestant Reformed Religion, by law established, to maintain the Laws of God in the Realm, and the True Gospel. It is all there in the Coronation Oath and the Act of Settlement, and both of these are the very cornerstone of the monarchy.

If, therefore, the Sovereign were to make a strong stand for the True Christian Faith and the True Profession of the Gospel in this Land, she would be fulfilling the very reason for which the monarchy exists. That is its role. And that is the Sovereign's role. And she is fully qualified to do it. I happen to know, for instance, on the authority of a source who is very close to the Queen, that Her Majesty not only believes in personal conversion to Faith in The Lord Jesus Christ, but that she has also had the experience of personal conversion. Therefore she has a profound and unquestionable reason for making such a stand, because she has the right that every True Believer has, of confessing The Lord Jesus Christ publicly before people. And for the simple reason that Jesus Himself said, "He, (or she) that confesses Me before men, the same will I confess before My Father which is in Heaven, and he (or she) who denies Me before men, the same will I deny before My Father which is in Heaven". Matthew Chapter 10 verses 32 and 33.

So the Sovereign has the same right as every True Believer in Jesus has, of confessing Him publicly before men. And furthermore, the Sovereign doesn't have to ask anybody's permission to do it, just as no True Christian has to ask anybody's permision to do it.

But there is another most profound reason why the Sovereign is fully qualified to make that stand, and that is, that God changed the course of the history on the monarchy to bring her to the British Throne for such a time as this. For when Edward VIII insisted on marrying a divorced woman, (Mrs Simpson), and then decided to abdicate, it was a Godly King, George VI, Her Majesty's father, that God caused to ascend the Throne. The Greatest Bible Teacher in the Realm said, in a Sermon, at that time, "The elder shall serve the younger in order that the purpose of God according to election might stand", which is a quotation from Romans Chapter 9 verses 11 and 12. If it was the purpose of God to change the election of Kingship *then,* it is certainly the purpose of God that Godly King George VI's daughter, now Queen Elizabeth II, who is a True Believer, should now occupy the

Throne for such a time as this. So in these three ways, at least, the Sovereign is fully qualified, indeed I would say, called, to give this Country the strident Christian Leadership, right from the top, that it so desperately needs. Such a strong lead, once stridently, and forthrightly given, could open the way for the conversion of the people of these islands to the genuine, New Testament Christian Faith, which is the only type of conversion which God Almighty is interested in, rather than to "the conversion of England" which Cardinal Hume and others say they have been praying for, for years, namely the "conversion", or "re-conversion" of England to Roman Catholicism.

God grant that the conversion of the British people to the True, New Testament Christian Faith is what we may yet see come to pass.

PARLIAMENT AND THE GOVERNMENT STILL PERSIST IN LEGISLATING DOWNWARDS: EVEN DISHONESTLY AND DECEITFULLY NOW.

But there is an urgent need now to face ourselves up with the question, "What do we see happening today to the contrary, and which is the direct opposite to that taking place?" Well, all the indications are that Parliament and the Government is, and deliberately intends to, continue to legislate downwards. For instance, the Home Secretary, Mr Kenneth Clarke, has proposed to relax the rules on children being allowed to be taken into Public Houses (March 1993). This can, in no sense, be seen, as upgrading the standards of behaviour. Quite to the contrary. Indeed, when this topic was tried at the bar of public opinion, the reaction was, "a lot of the parents won't be able to keep their children under control"; an argument which came up time and again. Many of the parents in the pubs frankly admitted they were unable to control their own children, let alone anyone else's! One mother said, "We're dead against children in pubs. We've never taken ours!"

A student from Southampton University thought that the passive smoking would be bad for children. He thought that the children would also be encouraged to drink. Then a couple who had spent nine years in the licensing trade said pubs were certainly not the right environment for children. "It is not exactly the way to bring them up, looking at people getting drunk". (From a Report published on the front page of "The Sunday Telegraph", March 21st, 1993).

And the Honourable Member for Bolsover was severaly critical of this proposal when it was first announced in the House of Commons. But despite all that, the Government continues to go in the direction of legislating downwards in this respect.

But there are signs that it continues to go in the direction of lowering the age of consent for male homosexuals to below the age of 21 also. Early in his premiership, Mr Major sent out signals that he was favourably disposed towards the campaign for homosexual rights. He received the campaigner, Sir Ian McKellen, at Downing Street very early this year (1993), and then sent a message of support to last year's relaunch of the Tory Campaign for Homosexual Equality. The Prime Minister has also told friends that he believes a change of the law on consent to be inevitable. (All the above is quoted from the "Sunday Telegraph's" Home Affairs Correspondent, Valerie Elliott, Sunday, February 21st, 1993).

It is true that the Prime Minister was being advised, in mid-February of this year (1993), to delay any move to lower the age of consent for male homosexuals for the time being. This was because ministers were urging him that it would be folly to raise such a contentious issue just now, and they pointed to the embarrassment suffered by President Clinton in the U.S.A. when he provoked howls of rage from Middle America, and from his Army Chiefs of Staff, by his instruction, just after his inauguration as President, to lift the ban on the recruitment of homosexuals to the United States armed forces.

It should be pointed out that in addition to these howls of rage which he provoked, the "Storm of the Century" battered the entire 2,000-mile stretch of America's East Coast during the weekend of March 13th, 14th and 15th (1993), as tornadoes, blizzards, and hurricane-force winds suddenly struck America's Eastern sea-board, and President Clinton was obliged to declare a national disaster in Florida, where the official death toll reached 14, and agricultural crops were wiped out in a state which was still recovering from last autumn's Hurricane Andrew, and where, now, at least two million homes were without electricity and so without heating, and where the whole of the Eastern sea-board, the most heavily-populated strip on the continent of North America, was brought to a standstill. (From a New York report published by "The Daily Telegraph" on Monday, March 15th, 1993).

This "Storm of the Century" suddenly came, as it were, from nowhere! Neither had there been any warning about it.

Eye-witnesses who were in Florida on holiday at the time, told me that there was something very unusual and awestriking about it. But I have already said more than once in my writings, and in my public addresses, that God uses His elements, His atmospheric forces, at times, to bring a Visitation of Judgment on a Nation. And I believe very strongly that that "Storm of the Century" which suddenly struck, as it were, quite "out of the blue" was a warning shot, fired from Heaven itself, across the bows of the new Clinton Administration because of the direction it was going in this "Gay Rights" issue. And that is to use Naval Language! But the question is did anybody point that out to President Clinton? Did Dr. Billy Graham, for instance? Or Dr. R.T. Kendall?

But Mr Major's decision to delay any move in this Country to lower the age of consent for male homosexuals is only temporary. It is but a postponement. There is no evidence whatsoever that there has been a change of heart on his part, or on the part of those Tory MPs who are exerting strong pressure to bring it about. The latest publication of the Conservative Family Campaign says in its Chairman's Message, "On this issue of homosexuality, pressure for further liberalisation will not of course go away". And in any case, even as I am writing this particular section of this booklet, it has been announced in a half-page, coloured, illustrated, article in "The Times", dated Monday, April 26th 1993, that "several hundred thousand homosexual rights activists filled the streets of Washington" the previous day, Sunday, "which has been billed as the biggest gay rights march in history, and one of the largest demonstrations ever held in the capital".

The article says that the President's strategy, at the moment, is to play down his support for gay issues. He distanced himself from the event, or appeared to, as he left Washington for out-of-town engagements. But the article goes on to say that, "he is not relenting on the issues in substance, especially his desire to allow gays into the military, — an initiative he took in his first days in office". He said on the Friday before he left Washington, "That *his support for gays,* (my italicising) was not born out of a special concern, but stemmed from a principled *libertarian attitude* (my italicising) and his deep-felt opposition to any kind of discrimination". So he has admitted that he has a support for gays. And sooner or later he is going to honour his election pledge and grant them what they are demanding, and what they have been so powerfully demonstrating for. And if that happens, I cannot bear to think what the *next* Visitation of Divine Judgment will be on the United States of America, for it will be far worse, and far more severe, and even more sudden than was "The Storm of the Century". You mark my words.

Lance Lambert, in commenting on the Election of Bill Clinton as President of the United States, said he thinks that that Election is, in itself, a Judgment on the United States, "certainly on the Christian side, and on the moral side", he said. We shall see.

He said, "An avalanche of moral evil is going to fall upon United States society". He says he does not think Bill Clinton realises for a moment the demonic forces which are poised to take advantage of him. He says President Clinton believes that he is broadening the American mind, making it more contemporary, more modern, cutting it off from what he feels to be the narrow-minded, straight-laced, moral majority attitude to things. So he wants to legalise abortion, he wants to legalise and free matters to do with homosexuals, lesbians, the gay society, and so on. He wants to free a whole number of other things, and in this he is joined whole-heartedly by his wife. He wants to, as it were, in his view, modernise American society, and make it contemporary, with a wide horizon. But Lance Lambert says he does not think that Clinton has any idea of the enormous interest of demonic forces in American society. Lance Lambert says that in the past, the United States, with all its faults, has been a spiritual bulwark in this world, for freedom. And indeed, not just for mere political freedom, but for Divine Truth, for what we might call Biblical Truth, and Biblical Standards, and it has been a centre and a funder, and an inspirer of Gospel Work. Lance Lambert says that in this she has taken the torch from Britain. For many years Britain, he says, was the centre of so much of this. But to Lance Lambert it seems that now the forces of darkness and evil want really to get right into American society. The fact is, he says, that all the time she has still been living on past spiritual credit, but that has now run out. When America was young, he says, she honoured the Lord, she obeyed Him, she loved Him. But when God gave her wealth, and status, and power, then she forsook Him, and she has been on a collision course with Him. Indeed, he says, the wind has been sown, and the whirlwind reaped. He says that even if a great spiritual awakening and revival comes, it will come in the midst of God's Judgments, not because of these Judgments being deflected. (From Lance Lambert's February 1993 Update Tape).

But since the Prime Minister of this Country, and his Government now always seem to wait to see what America is going to do, and then come into line with that, I dare to predict that before the end of this year (1993), or a little later, Mr Major, his Cabinet, and the British Government, will be going in the same direction as the Clinton Administration on this issue of homosexuality and the Gay Rights Movement. They will be yielding to all the strong pressures that there are, and will be giving way to them, and perhaps completely. And so they will be legislating downwards in this way also. And what severe Visitation of Divine Judgment on the British Parliament, on the Capital, and on the British Isles themselves will suddenly follow in the wake of that, may I ask? Are the British Isles and the United States of America destined to fall, and to go down together, I wonder? The answer is yet to be seen. But I think that even now, I can dimly predict from certain of the Prophetic Scriptures what that answer is going to be. And to quote the sombre and growling words of the late Sir Winston Churchill, "I have not always been wrong!"

But these are not the only indications that the Government and Parliament deliberately intend to continue to legislate downwards. Not by any means. It is now even being done, very subtly, by means of "the back door". This has been exposed, for instance, in a totally shocking Article which was published in the February 1993 issue of the magazine "Freedom Today", and was then taken up by the "Sunday Telegraph" on February 28th in a full-page Article which announced in its sub-title, "The Government is backing sex education policies whose ultimate aim is to destroy the family". And that sub-title asks the question, "Is there worse to come?" These Articles have also been confirmed, and then taken up, by Conservative Family Campaign letters and information leaflets.

I do not hesitate to state quite bluntly the totally shocking things which the Article in the Magazine "Freedom Today", the journal of the Freedom Association, brings right out into the open, despite the fact that when I first read it I was so repulsed that it made me sick. If the reader does not want to be likewise repulsed, then skip the next few paragraphs. I am merely reporting from the above articles exactly what has been going on. The British people ought to know.

The title of the Article in "Freedom Today" refers to what is going on as, "The growing scandal . . . ." It says in the first place, and I quote:- "The Guidelines of Sheffield Education Authority provide a fairly typical example of the sex education which the Government now *decrees* (my italicising) all children must receive". Notice it says *all* children.

Then comes a list. I quote again:-

(1) "Eight year olds are told how people get AIDS; why they need condoms, and to think whether their Mum or Dad has AIDS".

(2) "By 11, they are told why girls are called slags and boys studs".

(3) "At 12, pupils must 'recognise' the right to have sex with the partner of one's choice".

(4) "At 13, we move on to 'the pleasure of having sex with the partner of your choice'.

"The important thing is 'freedom to choose what you feel happy and comfortable with doing', and places to go for 'confidential' help if parents try interfering with it".

Then under the heading "What is taught?" there is this, and I quote again:-

"There is teaching about how to make sure your condom doesn't split. If sex is required for no more or less than orgasmic release — it is explained how to get this from oral sex. In case of accident, there is information about what to do when someone is pregnant and 'does not want help from the authorities'. Suggesting that everyone has AIDS anyway, at *age 14*, (my italicising) there are 'safety measures in dealing with accidental spillage of body fluids'. Marriage, 'family lifestyles', and parenthood are mentioned so that pupils know that there are *other* 'valid choices' — while the alternatives to homosexuality are discrimination, prejudice, and stereotyping".

This was what was, and is, going on under the guidelines of the *Sheffield* Education Authority. I apologise to the ladies for some of the language I have directly quoted. But some of you are mothers! You need to be told what goes on. It is *your* children who are being taught all this.

But next we come to *Gloucestershire* and to the *Gloucester* Local Education Authority. I have to warn you that the language I have to quote here is even more shocking. I quote direct from the Article:-

"One boy, Malachi Stone, described how a lady classroom visitor from the AIDS Department of the Gloucestershire Royal Hospital came to his classroom — a mixed class of teenagers of which he was a 15-year-old member — and wrote the following words on the blackboard:- Bonking, Screwing, Fucking, and Shagging. He said she filled the blackboard with such words. Then she proceeded to tell this mixed class of teenagers that many heterosexual couples have anal sex anyway. She told them that 50 per cent of local youngsters are already "sexually active" at 16. Then she told them about the "fun" condoms which are especially made for young people, and showed them how to put them on by getting the pupils into pairs, with one

115

holding up two fingers. Then she advised them to take a packet of them home and practise in the bathroom".

Again I apoligise to the ladies for having to shock you like this. But this is what goes on. You need to know. Some of you are mothers, I say. And this is what *your* children are being taught, and are being exposed to.

I now continue to quote from the Article:-

"The boy's parents complained to the headmaster of the school (Thosen Hill School), to the school governing body, to the Local Education Authority, and to the Department of Education. All these said nothing improper took place! And this, in spite of section 46 of the 1986 Education Act. This Act required that governors of schools ensure that sex education "is given in such a manner as to encourage those pupils to have due regard to moral considerations and the value of family life". It was also meant to offer some help to parents faced with "positive images" campaigns promoting homosexuality *from nursery to further education*". (My italicising). Parents were also granted the statutory right to appeal where they were unhappy about lessons, although governors had discretion over how to respond".

So that is what has been happening, and *is* happening, in Gloucester and in Gloucestershire. I come now to Hounslow. The "Sunday Telegraph" Article on February 28th of this year (1993), in addition to reporting what has been going on in schools in Sheffield and in Gloucester and Gloucestershire said that in Hounslow the area in which the writer of the Article, Patricia Morgan, lived, the Local Authority had produced a booklet which had a picture on one page of lesbians cuddling, and which referred to "new partners" — (note the word "partner" — not husband or wife). And it says concerning these "new partners", "it is more effective to practise safer sex every time, than to cut down on sexual partners", since being "faithful to one partner will only protect you (from AIDS) if that person does not have the virus".

I must confess that when I first read the shocking and repulsive statements made in all these Articles I formed the impression that it was Local Authorities and Local Education Committees that were going behind the Government's back to bring these iniquitous things about. But No. Not a bit of it. On a further reading I discovered that "stealthily, and unannounced, the Government decided that AIDS educations for 11 to 14 year olds is a compulsory part of the Science course laid down by the National Curriculum — by using the blunt, or, we might say, despotic instrument of *secondary* legislation. (My italicising). Here, having been granted the right to determine

116

what is to be taught in schools, the State can vary the content *at will* (my italicising) and could, by executive fiat, dictate that even necrophillia or cannibalism be taught if that was its wish. In turn, parents and teachers have no right to veto lessons or any control over material which may deeply offend their religious and philosophical beliefs, or any right of withdrawal for children. Instead, local authorities will have the right to prosecute schools or parents who fail to co-operate with their teaching". (Quoted from the "Freedom Today" Article, whose full title was, "The growing scandal of what is called 'AIDS Education'.") How iniquitous! How appallingly iniquitous.

So all that I have quoted so far as to what has been, and is, happening in Sheffield, Gloucestershire and Hounslow schools has been, and is being done under the name and umbrella of "AIDS Education". And by stealthy and unannounced means. So when the parents of 15-year-old Malachi Stone complained to the headmaster, to the school governing body, to the local education authority, and to the Department of Education, not only were they told that nothing improper had taken place, they were also told that it would have been perilous to protest by withdrawing their son from further sex education lessons: parents who take such action can be prosecuted by the local education authority! (Quoted from "The Sunday Telegraph" Article dated February 28th, 1993.)

That Article raised the question, "How has it come about that, under a Conservative Government which is apparently committed to supporting parent power, parents can now be prosecuted for seeking to uphold it?"

The answer is that it was a Minister of State who brought this about. It was Kenneth Clarke, when he was Education Secretary, the same Kenneth Clarke who now, as Home Secretary, has proposed that children be allowed into pubs! In November 1991, when he was Education Secretary, it was simply announced that AIDS Education would be added to the science curriculum, and this became law the following February (1992). And nobody noticed it! Nobody was aware of it! It was done by subtle means. Here is what happened. I quote again from the "Freedom Today" Article:-

"To satisfy the homosexual lobby, the Government had no need to face lengthy, argumentative and publicised repeal procedures to get rid of the offending laws (Laws to restrain the aggressive advocacy of homosexuality by local authorities, which had been a focus for outrage as what the Left see as a vast plan for repressive, patriarchal rule, as the previous paragraph points out.) This was at the time when Ian McKellan had told an anti-Clause 28 rally, "We must all be out and about, in the streets, in the classrooms

. . . promoting homosexuality". (Quoted from the same previous paragraph).

It was at the time, too, when he was due to have an interview with the Prime Minister at 10 Downing Street.

So the Article says:- "To satisfy the homosexual lobby, the Government had no need to face lengthy, argumentative and publicised repeal procedures to get rid of the offending laws. Conveniently, it could use the science curriculum to achieve this, *over the heads of Parliament,* (my italicising) — where AIDS has been the excuse to publicise promiscuous sex under the pretence of health education. *There was no consultation* (my italicising). It was not even in the original draft of the science curriculum. As Lord Stallard claims — (and I am still quoting the Article) — it was poked in at the end of the consultation period with the hope that it would not be noticed and would be implemented before anybody knew what was going on. Five little words simply appeared in the middle of a huge 40-page document. Slipping through, it leap-frogged Acts of Parliament which showed respect for the sensibilities of parents, teachers and governors, and surreptitiously removed fundamental rights of conscience — as the Government pretended nothing had changed".

So that is how it happened.

"Kenneth Clarke, who was then Education Secretary, issued the Order just before the Christmas Recess in 1991. In January 1992 an Early Day Motion was tabled against the Order, and it attracted cross-party support; but the Government did not allow MPs a debate, and the Order came into effect last autumn (1992)". Quoted from the front page of the "Evangelical Times", April 1993 issue.

That is what I mean when I say that the Government is now even legislating downwards by the back-door method. Or rather I should now say, By the back-hand method. It is despicable. Totally despicable. But that is the kind of Government we have got now.

Furthermore, what the Government has now so stealthily, subtly, and unannounced, introduced, is nothing short of legalised, Government-supported, and Government-sponsored child abuse. For much of this sex/AIDS education is given by bodies like the Brook Advisory Centres, AIDS charities, and the Terrence Higgins Trust, together with a recommended (so-called) organisation called, "AIDS Virus Education and Research Trust", AVERT for short. These Articles point out that the Department of Education's guidelines, on HIV/AIDS education, together with those of the AIDS Virus Education and Research Trust, contain not the smallest concession to moral considerations or family life. To the D.E.S., anal intercourse is just a reason to use condoms as "the only way to reduce the risk of infection". A.V.E.R.T. assumes that anal intercourse is normal. Both organisations positively advocate it. The procreative side of sex, i.e. having children, is not considered at all. Sex is just self-expression, where there is no such thing as deviances or perversion. There are no rules about it. No restrictions either. Condoms must be ever ready. Homosexuality is regarded in this teaching as the model for sex as pure recreation, not as buggery or as sodomy. That it is SIN doesn't even come into the teaching. And the National AIDS Trust even says, "There is no way that religious and moral beliefs should get in the way of safer sex education". In fact, as a Conservative Family Campaign Leaflet says, "The educational system in this country is being transformed into a means of distancing children from God". And again, "The problem is that the content of sex education affirms the immoral ethos, for example, propaganda for promiscuity, homosexuality, contraception, anti-marriage, fornication, and it encourages children to experiment with sex rather than buttressing children against these pressures. In short, the libertarians continue to exploit the mechanism of Sex Education to propagandise their value-system which is totally opposed to that of the vast majority of parents against their wishes, and in most cases without their knowledge. They aim to proselytise a generation of children so that in the next generations, their perversions are accepted as normal".

And the Government, by subtly and stealthily legalising downwards by the back-hand method is supporting and encouraging all this! It is legalised, Government-supported, Government-encouraged child abuse, I say.

It is true that Lord Stallard and others, including The Earl of Halsbury, The Baroness Cox, and the Lord Stoddart of Swindon have now tabled amendments to Clause 227 of the current Education Bill which are intended *firstly* to bring all sex education under the scope of the 1986 Education Act Number 2, and *secondly* to make schools give notice to parents about intended sex education, and to give parents the right to withdraw their children. (Quoted from information received in mid-April 1993 from the Conservative Family Campaign). According to this information, these amendments should be debated in the House of Lords on 27th or 29th April, or at the latest on 4th May (1993), but it is over a year after that iniquitous Order became Law. It is rather like closing the stable door after the horse has bolted. We wish Lord Stallard, The Earl of Halsbury, the Baroness Cox and The Lord Stoddart of Swindon, every success during that Debate, and we pray that, as a result, these amendments will be accepted and then become Law. But even if they do become Law, the question is, will they be implemented? With regard to the Broadcasting Bill and the law on T.V. Broadcasting which stated that freedom for evangelistic broadcasting without any restrictions or prohibitions should now be allowed, hours and hours were spent briefing the Peers who were involved, and then they stayed up late to ensure that that particular clause got through. The Bill was then passed onto the Statute Book and so became Law. But that part of the Bill was never implemented, and the Government, though urged to do so, would not take the necessary steps to ensure that it was implemented. So what guarantee is there, if these amendments become Law, that they will be implemented either? I would say, none whatsoever. So this subtly and stealthily Government-supported legalised child abuse will continue in our schools completely unarrested. It needs to be stated very strongly that Jesus said to His disciples one day, "It is impossible but that offences will come: but woe unto him, through whom they come. It were better for him that a millstone were hanged about his neck, and he cast into the sea, than that he should offend one of these little ones". Luke 17 verses 1 to 2. Spine-chilling words! Spine-chilling words indeed!

But they could be rephrased in this way today, "It is impossible but that offences will come: but woe unto Governments, Ministers of Education, Brook Advisory Centres, AIDS Virus Educational and Research Trusts, National AIDS Trusts, Terrence Higgins Trusts, D.E.S.'es, and all libertarians through whom they come". Jesus would unquestionably say today, "Woe to them all". Divine Judgment on them all is inevitable.

But let me point out that when Jesus went on to say, "It were better for him, (or for all these people) that a millstone were hanged about his neck, and he (or all these people) cast into the sea, than that he (or they) should offend *one* of these little ones", He said that, concerning just *one* of these little ones. But there are whole school-fulls of them, all over the Country! A whole generation of children and young people, in fact. The entire rising generation! We need to see the *ENORMITY* of it. It seems to me that there is going to be a colossal shortage of millstones!

And concerning all those through whom all the offences come, including Kenneth Clarke, the former Education Secretary, and Home Secretary, and now as this goes to print, Chancellor of the Exchequer, all those who so subtly and stealthily brought in that iniquitous Order by the back-hand method, and also all those who caused it, unnoticed, and undetected, to become law, which would include the Prime Minister and his Cabinet, and thus to cause such immoral havoc, confusion, misunderstanding, perversion and depravation amongst so many of the Nation's schoolchildren and school-going teenage young people, can we, or anyone, by any stretch of the imagination, say that a very severe form of the Judgment of God is not at all likely to come upon them?

In no sense can anyone say that.

John Major, as Prime Minister, when addressing a meeting in the Carlton Club on the evening of Wednesday, February 3rd of this year (1993), said in the opening paragraph of his address, "When I became leader of our Party … I set out my aim to create … a nation at ease with itself".

How can he, or his speech-writer, whoever that speech-writer was, talk about creating a nation at ease with itself when creating such a nation includes legislating deceitfully that all that kind of thing should go on? Furthermore, however can a nation possibly be at ease with itself *with* all this kind of thing going on? If the Prime Minister, his Cabinet, and this Government, refuse to repent of what they have done, and repeal that dastardly Order, and reverse the present policy of perverted Education to a specifically Christian Education policy, then I say to him, his Cabinet, and his Government very strongly, "In the Name of God, GO!"

THE NATIONAL SCANDAL OF THE LACK OF CHRISTIAN EDUCATION IN SCHOOLS.

Now I come to the next subject. And in view of what I have just written in the last few pages it is a very relevant one. Christianity in schools. And here another great national scandal has recently been brought to light. Early in March of this year, 1993, banner headlines both in the National Press and in the Church Press proclaimed: "Schools flout law on Christian teaching"; "Religious education law flouted by schools"; "The great education betrayal".

One of the Press Articles by Charles Hymas, an Education Correspondent, began with these words:- "Children are being left ignorant about the basic tenets of Christianity because schools and councils are flouting the law on religious education, according to an official inquiry". The same Article goes on to say:— "The investigation into the state of religious education in schools uncovered "disturbing" evidence that new syllabuses issued by education authorities fail to spell out what pupils should learn about God, about Jesus Christ and the Bible. None of the syllabuses complied in full with legislation that makes Christianity the main religion children should study". And a front page Article in the Friday, March 12th issue, (1993) of "The Church of England Newspaper" even says, "The report by the National Curriculum Council showed that all R.E. syllabuses for the past five years have been drawn up illegally". So Lady Olga Maitland, in a full page Article on Page 7 of that Newspaper says in her opening paragraph, "Children today are being cheated of the right to learn about Christianity, and the result is an appalling level of ignorance of basic knowledge of Christianity".

All this, therefore, means, that when, on the one hand, perverted and depraving teaching of our children about sex is being put across under the excuse of "Health" Education, nothing is being taught by way of Christian standards and moral behaviour to counter it. All that, has scandalously been removed.

But what does the 1988 Education Reform Act say? What are its requirements? To quote from Lady Olga Maitland's Article:- "The Act requires all new syllabuses to 'reflect the fact that the religious traditions in Great Britain are in the main Christian" (my italicising). She says, "The House of Commons endorsed this section of the Act by a massive majority of 27 on a free vote".

Or to quote Charles Hymas, the Education Correspondent, "the legislation makes Christianity the main religion children should study" (my italicising). And this was something which Baroness Cox and others fought long and hard for, during the passage of the 1988 Education Reform Act through Parliament, and particularly through the House of Lords. And this is the Law of The Land. And it is compulsory. And as the Law of The Land it should be obeyed by all concerned. In other words, it should be implemented.

But what, in fact, has been happening?

Lady Olga Maitland, the Tory MP for Sutton and Cheam, tells us, "Religious education advisers have carried out 'an act of massive civil disobedience — flagrantly disobeying laws which Parliament has laid down". (Quoted from an Article in the National Press dated 11th March 1993 by John Clare, Education Editor.)

So here, therefore, is yet another case where the law which has been enacted by Parliament and then placed on the Statute Book has not been implemented, but rather has been deliberately and wilfully flouted. I hereby propose, therefore, that a Bill be urgently passed in Parliament to enforce the implementation of all such laws which have been placed on the Statute

Book, and that heavy fines be imposed on all those who fail to do so, which could be used by the Treasury to help reduce our colossal National Debt.

The situation is this, therefore, that if it was the former Minister of Education, Kenneth Clarke, and the Government, who got that pernicious Order through by subtle, stealthy, and dubious means, and it was, then in *this* case it has been the Local Education Authorities, religious education advisors, some school governing bodies, and the schools themselves who have so seriously "got round" and violated the law. Lady Olga Maitland states in her Article, "The fact is that these bodies are being manipulated by religious education advisers, some of whom are deeply resentful that Parliament should pass a law giving primacy to Christianity within R.E."

And all that, I must add, against the rights of our British children to be taught Christianity. Lady Olga Maitland says, "My office has been deluged with letters from parents and teachers distressed that their schools are not teaching Christianity". "I have even received letters from young people", she says. "A 14 year-old girl wrote: 'Please can you help me? I have been forced to learn the Hindu religion for three years now. All we learn about is Hindus, Muslims and the Vishnu religion. I don't mind learning about other religions, but why can't I be taught about my own?' " And Lady Olga Maitland adds, "Why not indeed?" And I myself say the same thing. And especially when the Christian Faith is the only Faith that is valid.

For the Bible says, "Every man is brutish in his knowledge: every founder is confounded by his graven image: for his molten image *is falsehood* (my italicising), and there is no breath in them. They are vanity, and the work of errors: in the time of their visitation they shall perish". Jeremiah Chapter 10 verses 14 and 15. *Vanity,* may I point out, according to the Oxford Dictionary, means worthlessness, a worthless thing. And the word "vain", according to the same dictionary, means, "having no value or significance", "useless", "futile". And when it says, "In the time of their visitation they shall perish", it means, "In the time of their visitation *in Judgment,* in *Divine* Judgment, they shall perish". That is not what I say, but what *GOD* says. So what is the point of children spending all this time in schools, — in the case of this 14 year-old girl, 3 years! learning about other religions when God says they are worthless, useless, futile, valueless, and without any significance at all? What is the point, I say?

But to go on. All these disturbing Press Reports reveal that the investigation into the state of religious education in schools show that the local syllabus conferences which draw up Religious Education schemes are endorsing syllabuses up and down the country which give teachers in classrooms no idea at all of what to teach. So they seem to be left in an absolute quandary as exactly what to teach, and are waffling and wobbling about all over the place about what should be in the syllabus. On the one hand, government inspectors have found that many primary schoolchildren have no religious education lessons at all. In other schools it is humanism, Greek mythology, and even the role of witch doctors in tribal societies which are included in children's religious education. In Oldham, Lancs, a 40-page booklet for Oldham schools does not even mention God or the Bible! In the London Borough of Hounslow, Hounslow's syllabus lists seven "core areas" for study, Buddhism, Hinduism, Islam, Judaisim, Sikhism, Humanism, with Christianity thrown in for good measure! Lady Olga Maitland says that the syllabus for Sutton (her constituency) is a typical example of what goes on. "You have to turn through 32 pages before the word Christian is reached," she says. She says, "The syllabus has a take it or leave it approach, which puts Christianity alongside Judaism, Islam, Hinduism, Sikhism and Buddhism". "One religion", she says, "is regarded much the same as another". "Critics say the religious education of children has become a multi-faith mishmash", says Charles Hymas in his report.

And in Hartlepool, a Christian office worker, Josie Watson, had to withdraw her son Andrew, from religious education classes at his school in Hartlepool when she discovered that he was learning about ancestral spirits and witch doctors.!

Charles Hymas, Education Correspondent, says, "Most syllabuses were so vague it was impossible for the advisers to discover how much of the teaching in schools would be about Christianity!"

But why should everybody be in such an absolute quandary about this? Why should they all be "dancing about" like a cat on a red-hot hot-plate? Why all this vagueness in the extreme as to what should be taught? The answer is simple. If the legislation, the law of the land, makes Christianity compulsory as the main religion children should study, and it does, then it is the basics of the Christian Faith which need to be taught first and foremost. And since the Christian Faith is all about Jesus Christ, and has Jesus Christ at its very centre, and since it is all about being a follower of The Lord Jesus Christ, and about obtaining Eternal Salvation, and Eternal Life through Faith in Jesus Christ and through Faith in Jesus Christ *alone,* then it is the facts about

Jesus Christ which need to be taught first. And those are all found in the Bible. It is as simple as that. One of our Christian Hymns provides a perfect outline of what those facts essentially include. Its first verse puts it this way:-

"For My sake and the Gospel's go
And tell Redemption's story".

So it is all about telling Redemption's story, not about telling our *own* story, which is what the Archbishop of Canterbury talked about on the day of his enthronement. It is also what those who are involved in the so-called "Decade of Evangelism" seem to be talking about today. They talk about evangelism meaning going about telling *our* story. But it isn't. It is all about telling Redemption's story.

But they never talk about Redeption today, or the *need* for Redemption.

Then the words of that Hymn become more specific and detailed to show what telling Redemption's story entails. They go on to say:- "They preach His birth, His Life, His Cross, The love of His *atonement,* His Easter, (that means his Resurrection), His enthronement, (that means His Ascension up into Heaven where He was enthroned, and still is enthroned).

All that is fact. Historical fact. It all actually happened, here on Earth. It is all just as much fact, historical fact, as the life of King Alfred, as the history of Nelson and the Battle of Trafalgar, and as all the events which took place in the Second World War. And it should be taught as such. But the words of the Hymn go on later to talk about His Coming again to Judge the Living and the Dead, as do all the Creeds. They say,

"He comes, whose Advent Trumpet drowns
The last of Time's evangels —
Emmanuel crowned with many crowns,
The Lord of saints and angels".

And in the middle of the Hymn all this is referred to as, "Glad tidings of salvation".

You could not have a better outline to teach to than that which is so clearly set out in the words of that Hymn. It is an outline of the basic facts of the Christian Faith, the *central* facts; which cover the details about The Person of The Lord Jesus Christ, the Founder of the Christian Faith. And it needs to be stressed in all teaching that Christianity *IS* Jesus Christ. Nothing less than that. All these facts are so clearly set out in that Hymn because that was what always used to be taught and believed as being the basic facts of the Christian Faith, and so they were embodied in that Hymn. And you could not have a more simple outline, I say, than that, to follow. They should be given pride of place in any Christian teaching syllabus. And since the Moslem children and teenage young people are all taught very firmly and soundly about Hell and The Coming Day of Judgment, as well as about Heaven, and since this regularly enters into their conversation as an essential part of their outlook on life whenever they talk to me, why should not that be taught to our British children as well? I have to tell you, that if it isn't, then those British children who go to schools where Moslem children and teenage young people are present will soon be taught about Hell, and the reality of Hell, and about The Coming Day of Judgment and what will happen then, by the Moslem children themselves! I defy anyone to meet any Moslem who does not have a strong conviction about Hell and The Day of Judgment. Such a Moslem simply does not exist. Would to God every Christian had such a strong conviction about these two vital facts. It would change the behaviour of lots of them! And furthermore, when these two vital facts are taught in Moslem Mosques, there is no public outcry amongst those present, or from Ayotollas or Immans, the equivalent of our Archbishops, Bishops and National Leaders, that this is "fire and brimstone" preachings, either! The fact of Hell and The Coming Day of Judgment are an essential and fully accepted part of all Moslem teaching. So were they also an essential and fully accepted part of the teaching of the Christian Faith all down the centuries, from the days of Jesus and of the New Testament onwards. It is only in recent years that they have been tragically discarded. But that doesn't alter the fact that they are both, awesome Realities. Therefore they should be firmly taught. Both of them.

Then Lady Olga Maitland pointed out in her Article that a MORI poll in 1991 found that 57 per cent of 18 to 24 year-olds could not say what happened on Good Friday. Such is the abysmal ignorance today. But the same could be said about Easter and about Christmas. People need to be told all over again what Christmas, Good Friday, and Easter are all about. And people need to be told these things right where they are. And these things need to be proclaimed boldly, fearlessly and courageously in the multi-faith society in which we live. Christmas, Good Friday and Easter are not occasions for Archbishops and Bishops to make political pronouncements. They are rather occasions, of *all* occasions, for them to proclaim the basic facts of the Christian Faith, because people just don't know them any more.

Lady Olga Maitland's statement about what the 1991 MORI poll revealed, reminded me of what happened two Christmas's ago. I walked into an Indian Restaurant which I often frequent, and the place was decorated with Christmas decorations, which is unusual in what is, in fact, a Moslem-run Restaurant. One of the Moslem waiters, a 21 year-old, said, "I did this in honour of my Christian friend". He then led me to a table for me to have a meal. I said to him, "Everyone is talking about Christmas, everybody is making preparations for Christmas, everybody is busy buying presents for Christmas, but very few people these days know what Christmas is all about". He said, "I know". I had previously given him a Bible, so I said to him, "If you want to know what Christmas is all about, then I want you to read a certain chapter in your Bible". He said to me immediately, "Why don't *you* read it to me?" So I took out my pocket-Bible, opened it at Luke's Gospel Chapter One and I began to read at verse 26. And he was leaning over my shoulder following what I was reading. "And in the sixth month the angel Gabriel was sent from God unto a city of Galilee, named Nazareth, to a virgin espoused to a man whose name was Joseph, of the house of David: and the virgin's name was Mary. And the angel came in unto her, and said, "Hail, thou that art highly favoured, the Lord is with thee: blessed art thou among women. And when she saw him, she was troubled at his saying and cast in her mind what manner of salutation this should be. And the angel said unto her, "Fear not, Mary: for thou has found favour with God. And, behold, thou shalt conceive in thy womb, and bring forth a son, and shalt call His Name JESUS. He shall be great, and shall be called the Son of the Highest: and the Lord God shall give unto Him the throne of his father (forefather) David; and he shall reign over the house of Jacob for ever: and of his Kingdom there shall be no end". Then said Mary unto the angel, "How shall this be, seeing I know not a man?" And the angel answered and said unto her, "The Holy Ghost shall come upon thee, and the power of the Highest shall overshadow thee: therefore also that holy thing which shall be born of thee shall be called the Son of God. And behold, thy cousin Elizabeth, she hath also conceived a son in her old age: and this is the sixth month with her, who was called barren. For with God nothing shall be impossible". And Mary said, "Behold the handmaid of The Lord, be it unto me according to thy word". And the angel departed from her". Luke Chapter I verses 26 to 38.

Just as I finished reading that passage from Luke's Gospel, this young Moslem suddenly burst out with great enthusiasm, "That is no problem

127

to me. It is no problem to me that she could have a son without a human father. God is a God who works great miracles, and nothing is impossible to Him". To which I replied, "My dear young man, you believe more than the Bishop of Durham does"! And he smiled from ear to ear.

But then I said to him, "You see, it says twice over here, "He shall be called the Son of God — the Son of the Highest". And I said to him, "It was the angel Gabriel who said that. The angel Gabriel who was supposed to appear to Mohammed about 600 years later and said "God can never have a son, so Jesus cannot be the Son of God". And yet here, the angel Gabriel says twice over, "He shall be called the Son of God". This young Moslem waiter said to me immediately:- "It is good to see it in print"! You see, it was the Word of God read to him that did it, as he followed what I was reading. The message had gone home, and he began to see for himself what Christmas is all about.

Then, to what happened on Good Friday and the meaning and significance of it. May I put it this way:-

This Good Friday (1993), because I became very conscious of the fact that when Jesus said, "Go into all the world and preach the Gospel to every creature" — every creature including all those of other faiths — I sought ways and means of getting the Message and Meaning of Good Friday over to them, because I had become aware that some of them wanted to know. On going into an ordinary secular Card Shop I spotted an Easter Card which had a beautiful and very attractive picture, in colour, on the front of it, of The Risen Lord Jesus with arms outstretched towards any person looking at this card, and there were the marks of the nails in His hands and in His feet. Underneath this picture, on the front of the card, were the words, "Behold the Lamb of God which taketh away the sin of the world". John I verse 29.

I bought several of these cards and inside every one of them I wrote the following:

"He *has* taken them away. (The sins of the world).
Every single one of them.
He did it when He went to the Cross nearly 2,000 years ago.
Therefore they are not there any more.
Not any one of them.
This is what the Message of Good Friday is all about.
All *we* have to do is believe it.

But it had to be a *Person* who was sacrificed for our sins, not *an animal*".

(I wrote this, because I had become aware that those of another faith, sacrifice a lamb for each of their families at this time of the year. And on asking them why, they told me that it was in order that their sins might be forgiven).

So I wrote, "But it had to be a *Person* who was sacrificed for our sins, not *an animal*.

But it had to be a *Perfect* Person.

And the only Perfect Person was Jesus. He is the Only Perfect Person who has ever lived.

He it is therefore who is The Lamb of God.

When He went to the Cross, He put Himself in *my* place, — in *your* place, — as God's Provided Substitute.

We are all sinners. And God has said, "The Penalty for Sin is Death". But Jesus has paid that Penalty for us, so that we will never have to pay it, and so that we will never have to go to Hell, but can now go to Heaven.

I say again, all *we* have to do is to believe it.

And *when* we believe it, we will be made sure that we will never go to Hell but to Heaven.

This is The Truth. The Truth of God.

Believe it, and you will be Eternally saved, and your Eternal Destiny will be assured and made secure for ever.

And you will be sure also that you will have a Happy Easter!"

Having written those words inside each one of these cards, I took 9 of them, and handed them in turn to 9 of my Moslem friends, personally. The first thing that I have to say is, that each one of them, without exception, took the card and expressed very warm appreciation of it. Secondly, one of them said, "I will take it home and read it quietly when I get home." Another of them, a 15 year-old boy said, "I can't wait to see what you have written inside it". He has since told me with great glee that he has not only read all those words but that he has pinned the card up on his bedroom wall, "so that I can read those words again and again", he said, with his eyes shining.

A third one, a 17 year-old said, "I want to wait until I am alone, somewhere quiet, where I won't be interrupted, and then I can read it and take in what you have written". He has since told me he has invited The

Lord Jesus Christ into his heart. He is now reading the Bible most eagerly, "lapping it up" like a thirsty dog laps up water.

Furthermore, he is learning spiritual truths as a result of reading his Bible which it has taken some Christians years to learn. And I am told he is fast becoming a wonderful evangelist. He is one of those who is being taught of The Lord.

All this was going on in the Indian Restaurant which I have already mentioned. But just after I had handed out all these cards another man came in, a middle-aged man, who turned out to be a Pakistani Moslem. He sat down to have a meal. Shortly after, I had to leave. As I was leaving he got up and said, "Those were very wise words which you wrote in those cards. They are wise words, every one of them". I had not noticed, but one of the others had shown him the card that I had given him, and this man had read it. He walked with me to the door and out into the street. I said to him, "You encouraged me no end by what you said about the words I had written in that card". He repeated, "They are wise words. Very wise words, every single one of them". I said, "Do you believe them?" He looked me in the eyes, and with a voice charged with emotion he said, "Those words create faith. They create faith". I said, "Would you like me to write them out for you in a similar card so that you can have it as your own and keep it?" And again with a voice full of emotion he said, "That would be most kind of you. I would very much appreciate that". So I wrote the words out again in a similar card and gave it to him and he has been talking to me ever since, and has been asking me for more words from the Bible.

So don't tell me that you mustn't ever talk about the Message and Meaning of Good Friday and Easter, and of the other basic facts of the Christian Faith to people of other faiths and religions. Some of them are most eager to know.

If only the Archbishop of Canterbury, who has access to Television more than anyone has, were to proclaim these same simple, basic, and central facts of the Christian Faith which I have written in that card all over the United Kingdom by means of Television, look how many souls would be saved as a result! And that is what proclaiming the Christian Faith is all about — the eternal salvation of souls.

Would to God also that every Diocesan Bishop were to proclaim these simple, basic, and central facts of the Christian Faith throughout the whole of their Dioceses! That is their primary task when once they become

Diocesan Bishops isn't it? It would result in the eternal salvation of countless souls. How many souls would be saved in the Diocese of Liverpool for instance, if it were to be done all over the Diocese by the Diocesan Bishop of Liverpool? And how many souls would be saved eternally in the adjacent Diocese of Chester, if it were done by the present Bishop of Chester in the full Power of The Holy Spirit? I say again, that is what spreading the Christian Faith is all about, — the eternal salvation of souls.

And would to God that the same words which I have written in those cards were included in every school's religious teaching syllabus and then taught. To quote the words of the Pakistan Moslem, "Those words create faith". And surely that is what Christian Education amongst children and teenage young people is all about. It is about creating faith, and creating faith in The Lord Jesus Christ who is their one and only Saviour from sin, and from the eternal consequences of sin, and the one and only Saviour of the World. For rather than the content of such syllabuses giving attention to "Christian traditions", as the front page article in the "Church of England Newspaper" of Friday, March 12th, 1993, on the schools Religious Education debacle, at least three times over, weakly states, is the need, it is these simple, basic, and central facts of the Christian Faith which need strongly to be taught. Indeed it is all the major Cardinal Facts, without exception, which need strongly and clearly to be put across. Christian Education is not about "traditions". It is about facts. The facts of the Glorious Gospel of The Lord Jesus Christ, and it is these that need to be firmly embedded into the hearts and minds of all our children and young people while they are in the process of growing up. Lady Olga Maitland, at the close of her Article says, "Young people desperately need a moral framework to provide a code of behaviour". It is true that they do. But with all due respect, the Christian Faith is not merely about providing a moral framework — a code of behaviour by which to live, although it includes doing that. It does that in the process. Rather, the Christian Faith is all about equipping people for the whole of life, and then for the whole of eternity. What therefore these young people and children urgently need is the foundation of the Christian Faith to be well and truly laid in their lives while they are still young, and then for that foundation to be faithfully built upon. And the Bible says, "Other foundation can no man lay than that that is laid, which is Jesus Christ". I Corinthians Chapter 3 verse 11. That means that they urgently need Jesus Christ as the foundation, as the bed-rock, as the anchor if you like, in each one of their lives.

They need Jesus Christ *within*, for it is having Jesus Christ *within* which makes a person a Christian. Jesus described it as digging deep and building one's house, one's life, upon a rock, the rock Christ Jesus, which is Himself. Then I Corinthians Chapter 3 verse 12 goes on to say, that once that foundation is well and truly laid it needs to be built upon with gold, silver and precious stones, not with wood, hay and stubble. That means with imperishable things. And Jesus, at the end of His Sermon on the Mount, made it plain what that included when He said, "Whoever heareth these words of Mine and *doeth* them I will liken him unto a wise man, which built his house upon a rock etc". Matthew Chapter 7 verse 24.

So the Christian Faith, and Christian Education, is all about seeing that the right foundation is laid in people's lives, and then about building on that foundation all the sayings and teachings of Jesus and then putting them into practice. Nothing short of that. And indeed much more. It includes building on that foundation all the teaching of the New Testament Epistles and that teaching found in the Acts of the Apostles, and all the teaching found in the books of the Old Testament. It is not all about teaching mere "Christian traditions", whatever that might mean! Not a bit of it.

Then because Lady Olga Maitland said in her Article, "The local syllabus conferences which draw up Religious Education schemes are endorsing syllabuses up and down the country which give teachers in classrooms no idea of what to teach, and no indication of how much time they should devote to Christianity within Religious Education", and because she went on to say in her next paragraph, "The fact is that these bodies — (the local syllabus conferences which draw up Religious Education schemes) — are being manipulated by religious education advisers, some of whom are deeply resentful that Parliament should pass a law giving *primacy* (my italicising) to Christianity within Religious Education" may I say this:-

Christianity *should* be given primacy within Religious Education. There is no question about it. I say that quite unequivocally. Christianity stands on its own. It is quite unique. It should never be placed alongside Judaism, Islam, Hinduism, Sikhism and Buddhism as the Sutton syllabus, according to Lady Olga Maitland's Article is doing. And Christianity should be given primacy because it is the superior religion above all religions. I make no hesitation in saying that, no matter who may protest. Because the Bible says, "God has given the enthroned Lord Jesus a Name which is above every name; in order that at the Name of Jesus every knee should bow, of things in heaven, and things in earth, and things under the earth: and that *every tongue* (my italicising) should confess that Jesus Christ is *LORD* (my italicising) to the glory of God the Father''. Philippians Chapter 2 verses 9 to 11. And that includes every Moslem tongue, every Buddhist tongue, every Hindu tongue, every Sikh tongue, every Judaic or Hebrew tongue, in other words, every Jewish tongue, every Rastafarian tongue, or whatever tongue of any other religion or faith in the world, whether they like it or not. They will have no say in the matter *then*. They will all have to confess that Jesus Christ is LORD on that Day, because He *will* be. And there will be no doubt *then* that Christianity is superior to all other religions. Indeed it will be seen *then*, that Christianity stands on it own, that it is quite unique, and completely set apart from all the other faiths and religions of the world as the One and Only Way of Eternal Salvation. And it will be clearly seen *THEN* that the One and Only True Church of the Lord Jesus Christ on Earth is *NOT* the Roman Catholic Church, but rather, that that One and Only True Church of The Lord Jesus Christ on Earth is comprised *ONLY* of True, Bible-Believing, Born-Again Believers; of those who are truly Born Again of the Holy Spirit of God, in other words, and *ONLY* of those. And The Lord Jesus Christ Himself will clearly be seen, *THEN*, to be the Head of that One and Only True Church on Earth, and its *ONLY* Head. There won't even be any Pope there at its Head!

Furthermore, the Prophecies of the Bible say that the day is coming when The Lord Jesus will be king over all the earth: in that day shall there be *One* LORD, and His Name one''. Zachariah Chapter 14 verse 9. And as I have pointed out in previous pages, in that day all the other faiths and religions of the world, and which God Himself says are false, worthless, and entirely without significance, will be no more. They just will not be there. They will no longer exist. For that supreme reason, therefore, Christianity should unquestionably be given primacy, priority, and the supreme and superior place in all Religious Education.

It did when I was a boy. When I was a boy, the first period in school, from 9 o'clock to 10 o'clock, — one hour, — was devoted entirely to our reading of the Bible. We read steadily from the beginning of the Book of Genesis right through to the end of the Second Book of Chronicles in the process of time. And furthermore, the Bible was taught to us as the Authoritative Word of God. No teacher questioned it, or threw doubt upon it. We also read steadily through the pages of the New Testament from the beginning of Matthew's Gospel to the end of the Acts of the Apostles. We were also required to commit to memory, and then repeat in class, whole chapters of the Bible, including John's Gospel Chapter One, I Corinthians Chapter 13, Isaiah Chapter 53, Isaiah Chapter 55, Isaiah Chapter 35, Joshua Chapter One, Psalm One, Psalm Eight, Psalm Fifteen, Psalm Nineteen, Psalm Twenty Three, and Psalm Twenty Four. We were also required to commit to memory all of the Ten Commandments, plus the Apostle's Creed and the Nicene Creed, and then to repeat them in class. There were also regular set examinations on all the above teaching syllabus. Then in Services in Church, *as children*, we used to sing, on Sundays, all the Psalms set for the day in the Book of Common Prayer without exception, without omission, including all the lengthy ones, which were never abbreviated or shortened. In fact, I myself, used to look forward to singing these very long Psalms more than any of the others, because they took us through all the history of Israel and the marvellous Works which God did for them. In this way the Word of God was well and truly being sown in our hearts, and a good and solid foundation of Scriptural truth was being laid, for life. And nobody ever talked about "giving attention to Christian traditions", or "devoting our time to Christian traditions", or "the need to reflect mainly Christian traditions", which is all the front page Article of "The Church of England Newspaper" seems very weakly to be able to refer to, when it talks about Christian Education. It was something far more solid and far more substantial than that. And I might add that because of my father's influence, and because he was always talking about the Prophecies of the Bible, by the time I was thirteen I had read the Book of The Revelation in its entirety, at one sitting, at least twice, and the Book of Daniel at least once.

That is what I call thorough Christian Education. And it was all given to me between the age of 5 and 15! Oh that such an adequate teaching syllabus and form of Christian Education could be introduced into all the schools all over the British Isles today!

But the tragedy is that at the present time the direct opposite is true. Nothing whatsoever, so far, has been done to reverse the scandal of the law on religious education being flouted in our schools. The act of massive civil disobedience, referred to by Lady Olga Maitland in her Article, flagrantly disobeying laws which Parliament has laid down, and which therefore are the Law of The Land, continues, so far unarrested. This national disgrace therefore has not gone away. The illegality of all the religious education syllabuses continues. The nation's children continue to be betrayed. They continue to be cheated of the right to learn about Christianity. The religious education syllabuses continue to have no Christian content whatsoever. And in one school in North London that I am aware of, Dollis Junior School, Mill Hill, whose Headmaster is a devoted and totally dedicated Christian, and who has devoted Christian teachers on his staff, a fierce battle has been going on for well over a year now, because some of the School Governors and Local Authorities strongly object to the Christian ethos that has been created in their school. Parents have even been picketed at the school gates each day by these strong and persistent objectors, and the issue has been contested so fiercely at a series of Governing Body Meetings that it has had to be submitted to the Secretary of State for Education for a decision. So even where Christian teaching and influence is being put across in some of our schools it is being firmly resisted, and even sought to be removed by Local Authorities and members of school Governing Bodies. Hence Lady Olga Maitland, at the close of her Article says, "We are becoming a rootless and restless society with no spiritual and moral benchmarks". and I might add, certainly not a nation at ease with itself!

Whilst, therefore, the Government and Parliament show every sign of continuing to legislate downwards, and now even by stealthy, subtle, and devious means, the Local Education Authorities, the manipulating religious and education advisers, and even school staffs, are contributing strongly to the downward moral and spiritual slide, by blatantly flouting the Law of The Land which is design to counter that landslide. And who can possible say that God is not angry because of all this? The Prime Minister, John Major, said in his speech at the Carlton Club on Wednesday evening, February 3rd (1993), "Sometimes it seems that by removing just one brick, we may risk bringing the whole house down". He, or his speech-writer, whoever his speech-writer was, seems only to have been referring to changes that he sees may have to be made to Conservative Party philosophy, thought and outlook.

But we have not only removed just one brick, so far as the nation's spiritual and moral structure is concerned. We have removed the entire foundation, namely, Faith in God, Saving Faith in The Lord Jesus Christ, Teaching and Belief in the Bible, and all the Fundamentals and Basic Facts of the Christian Faith itself, and that, from the entire rising generation of our children and teenage young people. We have now lost and got rid of all this that was so precious to this country in the past. With the entire foundation now removed the bringing down of the whole house is now inevitable. I tell you that, unless those vital Christian Foundations are urgently and very speedily restored, and the whole structure of the Nation become thus strongly underpinned, total National collapse is bound to take place. And that, for our utter foolhardiness, will be seen, by all, to be the awesome and inevitable Judgment of God. His awful Nemesis will have struck again.

It is high time, therefore, that God's Ultimatum to Britain was Sounded Out.

THE DEVASTATING FLOODS IN AMERICA
A second severe warning shot from Heaven across the bows of the United States.
(Inserted in Mid-July (1993) by urgent request)

I said a few pages previously, that when President Clinton, in the U.S.A. gave instructions, just after his inauguration as President, to lift the ban on the recruitment of homosexuals to the United States armed forces and thus provoked howls of rage from Middle America, and from his Army Chiefs of Staff, the "Storm of the Century" battered the entire 2,000 mile stretch of America's East Coast during the week-end of March 13th to 15th (1993). It suddenly came from nowhere, quite out of the blue," and brought the whole of North America's Eastern sea-board to a standstill.

I said that I believed very strongly that that "Storm of the Century" was a warning shot, fired from Heaven itself, across the bows of the new Clinton Administration because of the direction it was going in the "Gay Rights" issue. I also said that if he and his Administration continued to go down this libertarian path I cannot bear to think what the next Visitation of Divine Judgment will be on the United States of America, for it will be far worse, and far more severe, and even more sudden than was "The Storm of the Century".

And I said, "You mark my words." But an even more devastating warning shot has since been fired from Heaven across the United States' bows. For exactly four months later, on Tuesday July 13th (1993) to be exact, headline news appeared on the front page of "The Daily Telegraph" announcing that the great Mississippi and Missouri rivers had burst their banks and as a result floods had devastated the entire agricultural heartland of the United States, washing away crops, destroying farms, and leaving 22 people dead and 30,000 people homeless. That front page report said that this was due to more than a week of freak torrential rains and thunderstorms. Notice they were described as "freak". In other words, as unusual. The report said there was still worse to come. This was indeed something far worse and far more severe as I had predicted.

Then if you please, on the very same day, I heard it announced to my horror on the 1 o'clock B.B.C. News Bulletin that Mr. Major had stated that he was going to give his full backing to unrestricted Sunday Trading. And that, in direct and deliberate violation of God's Fourth Commandment which says, "Remember that thou keep holy the sabbath day. Six days shalt thou labour and do all that thou hast to do. But the seventh day is the sabbath of the Lord thy God: in it thou shalt not do any work, thou, nor thy son, nor thy daughter, thy manservant, nor thy maidservant, nor thy cattle, nor thy stranger that is within thy gates: for in six days the Lord made heaven and earth, the sea, and all that in them is, and *rested* the seventh day: wherefore the Lord blessed the sabbath day, and hallowed it." Exodus Chapter 20 verses 8 to 11.

It was plain that by deliberately and wilfully violating this Commandment Mr. Major obviously intended to take yet another step downwards, and furthermore, was making it plain that he was going to cause his Government to legislate still further downwards and take the Country with it.

I was on my way, that afternoon of Tuesday July 13th, to the Fulham Y.M.C.A., of which I am Chairman, just after I had heard of the Prime Minister's retrograde decision and just after I had read the reports of America's devastating floods. I was due to Chair the monthly Executive Meeting there, and at every Executive Meeting we always begin with a Bible Reading and a time of prayer before doing anything else. I was wondering on my journey to Fulham what the Bible Reading should be. Then Psalm 2 and Proverbs Chapter One were brought to my mind. On arrival, and after the Committee Members had assembled, I told them about the devastating floods in the United States and about Mr. Major's decision to back unrestricted Sunday Trading. And I said, "That is yet another downward step that this Country is taking." Then I drew everybody's attention to the words of Psalm 2 as being very relevant to these two things, and I began to read it. It says:- "Why do the heathen rage, and the people imagine a vain thing? The kings of the earth set themselves, and the rulers take counsel together, *against the Lord,* and *against his anointed,* saying, "Let us break their bands asunder, and cast away their cords from us."

And I pointed out that President Clinton and Prime Minister Major are rulers, — rulers who today are taking counsel against the Lord, and against his anointed. His Anointed being The Lord Jesus Christ Himself.

I also pointed out that when they say, "Let us break their bands asunder and cast away their cords from us"; that means in modern language, "Let us throw over the traces. Let us have nothing more to do with things like God's Commandments. Let us break free from all such restraints."

Then I continued the reading. It says, "He that sitteth in the heavens shall laugh: the Lord shall have them in derision. *THEN*", and I repeated, "*THEN* shall he speak unto them in his wrath and vex them in his sore displeasure."

Then I said, "The Storm of the Century" which hit the United States just after President Clinton had given instructions to lift the ban on the recruitment of homosexuals to the United States armed forces almost immediately after his inauguration as President, was God speaking to the United States in his wrath? Furthermore, that these devastating floods in the United States which had just been announced that day was also God speaking to America in his wrath, and vexing them in his sore displeasure." And I asked, "Now that our own Prime Minister has decided to take yet another step downwards by announcing that he is going to back unrestricted Sunday Trading, whatever can we expect in terms of an equally devastating Judgment of God by way of God speaking to Britain in his wrath?" I said, "It does not bear thinking about. It has happened to the United States. Whatever is going to happen to us?"

But the floods in the United States have continued, showing that it is indeed something far worse and far more severe.

However, before I go on to recount about that, let me tell you what I then read to that Fulham Y.M.C.A. Executive Committee from the Book of Proverbs Chapter One. I began to read at verse 24. This is God speaking. He says, "Because I have called, and ye refused; I have stretched out my hand, and no man regarded; but ye have set at nought all my counsel, and would have none of my reproof: I also will laugh at your calamity; I will mock when your fear cometh; when your fear cometh as desolation, and your destruction cometh as a whirlwind; when distress and anguish cometh upon you. *THEN* shall they call upon me, but I will not answer; they shall seek me early, but they shall not find me; for that they hated knowledge, and did not choose the fear of the Lord: they would have none of my counsel; they despised all my reproof. Therefore shall they eat of the fruit of their own way, and be filled with their own devices. For the turning away of the simple shall slay them, and the prosperity of fools shall destroy them."

I broke off half way through this reading and said to everybody present,

"You will know that there was a Day of National Prayer in one London District last week. But what does verse 24 says?" It says, *"THEN shall they call upon me, BUT I WILL NOT ANSWER; they shall seek me early, BUT THEY SHALL NOT FIND ME."* And I said, "That is what happens when a Nation and a people have got themselves into this position that is described here in Proverbs Chapter One. And we, in Britain, have, in fact, got ourselves into that position and into that condition. And God Himself says here that He will not answer when they call upon Him. He even says He will laugh at their calamity when it comes."

I also said, "When did we last hear anybody proclaiming from our National Pulpits about "God speaking to a Nation in His Wrath, and vexing them in His sore Displeasure?" I said, "He is speaking to the United States right now in His Wrath. And with these devastating floods He is vexing them in His sore Displeasure. And we can expect Him to speak unto us, here in Britain, very soon in His Wrath, and especially as our Prime Minister has just made it plain that he intends to take the Country still further down-hill than we are going at the moment." I said, "These are very stern words that I have been reading. But we need to heed them."

Then I said, "But whatever way God is going to speak to this Nation of Britain in His Wrath, we, as Believers, should take comfort from the last verse of Proverbs Chapter One. It begins with a "BUT." And it is a big *"BUT."*

It says, "BUT whoso hearkeneth unto Me shall dwell safely, and shall be quiet from fear of evil."

I said, "That means that God is going to look after His people and keep them safe whenever the Coming Judgment descends and will give them peace of mind as they go through it all."

But I said earlier, however, that the Floods in the United States have continued.

By Saturday July 17th (1993), four days after that Fulham Y.M.C.A. Executive Committee, "The Times" Newspaper reported that it was now being called "the worst flooding in United States history." On another page in "The Times" on that same day huge black headlines declared that the Floods had now spread to cover an area the size of Great Britain, and the waters were still rising. That same night, July 17th, the B.B.C. announced on its midnight news that the floods in America were "of Biblical proportions." I am quoting the actual words which the announcer used. Strange words to be used by the B.B.C.! The floods were made even worse when the waters of the two great rivers, the Mississippi and the Missouri broke through flood defences and converged. Furthermore, more heavy thunderstorms were being forecast. By now, 6 million acres of prime farm land were under water.

By Monday July 19th Al Gore, the vice president, was describing the disaster area as "a new great lake" that has afflicted at least 20 million acres of America's most fertile farmland. (From a full-page report in "The Times" Monday July 19th 1993). And the "Daily Telegraph" reported on that day that the water was still rising an inch an hour. So it was obvious to all, by that, that it was something far more severe.

Then on Tuesday July 20th the "Daily Telegraph" said the flood waters were again sweeping through America's Mid-West and were swollen again by heavy rain and thunderstorms. By now no less than nine American States had been seriously hit. By now, too, 29 people had died in the floods, including a 12-year old boy. And a leading Article in "The Times" on Wednesday July 21st said, "The Great Flood is *more than* a natural disaster." (My italicising.) Indeed, it was reported in the "Daily Telegraph" on Tuesday July 20th, that one resident of the city of St. Louis, a Mr. Charles White, had said, "I guess you just can't mess around with the Big Boy up above." So somebody was acknowledging it was God!

That Tuesday, Tuesday July 20th, the third Tuesday in the month, was the day The National Council for Christian Standards held its monthly National Prayer Meeting, and I, as a Trustee, was expected to take part. The subject of the Floods in the United States came up. So did the Prime Minister's appalling decision to back unrestricted Sunday Trading. I suggested we should read Psalm 2. And when it was suggested that I myself should read it, I read the first few verses. So again I read the words, "Why do the heathen rage, and the people imagine a vain thing? The kings of the earth set themselves, and the rulers take counsel together, against the Lord, and against his anointed, saying, Let us break their bands asunder and cast away their cords from us."

I broke off there and said, "That is exactly what President Clinton has been saying, when he says he is all for the "Gay Rights" Movement and when he says he wants homosexuals to be recruited into the American armed forces. That is exactly what Mr. Major is saying when he said last Tuesday that he was going to back unrestricted Sunday Trading. Because these words mean, "Let us throw over the traces. Let's get rid of all these restrictive moral standards. Let us break free from God and from all God's regulations and commandments. Let us free ourselves from all such." That is what both of them are saying.

I then said, "So the following verses from Psalm 2 are God's answer to all that."

"They say, "He that sitteth in the heavens shall laugh." I said, "That is one of the very few verses in the Bible which speak of God laughing." I repeated, "He that sitteth in the heavens shall laugh: the Lord shall have them in derision. THEN shall he speak unto them in his wrath, and vex them in His sore Displeasure."

And I said, "He is speaking to the United States right now in His wrath. He uses his elements at times as his Instruments of Judgment. And that is what these devastating floods are all about, now engulfing no less than 9 States. And the waters are still rising, and more torrential rain is forecast. This is God speaking to the New American Administration and to President Clinton in his wrath, because of the way they are backing the "Gay Rights" Movement and because of other ways that they are taking the United States downhill in moral terms."

And I said, "I was horrified to hear, on the very day that these American floods were first announced in the British Press, that Mr. Major had stated that he intended to back unrestricted Sunday Trading." I said, "I am alarmed that he is taking yet another step downwards, and in so doing will take the Country still further downhill with him."

I said, "I am alarmed and horrified, because if God is speaking to the United States in his wrath right now in the way that he is, whatever is going to happen to us, here in Britain, when he speaks to *this* Nation in his Wrath?"

I said, "These are very stern words from Psalm 2, but we urgently need to be confronted with them." Everybody present could see that those words from Psalm 2 were speaking to the United States Situation today, and that they were also speaking to our own Situation here in Britain. And they all said so, with very deep concern written all over their faces, and indeed of alarm. We then turned to Proverbs Chapter One, which I read from verse 24. God is speaking. He says:- "Because I have called, and ye refused; I have stretched out my hand, and no man regarded; but ye have set at nought all my counsel, and would have none of my reproof . . . ."

I broke off here and said, "That is the position here in Britain today. We and our National Leaders have shut our ears to God. We and our National Leaders have even refused Him. We have indeed set at nought all His counsel, and would have none of his reproof or correction. Therefore what does He say?

He says, "I also will laugh at your calamity. (One of the other few occasions when the Bible speaks of God laughing.)

But notice He says, "I also will laugh at your calamity." So calamity is coming. Calamity is coming to Britain, not just to the United States.

I repeat. God says, "I also will laugh at your calamity; I will mock you when your fear cometh; when your fear cometh as desolation, and your destruction cometh as a whirl-wind; when disasters and anguish cometh upon you."

So we can expect to see desolation.

We can expect destruction.

We can expect calamity.

That is what God is saying here.

Because we've got ourselves into this position which is outlined in these verses.

And when desolation and destruction comes God will mock. That is what He says.

Did you know that God mocks?

When calamity comes God will laugh.

That is what He says.

And then we come to these most solemn and sobering words:-

"*THEN* shall they call upon me, but I will not answer; they shall seek me early, but they shall not find me." There will be nothing but silence. Nothing but a seemingly empty void.

And *WHY?*

The next verses give the answer:-

"For that they hated knowledge, and did not choose the fear of the Lord; they would have none of my counsel; they despised all my reproof."

That is WHY.

What a desperate condition for a Nation and a people to get itself in! But it was agreed at that National Council for Christian Standards Prayer Meeting that these verses from Proverbs Chapter One as well as the words of Psalm 2 are speaking precisely to our National Condition and Situation today.

This is *WHERE WE ARE!*

And I immediately had an urgent request from that Meeting to include all that I had said about Psalm 2 and Proverbs One and the American Floods, in this book. That is why I have inserted it here just before the book is due to go to print.

"Oh," but some people will say, including Peers of the Realm, "this is a lot of nonsense. How can you possibly say that such National Disasters as the American Floods are from God? And how can you possibly say it has anything to do with God exercising Divine Retribution? Disasters and Catastrophies like that have nothing to do with people's standing before God."

In answer to the last of these statements let me remind you of what Jesus Himself said. We read in Lukes Gospel Chapter 13 that, "there were present at that season some that told him, (Jesus), of the Galilleans, whose blood Pilate had mingled with their sacrifices. And Jesus answering said unto them, Suppose ye that these Gallilleans were sinners above all the Galilleans, because they suffered such things? I tell you, Nay: but except ye repent, ye shall all likewise perish.

Or those eighteen, on whom the tower of Siloam fell, (which was a national calamity then) and slew them, think ye that they were sinners above all men that dwelt in Jerusalem? I tell you, Nay: but except ye repent, ye shall all likewise perish." And Jesus would say the same about national calamities and about "natural" disasters, (so-called), today. And when He said, "Ye shall *all* likewise perish," He meant all. And "all" includes the Peers of the Realm. They are not in a category of their own, simply because they are Peers. They need to repent like everybody else or they, too, Jesus would say, shall all likewise perish. They are not exempt simply because they are Peers.

Then in answer to the first question "How can you possibly say that such National Disasters as the American Floods are from God and have to do with God visiting Divine Retribution?" let me say this. On the very day that I am writing this page, Saturday July 24th (1993), at the foot of three-quarters of a page in "The Times" giving the latest account of the American Floods, a report is printed which came from Washington. It says, "Nearly one in five Americans believe the Mississippi flooding is God's revenge against sinners." It says, "A Cable News Network/U.S.A. "Today" Gallup Poll asked a number of respondents whether "the recent floods in the Mid West are an indication of God's judgment on the people of the United States for their sinful ways." And that was the result; one in five Americans, it was reported, believe that it is.

143

So it seems that those who initiated that Gallop Poll were looking in the right direction for an explanation of those Floods.

But I ask. Who is there in the United States who will boldly and fearlessly proclaim in the words of Psalm 2, "This is GOD speaking to the United States in His Wrath, and vexing them in His sore displeasure?"

Will Dr. Billy Graham, who seems to have a close relationship with every American President?

Will Dr. R. T. Kendall?

At least we can say that there is one voice here in Britain that is bold enough to proclaim that!

MAASTRICHT

Then What about Maastricht?

Somebody who is in a strong position of Christian Leadership in this Country, and who knows the Bible pretty well, whilst discussing our tragic National Situation with me recently, said, "The Bible reveals that when a Nation forsakes God and turns its back on Him as we have done, two things inevitably follow in the wake of that apostasy. (1) It goes after other gods, faiths and religions; and (2) it engages in widespread sodomy, — in other words, in widespread homosexuality and lesbianism". My answer is, "All that is undoubtedly true. But the Bible reveals that a third thing happens. And that is, it starts going after and trusting in, False Alliances". Having forsaken God and Faith in Him, it no longer puts its trust in Him for everything. He is no longer even "in the picture". But it starts putting its trust in other confidences. And I believe Maastricht comes into that category. It is trusting in a False Alliance so far as Britain is concerned.

So what does the Scripture say about *this?* We must always go to the Bible for direction on such matters. "To the law and to the testimony" says Isaiah Chapter 8 verse 20. "If they speak not according to this word, it is because there is no light in them".

One of the first examples in the Bible of a Nation indulging in a False Alliance is the example of King Solomon . The First Book of Kings Chapter 3 verse 1 says, "And Solomon made affinity with Pharoah, King of Egypt". That is, he entered into a false alliance with him. To "make affinity", according to the Oxford Dictionary, means to "combine with", to "make a close connection with".

And in Solomon's case it was a retrograde step. It led to all kinds of trouble, including his marrying foreign wives who turned his heart away from following The Lord. It led to his going after other gods and religions, and to bringing into being a multi-religious society in his nation.

And God was so angry about this that He said that Solomon would lose his kingdom as a result. We read therefore, "Wherefore the Lord said unto Solomon, 'Forasmuch as this is done of thee, and thou hast not kept My Covenant and my Statutes which I have commanded thee, I will surely *rend the kingdom from thee* (my italicising). . . . Notwithstanding in thy days I will not do it . . . but I will rend it out of the hand of thy son". I Kings Chapter Eleven verses 11 and 12.

This was the Awful Consequence of Solomon doing this. But it all began with his entering into a False and Unholy Alliance. In his case, with Egypt. I need to state that the Judgment of God, in his case, was, he lost his kingdom.

The second example is that of good King Asa and the False Alliance which he entered into. In the early part of his reign, when an army of a million or more Ethiopians came against him, Asa cried to the Lord for help, and the Lord smote the Ethiopians in front of Asa and his people, and the Ethiopians fled. (See 2 Chronicles Chapter 14 verses 9 to 15). In other words, Asa was relying on the Lord at that time, and was looking to the Lord for deliverance. But later on in his reign, when Baasha, the wicked king of the Northern Kingdom of Israel, came up against Asa's Southern Kingdom of Judah, Asa entered into a False Alliance with Benhadad the King of Syria and asked him to come to his assistance. The Lord sent a Prophet, Hanani the seer, to rebuke King Asa for this. He came to him and said, "Because thou hast relied on the King of Syria, and not relied on the Lord thy God, therefore is the host of the King of Syria escaped out of thine hand. Were not the Ethiopians and the Lubims a huge host (army) with very many chariots and horsemen? Yet because thou didst rely on the Lord, He delivered them out of thine hand. For the eyes of the Lord run to and fro throughout the whole earth, to show Himself strong in the behalf of them whose heart is perfect toward Him. Herein thou hast done foolishly: therefore from henceforth thou shalt have wars". 2 Chronicles Chapter 16 verses 1 to 9. So God said to Asa that in indulging in a False Alliance and in trusting in it he had done foolishly.

And the Judgment of God in King Asa's case was, "From henceforth he would have wars".

And he did.

The third example is that of good King Jehoshaphat. In 2 Chronicles

Chapter 18 verse 1 we read, "Now Jehoshaphat had riches and honour in abundance". But then we read that he joined affinity with Ahab, the wicked King of the Northern Kingdom of Israel. In other words, he entered into a False Alliance with him. It was a False Alliance since Ahab was not walking with God, but was going against Him.

And God rebuked Jehoshaphat very serverely for this. We read in 2 Chronicles Chapter 19 verses 1-2, "And Jehoshaphat, the King of Judah returned to his house, (after the notoriously wicked King Ahab had been defeated and killed in battle against the Syrians), and Jehu the son of Hanani the seer went out to meet him, and said to King Jehoshaphat, "Shouldest thou help the ungodly, and love them that hate the Lord? therefore is wrath upon thee from the Lord". 2 Chronicles Chapter 19 verse 2.

So the Judgment of God on King Jehoshaphat in *that* case was, that wrath was upon him from the Lord.

But there was a *second* case as far as he was concerned. For we read in 2 Chronicles Chapter 20 verses 35 to 37 that he entered into a *Second* False Alliance, and this time with the wicked King Ahaziah of the Northern Kingdom of Judah, King Ahab's successor. These verses say, "And after this did Jehoshaphat King of Judah join himself with Ahaziah King of Israel who did wickedly: and he joined himself with him to make ships to go to Tarshish; and they made the ships in Ezion-geber". In other words, it was some kind of Trading Alliance, which also involved Ship-Building. A False Alliance involving Foreign Trade, which sounds very familiar today!

Then we read, "Then Eliezer, the son of Dodavah of Mareshah (another Prophet), prophesied against Jehoshaphat, saying, "Because thou hast joined thyself with Ahaziah (indulged in a False Alliance with him) the Lord hath broken thy works". 2 Chronicles Chapter 20 verse 37. It says, "And the ships were broken, that they were not able to go to Tarshish". The Lord smashed them, and the intended Foreign Trade came to nothing, because The Lord just was not in it. The Alliance was something He did not approve of. So His Blessing just was not on it. That was the Judgment of God in *that* case.

Is there a solemn and sobering lesson in this incident concerning Maastricht today? We need to ask that question.

But then we need to see what the Books of the Prophets have to say about a Nation or a people going after, and trusting in, False Alliances.

Take Isaiah Chapter 30 verse 1, for instance, "Woe to the rebellious children, saith the Lord, that take counsel, but not of Me, . . . that walk to go down into Egypt, — (to enter into a False Alliance, that means), and have not asked at My mouth: to strengthen themselves in the strength of Pharoah, and to trust in the shadow of Egypt". Isaiah Chapter 30, verses 1 and 2.

What is the Judgment of God on entering into such a False Alliance in this case?

Verse 3 gives the answer:- "Therefore shall the strength of Pharoah be your shame, and the trust in the shadow of Egypt your confusion".

With regard to Maastricht and trusting in the E.E.C. we could say of Britain today, "Therefore shall the strength of Delores be your shame, and the trust in the shadow of Brussels and Strasbourg your confusion". Furthermore, it is true to say, that Britain never took counsel of the Lord or asked at God's mouth about going into the E.E.C. Never once!

Or again, in Isaiah Chapter 31 verse 1, "Woe to them that go down to Egypt (or Brussels or Strasbourg) for help . . . but they look not unto the Holy One of Israel, neither seek the Lord!"

What is the Judgment of God in that case?

Verse 3 gives the answer:- "Now the Egyptians, (or members of the Council of Ministers and members of the European Parliament) are men, and not God . . . . When the Lord shall stretch out His hand, (in judgment), both he that helpeth, (that's the E.E.C.!) shall fall, and he that is helped, (Britain, and all the other member countries) shall fall down, and they shall FAIL together". That gives pause for thought! God will bring it down, and it will all come to nothing is what this is saying.

Then take the Prophet Jeremiah, for instance.

At the end of Jeremiah Chapter 2, the Prophet is remonstrating against the Southern Kingdom of Judah for relying on Egypt and Assyria as False Alliances. He says, in verse 37, "The Lord hath rejected thy confidences, and thou shalt not prosper in them".

So the Judgment of God in this case, was that God had rejected these False Alliances, these False confidences.

We need seriously to ask, "Is the Lord saying that to Britain today concerning Maastricht and the E.E.C." "The Lord hath rejected these thy confidences, and thou shalt not prosper in them?" It is a very sobering thought.

Then in Jeremiah Chapter 5 verse 10, in the second half of the verse, it says, "Take away the battlements; for they are not the Lord's".

Battlements are defences. Is that the reason, I wonder, why our defences have been cut to the bone and taken away? Is this The Lord's doing because they are not His? If so, that is another very sobering question indeed. And especially now that we have been reduced to one Royal Naval Dockyard!

147

Then Jeremiah Chapter 16 verse 5 says, "Thus saith the Lord ... 'I have taken away My peace from this people', saith the Lord, even loving-kindness and mercies".

So The Lord can take away His peace from a people. He can also take away His mercy. He can take away His Protection. And does so. And I believe He has.

Turning to the Book of Ezekiel. Chapter 16 is a very long chapter in which God rehearses the history of the whole house of Israel in pictorial form and then declares that Judgment is inevitable upon her for two reasons:-

    (1) For constantly going after the other gods and religions of the nations which were around her, and

    (2) For going after, and trusting in, False Alliances.

God declares in this chapter that he had taken the Northern Kingdom of Israel away into captivity and thus caused it to cease to be a Nation on account of this. So, — He said, at that time — will He do with the Southern Kingdom of Judah on account of the same thing. And He did do. They also ceased to be a Nation. That was the Judgment of God upon them in *those* cases.

Then concerning that Judgment, God said in Ezekiel Chapter 24 verse 14, "I the Lord have spoken it; it shall come to pass, and I will do it: I will not go back, neither will I spare, neither will I repent".

That tells us that when once God has pronounced His Judgment it is bound to come — Nothing can stop it. It is bound to fall upon those concerned.

Then in the Book of Hosea Chapter 7 verses 10 to 13, concerning a people which is under God going after False Alliances and relying on them, God says, "They do not return to the Lord their God, nor seek Him for all this. Ephraim, (the Northern Kingdom of Israel in this case), also is like a silly dove without heart: (that could be said of Britain), they call to Egypt, — (in Britain's case to the E.E.C.) — they go to Assyria" (Brussels, Strasbourg, Maastricht, the European Parliament, the Council of Ministers etc. in Britain's case). "When they shall go, saith the Lord, I will spread My net upon them; I will bring them down as the fowls of heaven: I will chastise them, as their congregation hath heard. Woe unto them! for they have fled from Me. Destruction unto them! Because they have transgressed against Me".

To which I would add, "Woe! Woe! indeed".

"It is a fearful thing to fall into the hands of the Living God". Hebrews 10 verse 31.

And if any reader should protest and say, "But all these Scriptures that you have quoted apply only to Israel", my reply would be, "Do they?" I repeat, "Do they?" I would remind you once again that I Corinthians Chapter 10 verse 11 says, "Now all these things happened unto them for examples: and they are written for *our* admonition, (my italicising), upon whom the ends of the world are come". You can't get away from that, now can you? That includes us!

Then about all that has been going on in Parliament concerning the Treaty of Maastricht for months and months now. What can we say? Maastricht has been an obsession as far as Mr Major is concerned. His Cabinet and the Leaders of the Opposition all appear to have been mesmerised by it. It is as if they have been driven powerfully along by some unseen Force. Furthermore, they all know full well that they have been going against the will of the British people. That is why the Prime Minister adamantly refuses to hold a referendum on it, despite the extremely strong demand for one. He knows full well he would lose. But what about that powerful driving force? Is there any explanation of this? I believe there is. And I believe it to be found in the Book of Hosea Chapters 4 and 5, and in certain other Scriptures. For instance, in Hosea Chapter 4 verse 10 it says "they shall commit whoredoms ... *because* they have left off to take heed to the Lord", and that statement is followed immediately in verse 12 by a directly related statement:- "The spirit of whoredoms hath caused them to err". So here we have a *spirit* operating. It is a spirit; the spirit of whoredoms. To commit whoredom is to go after a wrong relationship with someone, or something. It is to go after a strange relationship. And it is to be so mesmerised by it that it becomes an obsession. And by the time it has become an obsession a spirit takes over and the victim gets carried forward relentlessly and driven along by that spirit. Hosea Chapter 5 verse 4 even says, "the spirit of whoredoms is in the midst of them, and they have not known the Lord". So I have to say again, it is a spirit. The spirit of whoredoms. But I need to quote what the whole of verse 4 says. It says, "They will not frame their doings to turn unto their God: for the spirit of whoredoms is in the midst of them, and they have not known the Lord". So it is something that happens which is directly related to those who "have left off to take heed to the Lord". Hosea 4 verse 10, and who "will not frame their doings to turn unto their God". Hosea 5 verse 4. They get taken over and driven along by another spirit. There is a direct connection between these two things. The one

149

is the direct result of the other.

And furthermore, the Scriptures reveal that this can happen to heads of governments. For instance, Isaiah Chapter 19 verse 11 is talking about the princes, the rulers, the heads of government of Zoan and Noph in Egypt in Isaiah's time. And verse 14 of that chapter says, "The Lord has mingled a perverse spirit in the midst thereof; and they have caused Egypt to err in every work thereof". Verse 13 also says, "The princes of Noph, (the governing authorities) are deceived, they have also seduced Egypt".

So once again they were being influenced, directed, and driven, by a spirit, a perverse spirit. And it even says "The *LORD* had caused this to happen. "The LORD has mingled a perverse spirit in the midst thereof".

And the way Mr Major has adamantly and relentlessly been pursuing the Maastricht Treaty through the House of Commons against quite strong, legitimate opposition, even using the strong-arm tactics of the Whips at times, and all kinds of manipulations, manoeuvres, orchestrations, dubious, deceitful and totally despicable and disreputable means in order to get his own way as if he is totally obsessed with it, strongly suggests that there is another spirit at work, and that all this unseemly Parliamentary behaviour which has been so deplored by the British Press is a real sign that there is. And not only has he been going against the will of the British people by denying them their democratic right to determine the future of their constitution by a referendum, knowing full well he is going against them, he has been going against God. That is why he has found it such hard, tough, and frustrating going, all along the line. You don't need any other explanation than that. Indeed, to me, John Major is like Balaam in the Book of Numbers Chapter 22, going against God, with the Angel of The Lord standing in his way to block his path. And sooner or later some dumb ass will have his mouth opened by The Lord and will speak unto him and rebuke him!

In fact, at the time of writing this particular section of this booklet, (Saturday, May 8th, 1993), he and his Government have just suffered two most humiliating defeats. One, on Wednesday evening May 7th, when, in the House of Commons, it had to stage a climbdown to avoid certain defeat over the social chapter in the Maastricht Treaty, which, according to Mr Bill Cash, MP for Stafford, had now made the Bill incompatible with the Treaty, and had plunged the Government into uncharted waters, thus resulting in a matter of great constitutional importance.

This has also caused Mr Leo Price, QC, an expert on E.C. law, to say,

"There will be no successful ratification of this Treaty. it will therefore have to be renegotiated or allowed to die". And two, when the Government suffered a humiliating defeat in the Newbury by-election on Thursday, May 6th. And at the same time witnessed a disastrous performance in the local elections, when the Tories were routed, losing control of 15 councils, some of which they had held since as long ago as the 1880s, and when, of the 47 county councils in England and Wales, they now only run one, namely Buckinghamshire. Mr Major acknowledged after he had heard the results, that the Government had been given a "bloody nose" in the biggest test of national opinion since last year's general election. He said, "I understand that. I take note of that. We will learn by that". But I wonder if he sees, and understands, and has taken note of the fact that he has been given a "bloody nose" by God. Will he learn from *that,* I wonder?

The Government has been deceitful, devious, subtle and stealthy about many things. They have been guilty of stealthiness, deviousness and deceitfulness so far as putting the Maastricht Treaty to a vote from all the people of this Country is concerned, even though they know full well the British peoples' lives wil be altered irrevocably by it. Their main argument is that a referendum is not the way Britain does things. Parliament, the Government says, is the only trustworthy mechanism! They even claim that they have been given a mandate by the electorate to negotiate, and then to ratify the Treaty when it was not so much as mentioned in its Manifesto in the last General Election, or in any of the General Election Speeches. Cynical MPs know full well that that main argument of the Government is largely nonsense. It is sheer deception. After every State Opening of Parliament, and at the end of every gracious speech at that Opening, Her Majesty The Queen always concludes with the words, "I pray that the Blessing of Almighty God may be upon your counsels". But how can it be, with all this subtlety, deviousness, stealthiness, and deceitfulness going on? The Blessing of Almighty God just isn't on their counsels. It cannot be, when they handle affairs in that way. God's Blessing just is not on the Maastricht Treaty Debates, and has not been, all along. In no way. When they have handled affairs in the way that they have done. God's Blessing just is not on our National Economy either. And that is so, simply because God is saying, in the words of Haggai Chapter One verses 5 and 6, "Consider your ways. Ye have sown much, and bring in little: ye eat, but ye have not enough: ye drink, but ye are not filled with drink: ye clothe you, but there is none warm: *and he that earneth* wages earneth wages to put it into a bag with holes". (My italicising).

And again, in verse 9, "Ye looked for much, and, lo, it came to little: and when ye brought it home I did blow upon it. Why? saith the Lord of hosts, "*BECAUSE* of Mine house that is waste". *BECAUSE*, IN Britain's case, the cause of the essential, basic, New Testament Christian Faith has been completely abandoned in the Land.

I doubt very much, too, if God's Blessing is on our Nation's Manufacturing and Business Industry, with the collapse of Leyland Daf and the Swan Hunter Shipyard amongst the latest of a whole chain of our Industries that have been faced with having to close down. Thousands of smaller business have also had to "go to the wall". And God's Blessing simply is not on the Channel Tunnel Enterprise, with ever-increasing costs repeatedly delaying its opening, — over £10 billion being now the estimated cost, — over twice the original estimate. Neither is God's Blessing on our National Health Service, and particularly in London, and in the Midlands. Nor on our Coal Mining Industry with so many Coal Mines having to be closed down. Or even on our Judicial System. It is in total disarray.

And all this, is without question, *BECAUSE WE HAVE TURNED AWAY FROM THE LORD. THEREFORE THE LORD IS NOT WITH US.* Numbers 14:43.

I believe God is saying to Britain today, "I will go and return to My place, till they acknowledge their offence, and seek My Face". Hosea 5:15.

But the greatest deception of all, about the Maastricht Treaty, is this, that the Government, in a totally underhanded way, is covering up completely what is really going on, — and *has* been doing, — all along the line. It is high time, therefore, that this particular deception was bought right out into the open and was fully exposed. Maastricht and the E.E.C., as most people know by now, is all about a United Europe. But what they don't know is that the whole concept of a United Europe has been an idea and "vision" which originated in the Vatican from the very outset. That is the truth of the matter. And that is an historical fact. The Vatican has entertained this dream of a United Europe for a long time, and with a particular objective in mind. This is a fact which nowadays the Church of Rome takes very little pains to disguise. We can turn to history, first, to substantiate this. History is fact and cannot possibly be denied. And I am most grateful to Dr. David Samuel for many of the facts which are stated in the next few pages and which he has given me full permission to quote. He included them all in a Public Address which he delivered in London recently and which was then published. I have a full copy of it. He states that the historical fact is this, that over a hundred years ago, a proposal was made, for a European Council with the Pope at its head. The pretext for this proposal was the discordant and inflammatory condition of Europe. Its nations were continually on the brink of war. The question was being asked, "Can nothing be thought of to make so awful a calamity as war impossible? The answer given was "Yes". Means can be found. Let there be established a great European Council. And further, at the head of that Council, let there be some great moral authority". The proposers of this scheme said, "In the Pople we have precisely such a functionary". "This proposal", they said, "is a very specious one. It has come from the Roman side. We are likely to hear more of this proposal in time to come". And so we have done! A lot more! A certain Dr. J. A. Wylie wrote about this, over a hundred years ago, in a book entitled, "Which Sovereign — Queen Victoria or the Pope?" because this proposal was then a current subject of discussion in the London newspapers.

History has proved since that we have, indeed, "heard more of this proposal in time to come". The founding father of the European Community in the post-war era was Robert Schuman, a Roman Catholic. The Church of Rome is at present proposing his canonisation in recognition of that. Now with Maastricht, that proposal all seems to be coming to fruition. And here is the objective which the Vatican has in mind:- The "Sunday Telegraph" publicised an article on 21st July, 1991, which declared, "The Pope is not just bent on converting Great Britain; he has been making elaborate contingency plans over the last three years for the re-evangelisation of all Europe". And surprisingly enough the "Sunday Telegraph" entitled that Article, "Hatching a New Popish Plot". Those are not my words, but those of the "Sunday Telegraph". And when the Article said, "The Pope is not just bent on converting Great Britain," converting Great Britain means, converting Great Britain to Roman Catholicism. And when it refers to "the re-evangelisation of all Europe" it means the re-evangelisation of all Europe to Roman Catholicism, for by "evangelisation" the Church of Rome means making people Roman Catholics. This fact was born out by Father Forrest at the Brighton 1991 Conference when he said, "It is not enough to make people Christians. They need also to become Roman Catholics and so become members of the only one true Church on earth".

But where does the European Community and the Maastricht Treaty come in? The answer is that to the Church of Rome the European Community is its main engine, its main driving force, for re-Catholicising the whole of Europe, but not only the whole of Europe, but re-Catholicising all of Britain as well. It may well be remembered that when Mikhail Gorbachev was President of the Soviet Union, and then of what became Russia, he referred, in more than one of his speeches, to his vision of a Europe stretching from the Urals to the Atlantic. And then President Bush and Margaret Thatcher began to take up the same theme. Gorbachev at that time was referring to that kind of Europe as "a common European home". Then surprisingly enough, in December 1989 he visited the Pope in the Vatican City in Rome, on his way to meeting President Bush in Malta. He took the world by surprise in doing this. And there, behind closed doors in the Vatican City, he entered into some kind of union with the Pope, and the Pope with him. So atheistic Communism and Rome became united in some way. Or was it that the vision of "a United Europe stretching from the Urals to the Atlantic" became united in some way between the two of them? However that may be, "the Pope, Karol Woityla, is calmly preparing to assume the mantle which he solemnly believes to be his Divine Right, — that of the new Holy Roman Emperor reigning from the Urals to the Atlantic". (The latter quotation is also taken from the "Sunday Telegraph" Article of 21st July 1991). They are not my words.

But now we need to take this a step further. It needs to be clearly understood, and firmly grasped, that the Church of Rome is not merely a religious institution, it is a politico-religious institution. In other words, it is both political and religious. No other Church on earth has that characteristic.

And as both a religious and political institution, the Pope is acknowledged to be a Sovereign. People are wrong to think of him as just the same, as it were, as the Archbishop of Canterbury, just a religious leader. He is more than that. Much more than that. He is one who claims to be sovereign over all Christians, whether they be members of the Church of Rome or not. And furthermore, he is one who claims to have sovereignty over all countries, over all peoples, and over all rulers. His official titles ascribe him as "Father of Kings and Princes, the Vicar of Christ, and the Ruler of the World". This has been so, from the time of the Vatican's and the Papacy's inception, — from the time the Church of Rome and the Papacy came into existence. And that brings us to its early history.

Way back in the days of the Ancient Roman Empire there was the Roman

Empire itself and also the Roman Emperor. When these two were removed by the Barbarian Invasions, the Papacy and the Church of Rome took their place and succeeded them. But what succeeded them was a political entity. In no way did it resemble the Christian Church which was in Rome in the days of the Apostle Paul, and which was based fairly and squarely on the teachings and doctrines of the Apostle Paul's Epistle to the Romans. The Papacy, the Church of Rome, which came to take the place of the Roman Empire and of the Roman Emperor, was a political entity, I say.

And Cardinal Bellarmine, one of the greatest authorities on the Church of Rome, and one of the greatest Canonists who ever lived said, "The fundamental article of the Christian religion is the supremacy of the Roman pontiff". That meant every soul must be subject to the Pope, to the Papacy. But those who know their New Testament will know full well that in the days of the New Testament Church, and Churches, it was never the fundamental article of the Christian religion that the Roman pontiff was supreme. No such person as the Roman pontiff even existed then. No Roman pontiff ever existed until the Christian Church had been in being for over 300 years! So how could the fundamental article of the Christian religion ever be the supremacy of the Roman pontiff? All the fundamental articles of the Christian faith were laid down by The Lord Jesus Christ Himself in all His Teachings, and in all the New Testament Epistles. Furthermore, all the New Testament Churches, the Corinthian Church, the Galatian Church, the Ephesian Church, the Philippian Church, the Colossian Church, the Thessalonian Church, the Church which was at Rome in the Apostle Paul's day, the church which was at Jerusalem, and the churches which were in Asia mentioned in the Book of the Revelation, were all independent churches. There was no such thing as anybody holding supremacy over them all. Neither was such supremacy ever required by God, or by The Lord Jesus, who is the Only Head of His Church, for the simple reason that He, as The Head, exercised supremacy Himself over them all. There is only One Body of Christ, and there is only One Head, and that is Jesus, and He reigns Supreme over that One Body, and He ALONE. That is why many Christians and Church-going people say every Sunday in the words of the Nicene Creed, "I believe in ONE LORD, ... JESUS CHRIST. They own no other LORD.

Then regarding the Roman Church acknowledging the Pope to be Sovereign, it needs to be stated that a Sovereign is a King. With that in mind I was reading Isaiah Chapter 6 at the time I was writing this, and in verse 5 Isaiah says, "Woe is me! for I am undone: because I am a man of unclean lips, and I dwell in the midst of a people of unclean lips: for mine eyes have seen the King, the Lord of Hosts". He had seen the King, and it wasn't the Pope! Also the definite Article is used. It says, "*THE* King, meaning the *ONLY* King. There can never be two. And that King being referred to by the Prophet Isaiah is Jesus. John's Gospel Chapter 12 verse 41 testifies to this fact. It says, "Isaiah saw his glory, and spake of *Him;* that is, of Jesus. Furthermore, as I have frequently said in my writings, Zechariah Chapter 14 verse 9 says, the day is coming when "the Lord shall be King over all the earth", not the Pope! And the Epistle to the Philippians Chapter 2 verses 9 to 11 say of The Lord Jesus Christ, that "God also hath given Him a name which is above every name; that at the name of Jesus, (not at the name of the Pope!) every knee should bow, of things in heaven, and things in earth, and things under the earth: and that every tongue should confess that Jesus Christ is Lord, (not the Pope!) to the glory of God the Father". So how can the Pope possibly claim to have sovereignty over all Christians, and over all countries, and over all peoples, and over all rulers? And how can he claim to be the Ruler of the World? And yet he does. There is only one answer to this, and that answer is that it is usurped authority. It is not even designated authority, because never at any time, either in the days of the New Testament, or all down the centuries ever since, has The Lord Jesus Christ, the Only Head of His Body, the Church, appointed a Representative on earth to be Head of His Body and given him the title Vicar of Christ on Earth. Never! I defy anyone to say that He has. So why should Her Majesty the Queen, as the Sovereign of this Realm of Britain, or any world ruler, have to kow-tow and bow down to the Pope? Why *do* they? In the days of the New Testament Church no Christian worth his or her salt would ever bow down and declare, "Casesar is Lord". They would rather be thrown to the lions, or into the fire than do that. They fearlessly and unflinchingly proclaimed, "Jesus Christ is Lord, the One and Only Lord". So why do all rulers, including our own Sovereign, submit themselves in obeisance when they visit the Pope today?

Then as to the Church of Rome's claim that she, and she alone is the one and only true universal church on earth, outside of which there is no salvation, it needs to be firmly and clearly stated that that also is a spurious and false claim. There has been much reference in the National Press recently to this concept "the true universal church". The columnist, Clifford Longley, had an Article published in the "Daily Telegraph" on Friday, January 15th of this year (1993) which he entitled, "The search is on for the one true church''. This Article had to do with Anglo-Catholic clergy who are opposed to the ordination of women saying they would have to leave the Church of England and go over to another church. And in reference to that possible landslide, Clifford Longley said in his Article, "As the only show in town, Rome beckons". By saying that, he was implying, (to use his own language), that the Church of Rome is "the only show on the road". But that simply is not true. If the search is on for the one true church then, first of all, you have to turn to the pages of the New Testament to find it. The *true* church, and the *one* true church, is that which is totally and uncompromisingly faithful to all the teachings of Our Lord Jesus Christ and to all the doctrines and teachings of the New Testament Epistles with no other doctrines or teachings added. And the Church of Rome can in no way claim to be doing that!

Then *secondly,* the one true universal church on earth is that which comprises those who are truly Born-Again of the Holy Spirit of God as a result of hearing the Word of God Preached and the only Way of Salvation Preached and then Believing it. As a result of so doing they then become members of the One Body of Christ. The one true universal church on earth comprises of such people, and of such people only. No-one else is a member of the one true universal church on earth. And the one, true, universal church on earth most certainly does not consist of all the denominations, churches, and fellowships in the world, with unconverted people present in most of them, being amalgamated together in one great conglomerate in some form of so-called unity, and coming under one earthly head. In no way. The one true, universal church on earth consists of all those who have been eternally saved by hearing the Gospel of Salvation preached, and by believing it, and it consists of only those. And multitudes of such people all over the world, and in every country of the world, have been eternally saved without so much as coming near any Roman Catholic Church and without so much as being influenced by it. So how can the Vatican and the Church of Rome possibly say "There is no salvation outside the Roman Catholic Church?" That is manifestly and unquestionably the Devil's lie, and there is ample evidence in every country of the world to prove it. A person must be totally and absolutely blind in order not to be able to see that. How disillusioned and completely misled can people be?

All that, needs firmly and clearly to be stated. However, we have this terrible fact existing in the world, that the Church of Rome claims to be, (albeit falsely), the one true, universal church on earth; that it acknowledges the Pope to be a Sovereign; that indeed the Church of Rome holds that he rules over the whole world; that he therefore claims sovereignty over all Christians, whether they be members of the Church of Rome or not, and if they are not, all Christians who belong to any other churches must be absorbed into the Church of Rome and submit to the Pope as their head, because every soul must be subject to the Pope, to the Papacy. And the Pope also claims sovereignty over all countries, and over all rulers, and over all peoples, which is where the European Community, the Maastricht Treaty, and the position of Britain now come in.

As we all know by now, the Maastricht Treaty and the European Community, is all about a United Europe. As I have already stated, the Vatican has entertained this dream of a united Europe for a long time, for over a hundred years, in fact, on the pretext that the establishment of a great European Council, with some great moral figure, and authority, such as the Pope at its head, is the answer to a discordant and inflammatory condition in Europe whose nations are continually on the brink of war. Dr. J. A. Wylie in his book which I have already mentioned, entitled, "Which Sovereign — Queen Victoria or the Pope?" wrote at that time of the proposal that had been made of a European Council with the Pope as head, "This will be found a great stride towards grasping anew that temporal supremacy of Christendom which the Pontiff wielded in the Middle Ages". That, at that time, was language which more than hinted at the Restoration of the Former Holy Roman Empire, and if, as the Article in the 21st July 1991 issue of the "Sunday Telegraph" suggests, the present Pope, Karol Woityla, "is indeed, calmly preparing to assume the mantle which he solemnly believes to be his Divine Right — that of the new Holy Roman Emperor reigning from the Urals to the Atlantic", then that is what we are likely to see happening before too long.

Indeed, it is true to say that that kind of development is already well under way. For as Michael de Semlyn has said in his booklet, "Maastricht, Monarchy and Morality", "If the process of Maastricht is completed and we are committed to a federal Europe, the predominant religion of the confederation would be Roman Catholicism and its spiritual head would be the Pope, to whom all who profess the Roman Catholic faith owe allegiance, political, as well as spiritual". To that I would add that all the Continental Countries who are at present in the European Community, are Roman Catholic countries; — Germany, Belgium, France, Italy, Spain among them, for instance. The only exception is Britain which is a Protestant Christian Country by Constitution.

Michael de Semlyn also points out in his booklet that "among current leaders of Europe professing the Roman Catholic faith are Jacques Delors, the Dutch Prime Minister Rund Lubbers, (both of whom are Jesuit educated), Chancellor Kohl of West Germany, the Prime Minister of Spain Felipe Gonzales, former President Andreotti of Italy and former Premier Tadeusz Mazowieki of Poland". Some of these masquerade under the title "Christian Democrats". But it needs to be stated that "Christian" Democrats (so-called) are in every case Roman Catholics. But nobody ever says anything about this. Certainly The Prime Minister of this Country, and Douglas Hurd, the Foreign Secretary, and our other National Leaders who are negotiating the Maastricht Treaty never do. It, also, is swept quietly and subtly under the carpet. It is all part of the great deception which I referred to earlier.

Then Michael de Semlyn states in his booklet that Jacques Delors, the Dutch Prime Minister Rund Lubbers, Chancellor Kohl, Prime Minister Felipe Gonzales of Spain, former President Andreotti of Italy, and former Premier Tadeusz Mazowiecki of Poland, — these six European leaders, — are products of the Roman Catholic Social Movement. Then he says, "The Catholic Social Movement believes that there is no nobler task than the *unifying* (my italicising) of our continent". He also reveals this:- "Two internal commission reports which were submitted in February 1993 to E.E.C. President, Jacques Delors, argue "that ancient religious differences are at the heart of the conflict besetting the Maastricht Treaty on European Union. And religion, or at least *some kind of peculiar new Euro-spirituality inspired by Brussels* (my italicising) is the answer to the Community's political crisis". No mention has ever been made of that either. It has never entered into any public debate, either in the House of Commons, or in this Country. It has been quietly and subtly covered up. Michael de Semlyn comments, "There is no doubt as to the the nature of that spirituality, nor the importance of understanding the ancient religious differences referred to". By "the ancient religious differences" it means, of course, the ancient religious differences between Protestants and Roman Catholics, that is, between True, Bible-Believing, Holy Spirit Born-Again Christians and the Church of Rome.

And when that argument of those two internal E.E.C. Commission reports say that the answer to the Community's political crisis is "*some kind of peculiar new Euro-spirituality inspired by Brussels*" I strongly suspect that what is being argued is, that it must be of a multi-faith, multi-religious nature, to take account of all the various faiths and religions which have to be represented within the

E.E.C. And especially do I suspect that that is the case when they refer to it as "new", — "a *new* Euro-spirituality". And I notice that they use the term "inspired by Brussels", *NOT* "inspired by God"! And they are most certainly *not* talking about a Euro-spirituality based on the New Testament Christian Faith! So what are they talking about? I will return to that point a little later.

Michael de Semlyn goes on to say, "The European Community, from its inception, was an idea in the mind of the Vatican to re-Catholicise Europe, and into the bargain to re-Catholicise this country, Britain". And of course by "re-Catholicise" he means to make this Country and the whole of Europe Roman Catholic Countries once again. So once again the great deception which I have been referring to is being exposed. But of course, nothing has ever been said about this by our National Leaders, or in Parliamentary Debates about the E.E.C. and the Maastricht Treaty. They have never so much as mentioned that it is more than partly, all about making the whole of Europe, including Britain, Roman Catholic once again. Not even any of our Evangelical and Protestant M.P.s, or Peers of the Realm have.

Michael de Semlyn then adds, "Gullible Christians longing for unity have swallowed a red herring". He says, "This does not bode well for our freedoms. Having failed to conquer this Nation by direct assault in earlier centuries, the Jesuits (and the Vatican, which is my insertion) are now poised to attain their goal by means of the Ecumenical Movement and the "Maastricht Process".

Now it needs to be made quite clear that all that has been said and quoted above, ties in exactly with the Pope's and the Vatican's conception and intention of what they refer to as "World Evangelisation 2,000", as against the so-called "Decade of Evangelism" which is supposed to be going on in this Country, but which, at the moment of writing seems to be getting nowhere fast!

The Pope has stated that his aim in this "World Evangelisation 2,000 Project" is to present so many more million Christians from all over the world to the Lord Jesus Christ as a Birthday Present on the year 2,000. But it needs to be clearly and firmly stated that by "so many more million Christians" he means so many more million Roman Catholics. A Birthday Present about which The Lord Jesus would not be too well pleased, to say the least!

However, I need to repeat that to the Pope, to the Vatican, to the Church of Rome, to evangelise and to engage in evangelisation, and indeed, to engage in *World* evangelisation, is to make people Roman Catholics. There is no question about that. That was clearly stated at the Brighton 1991 Conference. Father Forrest, I repeat, said at the Conference, "It is not enough to make people Christians. They need to become Roman Catholics and so become members of the One True Church on Earth". Now in that respect it is very noticeable that the Pope, in his world-wide journeys, and in his many speeches in many Countries of the world, has never so much as Preached the Gospel of Eternal Salvation through faith in Jesus Christ alone, which is the essential New Testament Message of the Christian Faith. He has never so much as preached its central and crucial Message of The Cross, of why The Lord Jesus died there, i.e. to put away our sin, and the sin of the whole world. He has never once mentioned that our sins were Atoned for through the offering of the Blood of The Lord Jesus once and for all upon the Cross. Neither has he even so much as mentioned, let alone explained to the multitudes who flock to see him, what is The Way of Eternal Salvation, what is a Christian, and how a person becomes a Christian. He has never once proclaimed to them either, that they need to put their trust in The Lord Jesus Christ and in what He has done on their behalf on the Cross in order to be eternally saved. None of these basic, central, Scriptural facts of the real Christian Gospel are ever mentioned by him, let alone preached, in any, or all of his world-journeys.

No. All he is interested in, is the entire world being reached by the Roman Catholic Church and being brought into submission to him and to the Church of Rome.

Never forget that the Church of Rome holds that the Pope rules over the whole world, and so aims to actually bring that rulership and authority about. And of course, bringing everybody into submission to him and into what he and the Church of Rome hold (quite erroneously) to be the One True Universal Church on Earth with the Pope at its head, includes the necessity to absorb or re-absorb into their own fold the Protestant Christians from every other Denomination, — what they now have decided to call their "separated brethren", but whom they always previously called "heretics" during the days of the Glorious Reformation, and thus callously martyred so many of them by burning them to death at the stake, which the Church of Rome has never repented of.

To substantiate what I have stated in the above paragraph I have only to quote what one of their own leading Cardinals has said, Cardinal Heenan. He stated, when he was still alive, "Ecumenism does not mean pretending that all Christian Demoninations are equally true. It does not mean that the Roman Catholic Church has nothing more than other Churches. *The ultimate objective* (my italicising) of Ecumenism *is the reunion of all Christians under the Vicar of Christ"* (my italicising again). There you are, you see. You could not have it stated more clearly than that. That's straight from the horse's mouth!

Indeed, as Dr. David Samuel has stated in his public address entitled, "Rome's Strategy For England":- "Rome's aims are, and have always been, inimical (hostile) to the Protestantism of this (or any other) country. She is bent upon the overthrow and elimination of Protestantism (everywhere). The Church of Rome's object is to overthrow Protestantism and to reabsorb those Christians who belong to Protestant and Free Churches back within her own fold. She will use all the means at her disposal to bring about that particular objective". And I myself would add, that she has been very successful in accomplishing much of that re-absorption in recent years through the Charismatic Movement. And this, briefly, is how:- Both sides, — the Charismatic Movement, and the Church of Rome, have adopted a "set-aside" policy. And by means of this "set-aside" policy they have set aside the basic Doctrines and foundational tenets of the Christian Faith, Protestants included, and at the expense of these, have made the major factor one of experience only, the experience of receiving the so-called "baptism of the spirit". And it is on that basis, the basis of experience, not on essential Christian Doctrine, that some Protestant Christians are now saying they can unite with Roman Catholics who have had the same experience, and the Roman Catholics with them. It is all part of the great deception. And the Pope and the Vatican are now capitalising on this aspect of the Charismatic Movement to draw many gullible Protestant Christians back into their fold. The tragedy is, that that "baptism of the spirit" in many cases, is not the Baptism of The Holy Spirit, but is that of *another* spirit, a *deceiving* spirit. So these Protestant Christians have been, and are being, tragically deceived, misguided, and misled.

By this means, therefore, and by means of the Ecumenical Movement, the Churches Together Movement, the architects of ARCIC (where certain Evangelical Theologians betrayed the Evangelical Cause), and by other subtle and stealthy means), Britain has been slowly and surely de-Protestantised, and, in fact, re-Catholicised.

And it needs to be stated very firmly that it is all with the object of all Christians in this Country, in Europe, and everywhere else throughout the world, being united with the Church of Rome until eventually there is One World Church. And that is a most ominous factor, in view of the

Prophecies of Scripture, and particularly of the Book of The Revelation where it is clearly seen to be a *False* Church. But that is the way in which events are fast heading, European events included. And the only way you can be united with the Church of Rome is by submitting to the Pope, because it is of the very nature of the Papacy, as the Church of Rome itself states, that the Pope is a Sovereign. Therefore all must bow down to him. Rome therefore will brook no rivals at all. None whatsoever. Nothing and no-one must stand in its way. And as Dr. David Samuel says in his Address, "She will not be satisfied until Protestantism is destroyed in its doctrines, and in its institutions". But I myself need to add, this day, by way of strong protest to the Vatican, to the Pope, and to the Church of Rome, "But the doctrines of Protestantism and of the Protestant and Free Churches, are the True, Biblical, and New Testatment Doctrines of the Christian Faith, and always have been. And none can deny it. They are The Truth, — the Truth of God, and who can destroy the Truth of God? No-one. No Pope. No Vatican. No Roman Church. And no-one else either. No other Faith, either, can. Therefore all of you who are in the Roman Catholic Church need urgently to come into line with those doctrines in order to get yourselves into a right relationship with God, because there is only One Truth, and that is the Truth of the Bible.

Indeed, I say to you, right now, Pope of Rome, the Vatican, and Church of Rome, with all the force that I can muster, that, "You need to repent forthwith of all those false and un-Biblical doctrines which you now hold, and have held, all down the history of your Church, and with which you have misled countless millions all down the centuries. You need to stop immediately calling white black and black white in terms of saying that True Bible-Believing, Born-Again Christians are heretics and thus exterminating them or removing them by whatever means, and that you yourselves are the One True Church on Earth. And you need to do it promptly before the Lord Jesus Christ Himself, the One and Only Head of His Church, returns and rebukes you strongly for all the false doctrines and teachings which you now hold, as He rebuked some of the seven Churches which were in Asia at the time when the Book of The Revelation was written. And you need to do it *NOW*, before He removes your candlestick out of its place, as the Prophecies of the Bible, and particularly of the Book of The Revelation, say He is going to do, in any case".

Then to substantiate all that Dr. David Samuel has said in his Address

163

about Rome's Strategy for England it is only necessary to turn to the history of the Christian Faith in this Country. The historical facts speak for themselves.

In the first place, I am never tired of proclaiming that pure, New Testament Christianity came to this Country well over 500 years, that is, over half a century, before Augustine. It could have come direct from Pentecost, or very soon after Pentecost. Furthermore, it was within the period of the Roman occupation of Britain, which began in AD 43, that there arose a British Christian Church which sent its bishops to the early church councils. Furthermore, by about 563 AD it was an ardent and zealous Christian movement which was flourishing here in the north of England, in Scotland, and in Wales, and it was so full of fervour that it was spreading the Gospel to other parts of the British Isles apace. And it was an independent form of Christianity. It was free of all outside control. It was not in any way associated with the universal organisation of the papacy. It was for this very reason that Rome became deeply disturbed. She became deeply disturbed that this Christian Faith had been separately planted. She viewed with deep concern the fact that, from the very outset, it was independent of the papal throne. This was at the time when it had become the first care of the Bishop of Rome to see that all Christians in every country should be brought under one earthly head. The very reason therefore why Gregory the Great sent Augustine to England in 596 AD was to do this very thing. He was sent to bring about an effective union betwen the British Christians and what, in the Roman view, was the main body of the church. He therefore summoned a conference of the British Christian Bishops and Welsh representatives at the mouth of the River Severn. So the battle to make this Country a Roman Catholic Country had begun. But the British Bishops were not having any. When Augustine claimed to have supremacy over all Christians in Britain by virtue of his Roman commission they adamantly rejected his claim. When Augustine threatened that if they did not submit, the Saxon armies in England would be used to bring the whole influence and prestige of Rome against them, they saw Rome in its true light. She was out to get what she wanted by force of arms! That finished the matter as far as the British Bishops and Welsh representatives were concerned, and the conference broke up in enmity. All further efforts by Augustine were virulently repulsed. However the battle to make this Country a Roman Catholic Country continued throughout the succeeding years, and almost 100 years after Augustine's arrival, at the Synod of Whitby in 663 AD, because of the influence and betrayal of a woman, King Oswy of Northumbria's wife, by far the greater and more powerful part of the island now became associated with the papacy, and the rule of Rome became established.

This became the state of things up until the time of the Glorious Reformation. The historian G. M. Trevelyan wrote: "It cannot be denied that the decision of Whitby contained the seeds of all the trouble with Rome down the ages to come".

Then during the Period of the Glorious Reformation, England broke with the Papacy at the time of King Henry VIII. Archbishop Cranmer was one of the principle instruments in bringing about this severance of the power of the Pope in this Country. He knew that there could be no flourishing of Biblical Christianity and of Protestantism here until the power of the Pope in this Country was broken. Oh that we had such Archbishops today! And so it came about that after the reign of Mary, we broke away successfully from Rome. But as soon as we had done that, Rome exerted all her efforts to bring this Country back within her control and within her orbit. She stopped at nothing, she stooped to everything, burnings at the stake, the use of the rack and thumbscrew, hideous tortures, and then the Armada. A great army was marshalled under the Pope and Philip of Spain to come here, overthrow Queen Elizabeth I and put a Roman Catholic on the throne, destroy Protestantism, and overthrow the independence of this Country. The Pope even granted plenary indulgences to anyone who would assassinate Queen Elizabeth I. So much for his title, "Holy Father"! What kind of Holiness is this?

But Divine Providence over-ruled, when, concerning the Armada, God blew with His winds and they were scattered. It then became quite clear to the Church of Rome and to the Vatican, that this Country could not be brought back under the sovereignty of the Pope by force of arms.

However, Roman Catholic plots, conspiracies, and assaults continued against this Country and against the British Throne in terms of the Gunpowder Plot aimed at blowing up the King and Parliament, in terms of Archbishop Laud's attempt "to advance popery and alter the true Protestant Religion established in the Church of England" for which he was tried by Parliament, found guilty, and executed; and in terms of the attempt made by the Stuart King, James II, to bring this Country back under Roman dominance, which led to the "Glorious" and bloodless Revolution with the coming of King William of Orange and to the securing of the Protestant Throne.

Dr. David Samuel is therefore quite justified in saying in his Address, "The strategy of the Church of Rome is the same today as it was in the time of Henry VIII, in the time of Elizabeth I, in the time of the 18th and 19th Centuries, namely, to bring our church and nation back into submission to the papacy. Submission is the only term that Rome will recognise,'' he said.

The examples of that last fact are as follows:-

(1)   When Hurrell Froude and John Henry Newman went secretly to Rome in April 1833 to meet with Cardinal Wiseman to ask him on what terms the Church of England could be accepted back into the fold of the Church of Rome they were told by Cardinal Wiseman that the only terms were terms of submission. They would have to swallow the Council of Trent whole.

Dr. David Samuel comments on that:- ''You see Rome is consistent — always consistent''. But to that, I myself would add, ''But they have been consistently wrong. All down the history of their church they have been consistently wrong. And the Council of Trent in its entirety is wrong, consistently wrong''.

(2)   In this country, when the Ecumenical Movement took its rise in 1910 in Edinburgh and letters were eventually sent to the Pope to ask him if he would allow the Church of Rome to become involved in this ecumenical movement, the Church of Rome made it clear from the very beginning that the only terms on which it would accept people, and on which it would be reunited to the Protestant churches, were the terms of submission. It had no intention of changing its terms.

Those terms were, they stated, still submission to the Pope, acceptance of his sovereignty, and acceptance of all the teachings of the Council of Trent.

(3)   Then when Archbishop Runcie went in 1989 to visit the Pope in the Vatican, he found to his cost that the answer was the same. When he and Pope went into the Sistine Chapel and they read their communiques, at the end, the Pope made it abundantly clear. There could be no modification of the Papacy at all. Archbishop Runcie came back greatly embarrassed. The terms of the Vatican were still the same, and that is submission to the Church of Rome.

(4)   In the recent issue of certain Anglican clergymen considering going over to the Church of Rome because the vote in the General Synod went in favour of the ordination of women

Cardinal Basil Hume, having visited Rome for consultations about it, returned with the same answer. The terms would be that they would have to accept "the whole of the Menu". In no way could they select certain items on it and leave the rest.

To all those examples I must add this:- "Dr. David Samuel says in his address, "Then there is (in the Church of Rome) the question of bishop's titles". He says, "You probably have seen that the Church of Rome has recently written to the Prime Minister asking that territorial titles for its bishops be granted. That is, that a bishop no longer be known, for example, as the Roman Catholic Bishop of Leeds, but the Bishop of Leeds". He says, "It is very important to the Church of Rome, because she holds that the Pope rules over the whole world, and his bishops all exercise rule and authority over the territories by which they are known".

My own comment on that, is this. Presumably that applies to Liverpool as well. It is no longer the Roman Catholic Bishop of Liverpool, but the Bishop of Liverpool, which means he would take precedence over the present Church of England Bishop of Liverpool, David Sheppard. Is that the reason why the present Church of England Bishop of Liverpool never does anything on his own, but always "harnessed" to the Roman Catholic Archbishop? Is that yet another example of submission? And of the direction in which this Country is being taken?

All that *has* been going on, therefore, and all that *is* going on, means that the Church of Rome is manoeuvring itself into a position where it is poised to take the lead when the moment comes:-

(1) Europe.

(2) In Britain, if we dare to allow it.

and (3) Over the whole world when the One World Church becomes fully manifested and comes fully into being, and right out into the open.

That is what the Project "World Evangelisation" is leading towards. That is what it is all about. It is all about bringing into being, and establishing, a One World Church, with every Christian everywhere absorbed into Rome with the Pope as head.

And if what I suspect to be true is right, that the aforementioned, "some kind of peculiar *new* Euro-spirituality inspired by Brussels", is all about a merger or union into one, of all the various faiths and religions that there are in Europe, as the answer to what was described in that European Commission,

February 1993 Report, as, the Community's political crisis, because of "the ancient religious differences which are at the heart of the conflict besetting the Maastricht Treaty on European Union, then you would have a One World Religion comprising all faiths. And Dr. Habgood's push to get the Coronation Oath changed in order to unify an ecumenical and multi-faith society because the religious make-up of the country has changed so dramatically during the last few years, would be seen to be directly related to that self-same thing, and a major step in that direction.

And that would mean that with a One-World Church and One-World Religion a One-World Government would be only a step away.

Indeed, all the signs are, that that is already in being, *in embryo*. For instance, I regarded it as very significant indeed that Lord David Owen, whilst talking on the Radio during the evening of January 30th of this year (1993) about the break-down of the Peace Talks between Bosnia, Croatia and Serbia that had, at that time, just taken place, he suddenly announced that the matter would now have to be referred to "what is in effect *the World Parliament,* namely the Security Council". I am quoting his precise words. This is the first time I have ever heard The Security Council being referred to by a Senior Statesman as *The World Parliament.* David Owen seems to have "let the cat out of the bag" by his remark! Foreign Secretaries, and World Statesmen have no doubt regarded the Security Council as such, behind the scenes, but now, with David Owen's remark, it has been brought right out into the open. I regard his reference to The World Parliament as very significant in view of the Bible Prophecies.

Then also, if one considers what happened at the time of the recent Gulf War when almost every Country in the World was involved in one way or another, and was being consulted in a way that had never happened before in the whole of world history, and all under the umbrella of the Security Council and the United Nations, that, in effect, was a World Parliament, at least *in embryo.* And ever since then, the same procedure has been adopted whenever there has been a serious flare-up in any of the major trouble spots of the world. It is certainly true now, in the present situation in the Balkans.

So with a One-World Church, a One-World Religion, and a One-World Parliament already more than coming into being almost visibly, we are seeing the Prophecies of the Bible concerning these End Days in which we are living, and particularly those of the Book of The Revelation and of the Book of

168

Daniel, clearly being fulfilled and taking shape before our very eyes.

This means that the One World Ruler, about whom all those Prophecies prophesy, is likely soon to emerge onto the scene of human history. And the Bible calls him the Antichrist. And I myself consider that the European Community, with all its bureaucrats, bureaucracy, unelected European Parliament etc., to be an Anti-Christ System, if not *the* Anti-Christ System. And we should not be sucked into it. Not at any price. I believe there is a voice from Heaven saying, "Come out of her, My people, that ye be not partakers of her sins, and that ye receive not of her plagues." See Revelation Chapter 18 verse 4. "Come out". Not "go in".

So what should Britain do about Maastricht?

Well, the voice of the British people is clear enough. "The Times" National Newspaper has been campaigning strongly against it.

So has the "Daily Telegraph" National Newspaper.

The London "Evening Standard" has published strident articles against it.

Leading personalities in the Country, Baroness Thatcher, Enoch Powell, Lord Tebbit, Bill Cash MP, and Lord Cecil Parkinson amongst them, are all strongly against it.

The powerful "Freedom Association" under the Chairmanship of Norris McWhirter, C.B.E. has been writing and campaigning stridently against it.

Furthermore, Public Opinion Polls have voted very strongly against it.

For instance, the Maastricht telephone Poll launched by Lady Thatcher in February of this year (1993) attracted more than 90,000 calls in three months. More than 93 per cent of the 55,000 people who recorded their full names and data, voted "NO" to the question:- "Are you in favour of the Maastricht Treaty?" (Quoted from a report in "The Times", Friday, May 7th, 1993).

Then listen to the mounting pressure that has been exerted against it in Newspaper columns.

> (1) "Lord Tebbit on May 7th blamed the government's obsession with ratifying the Maastricht Treaty for its disastrous results at the Newbury and County Council elections." (From a report in "The Times" dated Saturday, May 8th). He said, "Unless the Prime Minister changes course, the Tories would lose the trust and affection of the British people. I do not think the County Council results were entirely disconnected with the widely held view that the government puts ratification of the

Maastricht Treaty above all else, and yet people do not understand why it should be given such priority", he said.

My own comment on that is, "But the Prime Minister needs to change course *GOD*-wards. That is what he needs to do above all else.

(2) The Leading Article in Saturday, May 8th issue of "The Times" said, about the Newbury and County Council election results:-

"Ministers' consistent dishonesty about the causes of the recession, their weasling words from Maastricht to Matrix Churchill, have turned the voters of Britain against them. On Maastricht, they are prepared to override the will of Parliament and determined not to test the will of the people".

To which I myself would comment:- So what has happened to "Government of the people, by the people, and for the people?" It just is not there any more.

(4) The the Leading Article in the "Sunday Telegraph" on May 9th said,

"Maastricht is economic nonsense. It hands political power to foreign bankers, and it will bring financial ruin on Britain. What is the point of carrying a Treaty whose positive merits the Prime Minister cannot explain? What is it for?

He does have a way out. He could call for a referendum. He could show that he trusted the people. He could say, "I understand the anxiety. I recognise that we have not convinced the voters about Maastricht. I now see that such an important change should not be made without, in the old phrase, the full-hearted consent of the British people. Let them decide. I am content to govern in the light of their choice". If he does not call a referendum, he is inviting a challenge to his leadership in the autumn".

(5) Then Paul Johnson said in an Article published in the same issue of the "Sunday Telegraph" on May 9th, and referring to "the disgraceful behaviour of the Whips over the Maastricht Bill', (his words, not mine);

"It is no accident that the Liberal Democrat victor in Newbury campaigned fervently for a referendum over Maastricht".

"A yawning gulf has opened between government and

170

people,'' Paul Johnson said.

"It is no accident either that, while Mr Hurd was wriggling in shame before the Commons over Maastricht's Social Chapter, Margaret Thatcher was holding a Press Conference citing an immediate acceptance of a referendum as the democratic way out of the Government's mounting difficulties. Mr Major should take Lady Thatcher's advice and concede a referendum. If he refuses, then he should go''.

(6) In "Letters to the Editor'' in "The Times'' on Tuesday, May 11th, Tony Paterson, Conservative Party Candidate, Brent, South, wrote:-

"The single way to allay public concern . . . as expressed in the election results, is to accede to the wish, repeatedly put in the Polls by the vast majority of those surveyed, for a referendum on Maastricht.

"After every party supported Maastricht at the last General Election which muzzled the Treaty's opponents, it is vital to hold a referendum on this issue''.

"The "Times'' campaign for a referendum, he wrote, "has been magnificent''. "There is public unease . . . about the policy of forcing Maastricht through Parliament in an unseemly and ruthless way. The Treaty would take away our independence as a nation without even asking our permission''.

Then the "London Evening Standard'' took up the cry. In an Article by Sir John Nott, published on Tuesday, May 11th, Sir John wrote:-

"It is up to politicians to listen'', said Mr Major after the Newbury and Local Government Election results were published.

"But'', Sir John wrote, "does this Government listen? I fear it does not. The Polls indicate a substantial majority of public opinion in favour of a referendum on Maastricht.'' He said the House of Lords is guardian of the British Constitution. And he raised the question, "Are they going to allow the British people their right to vote on this fundamental constitutional change?''

(8) This was followed by two letters in the "Times'' on Wednesday, May 12th in the "Letters to the Editor'' Columns. The first

was from Lady Margaret Fieldhouse who wrote:-

"When will the Prime Minister admit that one of the major causes for the trouncing the Tories received in both the local elections and the by-election in Newbury is his obsession with railroading the Maastricht Treaty through Parliament in a thoroughly undemocratic fashion? He does not seem to listen to what people are trying to tell him. The wretched Treaty is now discredited".

The second letter was from Mr Edward Barber, Treasurer, Labout Common Market Safeguards Committee, who wrote:-

"When people find out that Maastricht has handed economic policy over to unelected foreigners, both Europe and the Government are likely to become unpopular". And he was quoting from an Article by William Rees-Mogg which had been published in the "Times" on Monday, May 10th.

Then in addition to all this, Noel Malcolm, the Political Commentator for the "Daily Telegraph" said, after the Commons fiasco over the Social Chapter, "There is now some chance that it, (the Maastricht Treaty) may be smashed to smithereens in the courts".

And as long ago as Sunday, March 28th, Paul Johnson wrote, in an Article published on that day, in the "Sunday Telegraph":-

"The main argument used against putting the Maastricht Treaty to the vote of the whole people whose lives it will alter irrevocably, is that a referendum is not the way Britain does things. Parliament, it is argued, is the only trustworthy mechanism".

"Cynical MPs know this is largely nonsense," he went on. "The truth is, Parliament enacts much more legislation than its own creaking machinery can handle . . . . The public hardly comes into it at all, nor do the mass of MPs, except as lobby-fodder.

"Therein lies the case for the extra-parliamentary instrument of a referendum.

"The Maastricht Treaty will affect the daily lives of everyone in this Country, in many different ways, some of them unforeseeable. The Government has done all in its power, and used every torture known to the Whips, to hustle the Bill through and impose the closure. Only last week (3rd week in March) the Whips hauled supporters out of their beds of sickness in order to truncate discussion on one of the most important aspects of the Bill, *monetary union*" (my italicising).

Then he wrote this:

"When the consequences of Maastricht begin to hit the British people, the uproar which will follow will be historic, indeed, blood may well flow". That is not Enoch Powell writing that! That is historian Paul Johnson!

So there is no doubt whatsoever as to what the voice of the British people is saying. A vast majority of them are against it. I believe God Himself is against it. The very fact that the Prime Minister has had to rail-road it through Parliament in a thoroughly undemocratic and totally despicable, unseemly, and ruthless way, with the Government doing all in its power, and using every torture known to the Whips to hustle the Bill through, is evidence enough that he has been, and is, going against God. And the fact that he and his Government were so severely trounced at the Newbury by-election and at the Local Council Elections is evidence enough that God is against him.

Maastricht would mean that we, Britons, would lose all our freedoms. To have to submit to a Roman Catholic-controlled Europe with the Pope at its head would also mean that we, as an island and a group of islands, would lose the freedom from outside control that we have enjoyed ever since Henry VIII severed connections with the Pope and the Church of Rome at the beginning of the Glorious Reformation. With all that in mind, I say this:- It will not be very long now before the Promenade Concerts in the Royal Albert Hall begin. Every year, on the last night of those Proms, the following words are sung in an ever-rising, most inspiring crescendo:-

"When Britain first at Heaven's Command
Arose, arose, arose from out the azure main,
This was the Charter, the Charter of the Land,
And Guardian Angels sang the strain:-
"Rule Britannia, Britannia rules the waves,
Britons never, never, never shall be slaves".

And those words are sung with such outstanding enthusiasm, as encore after encore is called for, that they almost "raise the roof".

This is the voice of Britain being most emphatically expressed.

I guarantee that if those self-same words were sung in the Houses of Parliament today, or in the Palace of Westminster for instance, when all the members of the House of Commons and all the members of the House of Lords were assembled, the singing of those words would go off "like a damp squib". They would fall absolutely flat. And for the simple reason that

173

the Houses of Parliament, the House of Commons and the House of Lords together, no longer express the voice of the British people. Let all of our 56 million inhabitants rise up, and with one resounding voice, say "NO", to Maastricht. And let all those 56 million inhabitants rise up and declare in total defiance, with an equally resounding voice, and in unison:-

"Britons never, never, never shall be slaves". "No. Not to Rome. Not to Brussels. Not to Strasbourg. And not to the European Community. We shall remain FREE".

Thus let the Voice of Britain thunder and reverberate throughout the British Parliament, all over the Continent of Europe, as well as all over the British Isles. Let the British Lion once again arouse itself, even at this very late hour, and let it be the 56 million inhabitants of these islands, and not, *this* time, Sir Winston Churchill, who, with one voice, "Give the ROAR"!

So Maastricht and the E.E.C. is most definitely not the answer for Britain. Coming out, and remaining out, is. As I quoted earlier, the voice from Heaven is saying, "Come out of her, my people, that ye be not partakers of her sins, and that ye receive not of her plagues". Revelation Chapter 18 verse 4. And again, in II Corinthians 6 verse 17, which I believe the Holy Spirit is applying to us, as a Nation, as well as to Believing Christians, "Wherefore, come out from among them, and be ye separate, saith the Lord, and touch not the unclean thing: and I will receive you," which is the same principle as Revelation 18 verse 4. Furthermore, for Britain to continue going in the wrong direction as she has been doing for so long as if everything is normal, is not the answer for our Nation, either. Repentance is. And repentance means turning right round and going in the opposite direction, which would mean, for Britain, going in the right direction, and going the right way.

THE URGENT NEED FOR NATIONAL AND INDIVIDUAL REPENTANCE.

For instance, just before I started to write these last few pages I was told that arrangements are being made to call the Nation to God in prayer early in the Autumn, and that Her Majesty the Queen had been approached about this. That is good news indeed. But if the aim of that National Day of Prayer is going to be to ask God's Blessing on us, as a Nation, then there has got to be deep, and heartfelt repentance involved. Because, in no way, can God Bless a Nation, or indeed individuals, when there are things there that

174

provoke Him to anger and that arouse His fiery indignation, and cause Him to express His Strong Disapproval and Divine Displeasure.

Where our Nation is concerned, we need to repent of all the Anti-God and Anti-Christian Laws which have been passed onto our Statute Book for a start, and cause every one of them to be repealed, forthwith. (I have already written to the Queen about this as long ago as last November (1992).

We need too, to repent of all the ways that we have continued to legislate downwards since those particular offensive laws were passed onto the Statute Book in the Permissive '60s and early '70s.

That means we need to repent of giving support to, and condoning, the "Gay Rights" Movement, which is Sodomy, buggery, and lesbianism, and of bringing the age of consent down to 16 years of age and below.

We need to repent of abolishing corporal punishment and of disallowing any form of correction and the right kind of chastisement for the young.

We need to repent of all stealthy, subtle, devious, disreputable, and dishonest dealings in Parliament, together with all deceitful and back-hand methods that have been going on.

We most certainly need to repent of all the perverted and depraving sex education that is going on in our schools under the cover of so-called Health Education, and we need to see to it that it is all completely swept away.

We need to repent of all the multi-faith services and functions which have been going on in our churches and cathedrals which have thus defiled and polluted the Houses of God throughout the Land.

We need to repent of flouting the Law concerning Christian Education as the Supreme Faith to be taught in our schools.

We need to repent of trusting in False Alliances and in False Confidences, rather than trusting in God.

And we certainly need to repent whole-heartedly of failing to Preach The Saving Gospel of Our Lord Jesus Christ throughout the length and breadth of the Land by every means at our disposal, because of our fear of offending the other faiths and religions that are now here, in our midst.

These are but some of the serious and grievous things that we most urgently need to repent of, as a people, and as a Nation. No doubt others could draw up a further list.

But mark my words. No Blessing of Almighty God can possibly be bestowed upon these islands and upon its people while all these things remain unrepented of. In no way.

And then we need to recognise the days in which we live, in order to see the extreme *URGENCY* of doing this.

We are living in days when everybody is talking in terms of *ONE WORLD*. Politicians and Foreign Secretaries of the Major Nations of the world are speaking today of the need for *one-world* politics, *one-world* economy, a *one-world* consensus of opinion, a *one-world* security system, a *one-world* Army even, and a *one-world* unity.

The cry is for *the unificiation* of the world into one. The Statesmen of the World are therefore saying, "We need to move forward to *a new world order*. "Let's have *ONE* WORLD" is the cry.

At the same time, also, Forces are at work in the World today to bring about a *One-World* Faith, in addition to a One-World Church.

It was described as "a composite faith", and as a "cosmic universal religion" in a Main Article in a recent issue of "The Times", dated Thursday, May 20th (1993) and written by William Rees-Mogg.

And all this has extreme *prophetic* significance, because making the world one, with a one-world currency, one-world politics, a one-world security system, a one-world consensus of opinion, a one-world Foreign Policy, a one-world religion, the merging of all governments and parliaments into one so that you get a one-world government or a one-world Parliament, is all paving the way for a *One-World Ruler,* who, according to the Book of the Revelation Chapter 13 will ultimately be the Anti-Christ — the Beast of Daniel Chapter 7 — the Man of Sin of 2 Thessalonians Chapter 2 verse 3.

And things are fast shaping up that way — to bring him on to the scene. We can see it all happening. And of course, Maastricht and the European Community are a major step in the direction of establishing that *One-World* Government or Parliament. That is why I have said I believe the European Community is an Anti-Christ System, if not *the* Anti-Christ System. That is the reason why also we should not go in, but come out.

THE CLIMAX OF THE AGES.
How near are we to it?

But the fast moving events which we see happening in the World today, — on the Continent of Europe, for instance, and in the Middle East, — are strongly indicating to us that we are fast heading also towards the Grand Finale of World History, — to the Consummation of all things, to the Climax of the Ages. And that is going to come to a head in Jerusalem. That is what all the relevant Prophecies of the Bible teach.

And all the various countries and personalities which are related to the fulfilment of those Prophecies are fast emerging onto the scene of human history. I quote, for instance, present day Iran which is Biblical Persia, Ethiopia, Libya (Gadaffi's lot!), Syria, the Lebanon, Jordan, and of course Israel, among several others.

And I said on an earlier page, that every decadent society ultimately comes to an end. And I said, "Britain today is unquestionably a decadent society". And throughout the whole of this booklet I have provided an abundance of evidence to prove it.

But then I said, the decadent society is replaced by a more robust and strong society. And I said, the question arises, Where is there a society which will replace the now decadent United Kingdom Society? And I said the answer may well be revealed in these concluding pages.

Then in conjunction with that, I must add, that my study of all the Scriptures reveal, that when all that takes place in the life of a Nation which has taken place in our Nation to bring it so low and away from God, then The Lord stirs up the spirit of certain super-powers against it. He did it, for instance with the Assyrian Empire, then with the Babylonian Empire, then with the Medo-Persian Empire, then with the Grecian Empire, then with the Roman Empire when the Nation of Israel, at various stages of its history turned away from God and rebelled against Him. The Bible says "The *Lord* stirred up the spirit of these various Empires or Super-Powers against the Nation of Israel".

Concerning the Northern Kingdom of Israel, for instance, when it turned away from the Living God and went after other gods, the Bible says, "And the God of Israel stirred up the spirit of Pul, King of Assyria, and he carried them away captive". I Chronicles 5:25.

Then concerning the Southern Kingdom of Judah when they went after other gods and committed spiritual fornication, the Bible says, "Moreover the Lord stirred up against Jehoram the King of Judah the spirit of the Philistines, and of the Arabians . . . and they came up into Judah, and brake into it". 2 Chronicles Chapter 21 verse 16.

It says The *Lord* did it. The *Lord* stirred up the spirit of the Philistines against them. Today, people say, they brought the judgment upon themselves. But that is not what the Bible says. It says The *Lord* brought it. And I must be true to the Bible.

The Question is, "Is there, today, a Super-Power whose spirit the Lord could stir up against us?" Let us look around the Nations of the World for a brief moment and see if there is. Would it be China, for instance? The Dalai Lama, in his address to members of the British Parliament recently, pointed out that its rapidly growing economy would make China "the next Super-Power, *armed with* nuclear weapons". (My italicising). From William Rees-Mogg's report in The "Times", Thursday, May 6th, 1993.

But I don't think it would be China.

Could it be a European Super-Power? I don't think so. The nations of Europe are in disarray at the moment, and are totally perplexed at what to do about the Balkans situation. And Russia, *at the moment*, and I repeat, *at the moment,* is no longer a Super-Power. But it needs watching.

What have we then?

Well I'll tell you. There is emerging on the scene today — almost un-noticed it seems to Western eyes, — *a Middle East Super-Power.* And that Super-Power is *Islamic.*

Those are the exact words which I delivered to the British Foreign Office Christian Union by way of Warning as long ago as Tuesday, January 28th, 1992. This was in an Address entitled. "The Key Scriptures relating to the Middle East Situation as we see it today, and the Key Scriptures relating to today's Situation in Israel" which was delivered in two parts on two successive Tuesday's, at that Christian Union's request.

And then, almost a year later, on Saturday, January 2nd, 1993, it was reported in "The Daily Telegraph" that Shimon Peres, Israel's then Foreign Minister, had said that "Radical Islam was a deadly threat to world peace". The Report said, "Communism may be dead, but according to Israel the world faces a deadly new challenge — the rise of Radical Islam *sponsored by Iran"*. (My italicising). I repeat, "sponsored by Iran".

"The new monster," the Report went on to say, "had spread its tentacles throughout the Middle East and North Africa, and it could be stopped only by concerted action by the West, Israel, and countries in the Arab world, such as Egypt and Jordan, which were most threatened by Islamic fundamentalism".

Then, as I had reported in my Address to the British Foreign Office Christian Union, the "Jerusalem Post" had been carrying big, black, headlines saying, "FUNDAMENTALIST ISLAM IS ON THE MARCH". A further report had said, "The one really significant factor in the Middle East today is *the* growth of Islamic Fundamentalism". (My italicising).

It said, "As it sweeps the whole of the Middle East Region the consequences of it will be *ENORMOUS*" (my italicising).

I said at the British Foreign Office at that time, "Warnings therefore need to go out".

I reported during that Address also, that a well-educated and secular young Israeli-Arab had even said during discussions on religions in the Middle East at that time (January 1992), "The World will become Moslem: with *One* Moslem Ruler". That was quoted directly from the January 18th, 1992, issue of the "Jerusalem Post International Edition" Page 13.

I said, "That statement really made me sit up". And I said I was obliged to ask myself the question, "Will the Coming World Ruler, the Anti-Christ that the Bible talks about, be a Moslem, a Fundamentalist Islamic Ruler? Another Saddam Hussein, for instance? I said, I myself have believed for some time now, from my understanding of Daniel's Prophecies, that he will be a Middle East Figure, not a European.

Then, furthermore, Lance Lambert, in his February 1993 cassette-tape update, said, "Islam, by its very nature, intends to take the whole world". He focuses attention on Iran as its pivotal point. And that is highly significant from a Prophetic point of view, because Iran is ancient Persia, — *Biblical* Persia, who were numbered in those days among the Chaldeans. I will be returning to that point a little later on.

Lance Lambert says in his February (1993) up-date, "In Iran, its leaders, its Mullah's and its Ayattolah's, have been openly calling for a Third World War against the West".

So I ask immediately, "Is this The Lord stirring up the spirit of Iran against the West?"

It is a question that needs to be asked.

Lance Lambert goes on to say that they have their eyes upon the West, and particularly on the United States of America, but, in fact, upon the whole of the West, and upon Western Civilisation. And he says, Israel, of course, is included in their eyes as a foundational part of this Western Civilisation.

He repeats that Iran's leaders, its Mullah's, and its Ayattolahs have been calling for a Crusdade, a Third World War, against the West. And he says they call the Twenty First Century the Islamic Century. And may I myself add, the Twenty First Century is now less than 7 years away.

Lance Lambert says they believe that Allah has finally destined that Islam will conquer the world. He says it is not merely Moslem nations, and not even nations with a powerful Moslem minority that they are out to conquer. They are calling for the conquering of the Whole World for Islam. He says, "Nor should we be surprised at this, for Islamic theology, has, from the very beginning, declared that Allah has given, in the revelation through Mohammed who *they* say was the final greatest Prophet, that the World will submit to the Truth as he gave it through Mohammed". And of course, it has been, from the beginning, submission by force, which also means, by force of arms.

We need to know, therefore, that there is this whole New Spectre, this Monster, *more* than emerging on the horizon in the Middle East today. And it is Fundamentalist Islam with its centre in Iran, and being fanned into a flame by Iran.

Furthermore, there is no doubt but that the strongest *Anti-Christ* — and *Anti-Christian* Force in the World today is Fundamentalist Islam. Therefore it is from Fundamentalist Islam that The Anti-Christ, the Beast, the Coming World Ruler could well emerge.

And Lance Lambert says, the blindness, not only of the Western World, but of the whole of Christendom to the true nature of Islam is amazing.

Then he goes on to say that the most serious and sombre development in the Middle East today can be said without any hesitation to be the growing development of *Iran* as a Middle East Super-Power. A "Times" Leader said on Tuesday, May 25th (1993) "Iran is again spreading violence throughout the Middle East".

So there you have the answer to my question, "Is there, today, a Super-Power whose spirit The Lord could be stirring up against us and against the Western World?" And the answer is, that there is. It is Fundamentalist Islam led by Iran.

And to further substantiate that, Lance Lambert goes on to say in his February 1993 up-date tape, "Iran is now in the throes of a massive multi-dollar rearmament programme". "Her plan is for a two-year consolidation period. During that time she will be re-developing all her defensive and offensive weapons, plus her army units and battalions. She has literally two years, and maybe less, before she develops a nuclear device. During this two-year consolidation period also fulfilling her re-arming and military preparation, she is forming a confederation of Islamic States. These Islamic States would include countries like Pakistan, Afghanistan, the ex-Soviet Muslim areas of the Soviet Union, such as Kazakistan, Turkmanistan, and Azerbaijhan, all of which border on Iran. And some of them already have nuclear weapons. Then soon after this two-year consolidation period is over, a holy war, a jihad is being contemplated in which this confederation of Islamic States would participate, but it would be led by Iran, because Iran wants to be the leader of this confederation, and therefore of this holy war.

And all this has been going on when, first, the Bush Administration announced as long ago as Wednesday, 29th January 1992, that it intended to halt production of nuclear bombs indefinitely. And I warned in my Address to the British Foreign Office the day before, that I could see quite clearly that that will mean that this Emerging Middle East Super-Power will be able to hold the West, including Britain, to ransom when once they have gained nuclear superiority, if we don't watch it. They will be able to say, "Do this — or else"! And I said then, in the British Foreign Office, "WE NEED TO BE WARNED".

But since then, Britain and the United States of America have continued to cut down their defences and have been cutting down their Armies, Navies, and Nuclear Weapons to the bone. And now the Clinton Administration has not only continued to close down America's military and naval bases both overseas and at home, but has decided to "kill off the 'Star Wars' anti-missile defence programme". That caused former President Reagan to react immediately, and say "If the new administration in Washington thinks we are no longer at risk from incoming missile attacks they need to open their eyes and take a long, hard look at the World". From a "Daily Telegraph" Report, Monday, May 17th, 1993.

To which I would say, "I should think so".

While all this was going on, my attention was drawn to two verses in the Book of the Prophet Habakkuk Chapter 1. Verse 6 is God speaking. It says, "Lo, I raise up the Chaldeans, that bitter and hasty nation". And Habakkuk, the Prophet said in verse 12, "O Lord, thou hast ordained them for judgment; and, O mighty God, thou hast established them for correction".

And after I had read those words I made a pencilled note, in red, which said, "This surely could apply also to present day Iran, which is ancient Biblical Persia who were, in Habakkuk's day, numbered among the Chaldeans. In other words, it applies to the Rising Middle-East Super-Power. God has established them *for correction*.

    (a)   of the Western Powers;

    (b)   of the United States of America".

Solemn thought!

The big question now is, Where is all this Heading?"

What is it all Leading Up To?

First, it is all leading up to a Major War in the Middle East brought about by Fundamentalist Islam when that confederation of Islamic States has been formed, with Iran as its pivotal-centre or nucleus. They will call it a holy war or jihad. Lance Lambert says, "This Islamic holy war will be a jihad or holy war of huge proportions such as the world has not seen since the Crusades and even actually greater than that. And it will be led by Iran".

Second, its aim will be the Liquidation of Israel. Islamic Fundamentalist Leaders have been saying all along, "There can be no Jewish State". "It has to be Liquidated. And Jerusalem has to be liberated. It is *OURS*. It must become the Islamic Capital of the Middle East. In fact it must become the Islamic Capital of the World". Fundamentalist Islam has been saying that for years. They could do no other, according to Islamic Theology. This has been Islamic Theology for years.

It is a major part of their plan to conquer, and then to rule the World.

And incidentally I need to insert here, that when the Moslem Mosque in Regent's Park was originally opened it was declared at its Opening Ceremony that the object was, that in a measurable distance of time (10 years, they said then) — London would become the Islamic Capital of Europe. This also is part of their plan to conquer, and then to rule the World.

But to rule the World is what *they* think! And Jerusalem, and the capture of Jerusalem is the Bottom Line in all this. The Crunch Point therefore, is Jerusalem.

And here I bring all this into line with the Prophecies of the Bible. Because the Prophecies of the Bible reveal that Jerusalem is going to be the Culminating Point in World History, and that everything will come to a head there.

But the Prophecies of the Bible also reveal that so far as Almighty God and His Divinely Revealed Purposes are concerned, *Jerusalem is not negotiable.* In no way.

Throughout all the pages of the Bible, God Himself refers to Jerusalem as "The Place that I have chosen to set My Name there, and to set My Name there *for* ever". I could quote umpteen passages of the Bible where God himself says this.

Moreover, He says in Ezekiel Chapter 5 verse 5, "Thus saith the Lord God, 'This is Jerusalem. I have set it in the midst of the nations and countries round about her'." Notice he says "*I* have". "*I* have set it there in the midst of the Nations and countries round about her". So that tells me it is *God's*.

But that is also what the Bible says. For the Prophet Daniel refers to it in Daniel Chapter 9 verses 16 and 18, and in verse 19 also as, "*Thy* city, and to "the city that is called by *Thy* Name", and to "Thy city and *Thy* people which are called by Thy Name".

So these mighty Fundamentalist Islamic Forces, when they *do* come against Jerusalem, God's own city, are going to come into a mighty collision with Almighty God!

But that is exactly what the Bible says. Indeed, God Himself says, in Zechariah Chapter 12 verse 9, "It shall come to pass *in that day* that I will seek to destroy all the nations that come against Jerusalem". And when God says, "It shall come to pass", it shall come to pass! It is going to happen. How Spine-Chilling!

So Jerusalem is never going to be the Islamic Capital of the Middle East, or the Islamic Capital of the Whole World. That is for sure. God says it isn't.

But, however, those armies *are* going to come against Jerusalem. For the first part of Zechariah Chapter 12 is talking about a time when armies will be in the siege against Jerusalem and against Judah (the surrounding district, what is *now* referred to as "The West Bank".) (See in particular Zechariah 12 verse 2). But I will be quoting other Bible Prophecies a little later.

So this invasion of Israel by armies *is* going to happen, and Jerusalem is going to be besieged.

But WHEN? That is the question.

It *could* be soon after two years. Because, as we have seen, Iran is engaged in a two-year consolidation period in which to build up her armies and to form a confederation of Islamic States. Iran has also described the Twenty-First Century as the Islamic Century. So it could be within the next 7 to 10 years.

But the Bible Prophecies say something more specific than that.

God says, for instance, in the Book of the Prophet Joel Chapter 3 verse 13, it will be at the time when the wickedness of the nations, of the world, is great. When it has peaked, in other words: when it has come to a head; when it is ripe for Judgment.

And it must almost have peaked right now! Even world-wide. All that I have written in the previous pages of this book provides abundant evidence that it has peaked in this Nation of Britain. But so it has, world-wide.

God always Judges when the wickedness of man and of Nations has come to the full. He did it, at the time of the Flood. He did so again at the time of Sodom and Gomorrah. And He is going to do so again, at the time when He will gather the Nations to battle against Jerusalem. Have no fear.

And this is where I need to begin to Sound Out God's Ultimatum to the whole world. For God never judges, except He first warns. And He is warning right now, through these pages.

He is warning the Nations, and the whole World that they should Repent, while there is still time. And it needs to be deep, and heart-felt Repentance.

So that is the *first* answer, from the Bible, as to *WHEN* these things will happen. It will be when the wickedness of the world has come to a head, has reached its peak.

That these things are, indeed, going to happen is further confirmed by what God says in the Book of the Prophet Zephaniah Chapter 3 verse 8 and the second half of the verse. I quote. This is *GOD* speaking:-

"For My *Determination* is to gather the nations, that I may assemble the kingdoms, to pour upon them Mine Indignation, even all My Fierce Anger; for all the earth shall be devoured with the fire of My jealousy".

A VERY ARRESTING STATEMENT INDEED!

This is very strong language:

God says, "My *Determination* is to do that". "Gather the nations — assemble the kingdoms".

SO *NOTHING CAN STOP IT.* IT WILL HAPPEN.

And that is what God is saying *NOW*.

And you will notice that what God says, is not limited to Islamic Nations.

This is a recurring theme throughout all the Prophecies of the Bible concerning the Last Days — *that God will gather the nations.* And I believe all the signs tell us abundantly clearly that we are now living in the last days.

But now we come to the *second* answer from the Bible as to *WHEN* these things will happen. We find that answer in the Book of the Prophet Joel Chapter 3 verses 1 and 2. Again this is *GOD* speaking. I quote:-

"For behold, in those days, and in that time, *WHEN* I shall bring again the captivity of Judah and Jerusalem, I will *ALSO* gather all nations, and will bring them down into the Valley of Jehoshaphat, (which is just outside Jerusalem) and will plead with them there for *MY* people and for *MY* heritage Israel, whom they have scattered among the nations and parted *MY* Land".

And when it says, "I will plead with them there", it means plead with them *in Judgment.* So this is where I need to *continue* to Sound Out God's

Ultimatum to the Whole World.

Furthermore, I don't need to tell you that God has been bringing again the captivity of His People Judah and Jerusalem who have been scattered among the Nations, for a long time now. You have seen it on television. It has been happening at least since the Balfour Declaration, and is constantly being referred to as "The Return of the Jews". And the Jews stem from the tribe of Judah. And this Prophecy is talking about God bringing again the captivity of His People *Judah.*

And it has been happening for a long time now, and increasingly so since the Declaration of The State of Israel in 1948.

But today it is increasing apace.

Then, please notice, God refers to The Land of Israel in Joel Chapter 3 verse 2 as *My* Land. I quoted this in my Address at the British Foreign Office, and I said, "All Foreign Secretaries all over the World, and all World Governments and World Authorities please note. God says of Israel, 'It is *MY* Land.' So you need to Watch It, all of you!"

God also refers to Israel in the same verse as "*MY* people — and *MY* heritage". "So woe betide anyone", I said, "or any Nation of the World who harms them — or any group of Nations who harms them! You need to be WARNED!"

So that is the *second* answer as to *WHEN* all these things will happen. God states it very specifically in Joel Chapter 3 verses 1 and 2. It will be *WHEN* He shall bring again the captivity of Judah and Jerusalem. And it is already happening, and happening apace. It is *THEN* that God will *also* gather all nations." And notice that God says "*all* nations," not *some* of them. And when God says *all,* He means *all.* All without exception.

Such Prophecies tell us *WHERE WE ARE* at this Dramatic Moment of World History.

We must be almost there! At the Climax of the Ages. We must be almost within a hair's-breadth of being there!

And woe betide any — who have parted God's Land, or divided it up in any so-called Middle-East Peace Process *THEN.*

I said all that, also, during my Address at the British Foreign Office. I did not pull any punches! And never will!

And now I need to come to this Major Point:-

In order that the Bible Prophecies concerning the events that are due to happen in the last days might be fulfilled, *Israel had to become a Nation once more.* All Scriptural Prophecies relating to the events of the Last Days always pre-suppose Israel as a Nation *back in their Land.*

I said during my Address in the British Foreign Office, "All Foreign Offices throughout the World, are you listening? Yasser Arafat and the P.L.O., are you listening? All Arab Countries in the Middle East, are you listening? Saddam Hussein, are *YOU* listening?

Hands off Israel, therefore, all of you!"

And that brings me to the *third* answer from the Bible as to *WHEN* these things will happen. And to do that, I need to turn you again to the Book of the Prophet Zephaniah Chapter 3 verse 8, and the second half of the verse, and in order to be concise. This is *God* speaking, "For My Determination is to gather the nations, that I may assemble the kingdoms".

What to do?

The verse tells you:-

"To pour upon them Mine *Indignation,* even all My *Fierce Anger*". That is what to do.

"For all the earth shall be devoured with the Fire of My jealousy".

That is a very grim statement indeed about the Judgment of God which is very soon to come on the Nations of the World. But it needs to be made.

And this is where I need to Sound Out *yet again* God's Ultimatum to the Whole World. If ever there was a time when deep, heartfelt, genuine, Repentance of all sin World-Wide was needed, this is *IT.*

And this leads me to turn your attention to Isaiah Chapter 63 verses 1 to 6 for elaboration. But I can only pick out key verses in order to be concise. I have to leave the reader to read the whole chapter.

Verse 3 says, "I have trodden the winepress alone; and of the people there was none with me: for I will tread them in Mine anger, and trample them in My fury; and their blood shall be sprinkled upon My garments, and I will stain all My raiment". Then look at verse 4. "For the day of vengeance is in Mine heart, and the year of My redeemed is come".

Here we have *Two Things* clearly stated:-

    (1) The Day of Vengeance.

    (2) The Year of My Redeemed.

What are they all about?

The Day of Vengeance means, The Day of God's Vengeance on all His People Israel's enemies. The Year of My Redeemed means The Year when He will Redeem or Deliver His People Israel from the hands of their enemies

186

and bring about their *spiritual* birth as a Nation.

Jews all over Israel today, and indeed, all over the world, are talking about "the Redemption of Israel", although in their present state of unbelief they don't know what it means. But at least that is what they are talking about, and writing about. They are writing about it in "The Jewish Chronicle," in "The Jerusalem Post," and in other Jewish Newspapers, Books, and Magazines.

And so verse 5 of Isaiah Chapter 63 goes on:-

"And I looked, and there was none to help; and I wondered that there was none to uphold: therefore Mine own arm brought salvation unto Me; and My Fury, it upheld Me. Verse 6. "And I will tread down the people in Mine Anger, and make them drunk in My Fury, and I will bring down their strength to the earth".

That is a further statement about The Day of Vengeance that is soon coming.

And please notice that the phrases, "treading down the winepress" and "treading in the winefat", in Scripture, is the language of Diving Judgment — and in *this* case, Divine Judgment on the Nations.

That is what it means when it says in verse 3, "for I will tread them in Mine Anger, and trample them in My Fury", and in verse 6, "And I will tread down the people in Mine Anger, and make them drunk in My Fury, and I will bring down their strength to the earth". The Book of the Revelation Chapter 14 verses 14 to 20 gives a similar picture. I advise the reader to read it. The Question is, "Who is the *them?*" "I will tread *them* in Mine Anger". And who is "the people"? "I will tread down *the people* in Mine Anger"?

The answer in both cases is, It is the enemies of God's people Israel. The nations that God has gathered, the kingdoms that He has assembled against Jerusalem to battle at the time of The Day of Vengeance.

So the *next* thing which must shortly come to pass in God's Revealed and Stated Programme in World Affairs, and in Middle East Affairs in particular, is The Day of Vengeance that is coming soon, and The Year of His Redeemed. Both of them are ahead of us, and maybe close ahead of us. And the Prophecies of the Bible reveal that they both happen together. They are inter-connected.

Then as to the *fourth* answer from the Bible as to WHEN these things will happen I would turn your attention to the Book of the Prophet Zechariah Chapter 14 verses 1 to 3, where again it is *GOD* speaking. And He is speaking concerning Jerusalem, as to what will happen concerning it at the end of the Last Days:-

"Behold, *the Day of The Lord* cometh". Note that phrase.

"Behold, the Day of The Lord cometh, and thy spoil, (Jerusalem) shall be divided in the midst of thee. *FOR* I will gather *all* nations against Jerusalem to battle" etc.

There you are again, you see. It is all part of God's Revealed and Pre-Stated Programme for the Middle East Situation and Scenario today. Everything is going to come to a head in Jerusalem. That is God's Pre-Stated Plan and Purpose. The History of the World is going to come to a head in Jerusalem. And nothing can stop it. And it is ahead of us. And maybe *immediately* ahead of us.

But *then* what will happen?

Verse 3 of Zechariah Chapter 14 tells us.

And here we come to the *fifth* answer from the Bible as to WHEN these things will happen.

"*THEN* shall the LORD go forth, and fight against those nations, as when He fought in the day of battle". What is being referred to, is The Lord's Intervention on behalf of His People Israel.

That is *The Day of God's Vengeance* on the enemies of His People Israel, in order to break their yoke from off Israel's shoulders finally and for all time.

But it is also The Year of The Lord's Redeemed.

And I said in my Address at the British Foreign Office, "It behoves The British Foreign Office to ensure that they are not on the wrong side when this happens, but on the right side! And it behoves The British Foreign Office to ensure that Britain itself, as a Nation, is not on the wrong side when this happens, and especially as God has said "I will gather *all* nations against Jerusalem to battle". And "*all*" means "all".

So here I need to Sound Out God's Ultimatum to Britain, and in no uncertain way.

I said in my Address to the British Foreign Office, "I am here, today, to *WARN YOU*. You won't be able to say after today that you haven't been warned!!" And the Chief Legal Advisor on Middle East Affairs, (who is a Christian) to the Prime Minister and to the Foreign Secretary was present when I said this. I said, "It is vital that the British Foreign Office be fully informed about these things, and that it be well and truly in line with what *GOD* is doing where World Affairs and Middle East Affairs are concerned, and that it be well and truly in line with The Divinely Revealed Purposes of

188

God for Israel and for the Nations of the World". But it is vital also that the Nation of Britain itself be fully informed about these things, and that as a nation it be well and truly in line with what *GOD* is doing where Middle East Affairs, and particularly where Affairs Regarding Israel are concerned.

Britain must never line herself up with other Nations against Israel. If she does, the consequences will be *DIRE* in the extreme. It will mean Destruction. And she will most certainly cease to be a Nation. And that will be the outworking of the Judgment of God on all her terrible sins. So once again I need to Sound Out God's Ultimatum to Britain. She must not, on any account, be amongst the nations and amongst the kingdoms that God is going to assemble and bring against Jerusalem to battle when that time comes. And that will mean that she will have to be free of any United Nations commitment against Israel and free of any such commitment that might be made against Israel by any World Parliament. Britain must be quite independent and free.

And now I return to Zechariah Chapter 14 verses 3 to 4 in order to come to the *fifth* answer from the Bible as to *WHEN* these things will happen. Let me repeat what it says:-

"*THEN* shall The Lord go forth, and fight against those nations as when He fought in the day of battle. And His feet shall stand in that day upon the Mount of Olives which is before (in front of) Jerusalem .... "

Then to verse 5, the second part of the verse:-

"And the Lord my God shall come, and all the saints with thee".

Then to verse 9:- "And the Lord shall be King over all the earth". *Not* some Fundamentalist Islamic World Ruler! And The Lord, as King, shall be reigning from Jerusalem, as other Prophetic Scriptures say, having devastated all His, and Israel's enemies.

The Day of Vengeance will have come, and will have been accomplished.

Meanwhile, His People Israel, will look upon Him whom they have pierced and will recognise Him as their Messiah, and will Repent of what they did to Him on the Cross. And this will lead to The Spiritual Rebirth of The Nation of Israel *as Romans Chapter 11* prophesies, and as Prophecies in Isaiah, Jeremiah, and Ezekiel prophesy.

Jesus will, at that time, usher in His Glorious Messianic Age, when the Earth will be filled with the Glory of the Lord as the waters cover the sea, when the kingdoms of this world shall have become the Kingdom of Our Lord and of His Christ, and when the Scriptures reveal that Jerusalem will be The Central Place of Worship for the Whole World, and Jesus Christ, as King, will reign for ever and ever.

So the *fifth* thing which will happen according to God's Divinely Revealed and Pre-Stated Programme for the Last Days is that The Lord Jesus Christ is to Return to Jerusalem.

That is the Crunch Point towards which everything else is heading. That will be the Great Climax of Human History — the Culminating Point of Human History. And His Return to Jerusalem will be *WHEN* God has gathered *all* nations against Jerusalem to battle. Because His Return will be to Intervene on God's People Israel's behalf against His and their enemies. So it will have to do with The Destiny of Israel and with their Spiritual Birth as a Nation.

So there we have the *fifth* thing that will happen.

But listen! At some stage between now and then, this Anti-Christ, Anti-God, World Ruler will emerge onto the human scene.

He is referred to in Daniel Chapter 7 verse 25 as someone who shall speak great words against God Most High. So he is Anti-God. He is also referred to in that verse as someone who shall wear out the saints of God Most High. That means he is Anti-Christian and Anti-Israel, because the term "the saints of the Most High" here, refers to the saints in Israel, the godly and believing remnant. He is referred to also in that verse as someone who shall think to change times and laws, and he will be allowed to do that for a time.

He is referred to in Daniel Chapter 11 verse 36 as someone who shall exalt himself, and magnify himself above every god, and shall speak marvellous things against the God of gods, and in verse 37 as someone who shall not regard the God of his fathers, nor regard any god: for he shall magnify himself above all".

In verse 38 he is referred to as someone who will honour the god of forces, which I take to mean armies. It also says of him in that verse, "a god whom his fathers knew not shall he honour with gold, and silver, and with precious stones, and pleasant things".

Verse 39 says of him, "Thus shall he do in the most strong holds with a strange god, whom he shall acknowledge and increase with glory". So he will be an acknowledger of a strange god who he will greatly honour and magnify. And that verse even says, "And he shall divide the Land for gain", which is very significant if it means he shall divide the Land of Israel for gain, especially in view of the present so-called Peace Talks that are taking place.

Other verses in this chapter say he shall be "against the holy-covenant", see verse 28 for instance, which means he will be Anti-Jewish. And verse 32 speaks about others who shall do wickedly against the holy covenant whom he will corrupt by flatteries.

And there are implications in this chapter that he will enter into an Unholy Alliance with a certain negotiator and they shall speak lies at one table (see verse 27) which might have something to do with the statement in verse 39 "and he shall divide the Land for gain". And also with the so-called "Peace Process".

Now before I go any further I need to say that I am well aware that there are those who argue that the "Beast" referred to in Scripture is a System and not a Person. To that I would rejoin that it is both. For instance, the great image which King Nebuchadnezzar saw in his dream, as recorded in Daniel Chapter 2, was a System, a System of World Rulership. It was the Babylonian Empire in the first instance, which is described in verse 37 of that chapter as "a kingdom, power, and strength, and great glory." But Nebuchadnezzar, as a person, was at the head of it. God, in His revelation of what that dream meant said to Nebuchadnezzar through the Prophet Daniel, "Thou art this head of gold". So it was a System headed up by a Person, Nebuchadnezzar, — the Babylonian System of World Rulership, of World Government, of World Empire in fact. Likewise, Nebuchadnezzar was shown in this dream of his that after him there would arise another kingdom, and then a third one "which shall bear rule over all the earth." See verse 39. And then he was shown that there would be a fourth kingdom which eventually would be divided into ten parts. See verses 40 to 44. These kingdoms, or systems of world government, or empires, we now know from Daniel Chapter Eleven, and from history itself, were the Medo-Persian Empire, the Persian Empire, the Greek Empire, and then the Roman Empire. But each one of them was headed up by a Person.

King Darius the Mede, for instance, headed up by the Medo-Persian Empire in his day. Cyrus King of Persia later headed up the Persian Empire. Alexander the Great headed up the Greek Empire in his day. And the various Caesars headed up the Roman Empire when that System of World Government came into being. In fact, every System of World Government, World Rulership or Empire, has been headed up by a Person. So I say again that when the Scriptures refer to the Beast it is not just a System that is being referred to, it is both a System and a Person, and the System is headed up by that person. Furthermore, in Scripture the Beast is always referred to as "he" in the singular. And the "he" in every case is always a Person, whether he is heading up a System or not. So much therefore for that argument.

But to continue with what the Scriptures have to say about the Beast.

When we come to the Book of the Revelation we are given a much clearer picture. Chapter Eleven, Chapter Thirteen, and Chapter Seventeen are the Key Chapters. We are confronted in these chapters by something quite sinister. In Revelation Chapter Eleven verse 7 for instance, this person is referred to as, "the beast that ascendeth out of the bottomless pit." So he is due to come up out of the bottomless pit. That is where he is now which is sinister enough in itself. Then in Revelation Chapter 17 verse 3 an Angel shows the Apostle John "a scarlet coloured beast, full of the names of blasphemy, having seven heads and ten horns." Then in verse 8 of Chapter 17 the Angel explains to the Apostle John a little more about who this beast is, and again it is something very sinister. The Angel says to John, "The beast that thou sawest was (he existed, that means) and is not; (he does not now exist, that means), and shall ascend out of the bottomless pit, and (then) go into perdition." So again it is referring to someone who ascends out of the bottomless pit. In other words, the Angel was referring to someone who had been in existence on earth before the Apostle John's day and to someone who was no longer in existence on earth in the Apostle John's day because he is now in the bottomless pit, and to someone who will exist on earth again, at some stage, after he has ascended out of that bottomless pit.

The implications of all this, therefore, are very sinister indeed.

The Angel refers to him again in the second part of that verse 8 as, "the beast that was, and is not, and yet is." And the Angel says that, "they that dwell on the earth shall wonder when they behold this beast that was, and is not, and yet is." That is, The Angel says, "those whose names were not written in the book of life from the foundation of the earth" shall wonder at him.

But when we turn to Revelation Chapter 13 we learn still more about him, which increases the sinister description of him.

The Apostle John is on the Island of Patmos. And he says in verse 1, "And I stood upon the sand of the sea, and saw a beast rise up out of the sea, having seven heads and ten horns, and upon his horns ten crowns"

192

(which indicates that the ten horns are ten kingdoms). And John says, "And upon his heads the name of blasphemy." This agrees with the Prophet Daniel's description of the beast.

So it is a blasphemous person, which means he is against God, — Anti-God. He blasphemes against Him.

And when the Apostle John said, "I saw a beast rise up out of the sea," because the Isle of Patmos is in the Aegean Sea he must have seen him rise up out of the Aegean Sea, and that could have significance in itself, because not only is Patmos a Greek Island, it is also quite close to the coast of Turkey. And Turkey, a few hundred years later, became the seat of the Ottoman Empire, which was Islamic.

Whatever the significance of that might be, because John saw this beast rise up out of the sea, which was either the Aegean Sea or even the Mediterranean, that is why I believe it is a Mediterranean or Middle East figure or person that is being referred to, and not a European.

But then the Apostle John says in verse 3, "And I saw one of his heads as it were wounded to death, and his deadly wound was healed."

Then in verse 12 he refers to him again as "the beast whose deadly wound was healed."

Then in verse 14 we are told exactly how he received that deadly wound so that he was wounded as it were to death. It says he "had the wound by a sword, and did live."

So he is a person who was killed by a sword, (no doubt in battle).

That is why the previous verses which I have quoted say "he is not". In other words, "he no longer exists". But those verses also say, "he *will* exist." In other words, he will come to life again, and will live. But that will be when he "ascends out of the bottomless pit."

So there is no doubt but that he is a sinister, Satanically supernatural being. That is why Revelation Chapter 13 verse 3 says that "all the world wondered after the beast" who was wounded to death and his deadly wound was healed.

Furthermore, to emphasize that he is Satanic in origin, verse 2 of Chapter 13 says, "And the dragon (which is Satan) gave him his power, and his seat, and great authority." The "seat of the beast" is also referred to in Revelation Chapter 16 verse 10, and that same verse refers also to "his kingdom" "the kingdom of the beast," which must mean a location, an area. And this kingdom is Satanic.

193

Moreover, Revelation Chapter 13 verse 7 says, "And power was given him over all kindreds and tongues and nations" which means he is to be a World-Ruler — the One-World Ruler. And his "seat" is a seat of authority, a "centre" from which to exercise his power with great authority.

And we even read in Revelation Chapter 17 verse 17 that "God hath put it in the hearts of the ten horns (kingdoms) to fulfil his will, and to agree, and give their kingdom unto the beast, until the words of God shall be fulfilled."

So take heed, all you E.E.C. Countries, in case this should be referring to you!

Take heed, I say. God has put it into your hearts to give your kingdom unto the beast!

Then before I proceed further with an added exposition of Revelation Chapter 13 I need to say at this stage, from the Scriptures, what will be *the end* of this grim and evil person.

The Prophet Daniel says, in Daniel Chapter 7 verse eleven, "I beheld even till the beast was slain, and his body destroyed, and given to the burning flame." And this agrees with what we read in Revelation Chapter 19 verse 20: "And the beast was taken, and with him the false prophet that wrought miracles before him, with which he deceived them that had received the mark of the beast, and them that worshipped his image. These both were cast alive into a lake of fire burning with brimstone."

And his Victor, of course, as the previous verses show, is none other than The King of Kings, and Lord of Lords, The Lord Jesus. See Revelation Chapter 19 verse 16, for instance.

But to return to Revelation Chapter 13 and to what else it has to say about the beast. In verse 2, as I have already said, we are told, "and the dragon, (that is, Satan) gave him his power and his seat and great authority." So he is undoubtedly a Satanic person, a powerful Satanic person.

Then in verse 3 the Apostle John saw that one of his seven heads was, as it were, wounded to death; and his deadly wound was healed: and all the world wondered after the beast".

Then verse 4 says, "And they, meaning all the world, worshipped the dragon, (Satan) which gave power unto the beast". In other words they were now Satan-worshippers, and that is the way the world is going more and more at this present time.

Then verse 4 goes on to say, "and they worshipped the beast" who

194

we have already seen is a powerful, Satanic, blasphemous person.

Then verse 4 says, "And they worshipped the beast saying, "Who is like unto the beast?" "Who is able to make war with him?"

So he is a world-wide Object of worship — a powerful, Satanic, blasphemous world-wide Object of worship, and also a powerful, Satanic person of War.

Verse 5 says, "a mouth was given him speaking great things and blasphemies" which ties in with Daniel's description of him in Daniel Chapters 7 and 11.

And verse 6 says, "and he opened his mouth in blasphemy against God, to blaspheme his name, and His tabernacle, (The Temple), and them that dwell in heaven".

Then verse 7 says, "And it was given unto him to make war with the saints, and to overcome them". That also ties in with Daniel's description of him. So he is Anti-Christian if "the saints" means Christians here, and is out to exterminate them, to martyr them. If "the saints" also means the believing Jewish remnant, and it could well do, then he is Anti-Jew also.

Then verse 7 goes on to make the startling statement, "And all that dwell on the earth shall worship him, whose names are not written in the book of life of the Lamb slain from the foundation of the world". That means all but Truly Believing Christians will worship him. So once again he is seen to be a World-Wide Satanic, blasphemous, War-like Object of Worship.

So much, then, for the Apostle John's description of the Powerful, Satanic Figure in Revelation, Chapter 13, whom we can now refer to as the *first* beast.

Because from verse 11 of that Chapter onwards the Apostle John gives a description of *another* beast that he saw. This one was coming out of the earth and had two horns like a lamb, but he spoke as a dragon. So he also is Satanic. And verse 12 verifies that, because it says, "he exerciseth all the power of the first beast which was before him". And we were told with regard to the first beast in verse 2 that it was the dragon, Satan, who gave him his power. So this second beast, or person, is Satanic also. In other words, he is of the Devil, as was the *first* one.

Then we are told in verse 12 that this second person who was of the Devil "caused the earth and them that dwell therein to worship the first beast, whose deadly wound was healed. So here you have a joint confederacy, which is Satanic in origin, conspiring and working together to bring about World-Wide Satan Worship. Nothing short of that. It is a blatant counterfeit of the worship of Almighty God and of His Son, The Lord Jesus Christ, and is a complete substitute for it.

That is the kind of World, the World is going to be, before the Glorious Return of Our Lord and Saviour Jesus Christ, according to these Prophecies. We see it all taking place around us, in embryo, so to speak. Satanic images, and pictures, and activities are everywhere, and on the television screens and in the cinemas, and in plays on theatre stages also. They are even in our schools. That is the way the world is being taken, and *will be* taken at this present time, and by evil, Satanic Forces. This Prophecy says so.

Then we are told in Revelation Chapter 19 verse 20 that this second person, or beast, is described by God as "The False Prophet". He is referred to as "The False Prophet" again in Revelation Chapter 20 verse 10. So that, in a way, identifies who he is.

But let me return to Revelation Chapter 13. Verse 13 says, "he doeth great wonders, so that he maketh fire come down from heaven on earth in the sight of men".

And verse 14 says, "he deceiveth them that dwell on the earth by the means of those miracles which he had power to do *in the sight of the beast*" (my italicising). So he is a great Satanic deceiver, and he is *false*.

This should be warning enough for those today whose only thought seems to be to go chasing after "Signs and Wonders". I myself have seen very clearly that at least some of the miracles of healing that have been taking place in the "Signs and Wonders" Ministries have been brought about by such things as hypnotism, enchantments, and sorcery, and that there is another spirit at work amongst it all which is not the Holy Spirit. The Apostle John in his First Epistle Chapter 4 verse 3 refers to it as "the *spirit* of anti-Christ" which he said was even *then* already in the world. In verse 6 of that Chapter the Apostle also refers to "the *spirit* of error". So we need to be very much aware today that there are *other* spirits at work besides The Holy Spirit, and that they are *evil* spirits and *deceiving* spirits, and that they can work miracles and do wonders, even giving to gullible people a False Baptism which is not the Baptism of the Holy Spirit but a Counterfeit of it. And we need constantly to be reminded these days that Jesus repeatedly said to His disciples, "Take heed that ye be not deceived". Yet despite all these warnings of The Lord Jesus I am afraid many gullible Christians today are, indeed, being deceived, and certainly in Charismatic Circles. Why is it, I often ask myself, for instance, that since The Lord Jesus said, in John Chapter 16 verse

13, that "when He, the Spirit of Truth is come, He will convict the world of sin, and of righteousness, and of judgment", why is it, I say, that you never hear of people being convicted of sin when they are supposedly "baptised in the Spirit" in Charismatic Circles? It never once seems to be mentioned, and it raises the question, "Is it a genuine baptism of the Holy Spirit?" Or, "is it a baptism of some *other* spirit, and especially where 'speaking in tongues' is concerned?" Because all occult Movements can produce "speaking in tongues"; even Moslems and Hindus and Buddhists can "speak in tongues"!

So "speaking in tongues", is in no way, the essential evidence that a person has been genuinely Baptised by The Holy Spirit. Furthermore they never seem to be convicted of judgment in these Charismatic Circles. They certainly never talk about it. So we need to hear the warnings of The Lord Jesus all over again. "Take heed that ye be not deceived"; and that ye be not "taken in". We should rather "try the spirits whether they are of God". I John 4 verse 1.

But now we come to a tremendous Crunch Point so far as this *second* person, or beast is concerned. It goes on to say in verse 14 of Revelation Chapter 13, that this second person, this beast, "says to them that dwell on the earth, that they should make an image to the beast, (the *first* beast) which had the wound by the sword, and did live, and he had power to give life unto the image of the beast, that the image of the beast should both speak, and cause that as many as would not worship the image of the beast should be killed". Revelation Chapter 13 verses 14 and 15.

So here, all True Christians are being confronted with a repetition of the situation when, in the Prophet Daniel's time, King Nebuchadnezzar, of Babylon, set up an image in the plain of Dura in the province of Babylon, "and commanded that everyone should fall down and worship this golden image that he had set up, and whosoever falleth not down and worshippeth this image, shall the same hour be cast into the midst of a burning fiery furnace". See Daniel Chapter 3. It is a repetition of exactly that situation. Only in the case of Revelation Chapter 13 what is added, is this:-

"And he, (the second person, or beast) causeth all, both small and great, rich and poor, free and bond, to receive a mark in their right hand, or in their foreheads: And that no man might buy or sell, save he that had the mark, or the *name* of the beast (my italicising) or the number of his name". Revelation 13 verses 16 and 17. And verse 18 says:- "Here is wisdom. Let him that hath understanding count the number of the beast: for it is *the number of a man* (my italicising). And his number is Six hundred three score and six''. Which is 666.

Therefore, at this point, I need to Sound Out God's Ultimatum to every Truly Believing and Born-Again Christian. For God delivers an extremely strong warning concerning anyone who shall worship this first beast, or his image, when he emerges onto the human scene. And that very strong warning is given in Revelation Chapter 14 verses 9 to 11. And it says:-

"If any man worship the beast and his image, and receive his mark in his forehead, or in his hand, the same shall drink of the wine of the Wrath of God, which is poured out without mixture into the cup of His Indignation; and he shall be tormented with fire and brimstone in the presence of the holy angels, and in the presence of the Lamb, (The Lord Jesus) and the smoke of their torment ascendeth up for ever and ever: and they have no rest day or night, who worship the beast and his image, and whosoever receiveth the mark of his name''.

I am only quoting the Bible!

This is a devastatingly strong warning. And it is repeated several times in the following chapters of the Book of The Revelation. I am well aware also that there are those who have been saying, "Oh, but the True, Believing, Born-Again Christians will no longer be here on earth at the time of The Anti-Christ. They will have been taken up to be with The Lord before he comes''. I have to challenge such a statement. Because why would God Almighty have to deliver such a devastatingly strong warning against any person worshipping the beast, or his image, or receiving his mark or his name, if they are not going to be here at that time?

Having read the Book of the Revelation at one sitting umpteen times, together with the Book of Daniel, I believe the direct opposite is the case. I believe they will still be here, and that they will need to be bold and courageous enough to make their stand as did Shadrach, Meshach and Abednego in Daniel Chapter 3, and proclaim boldly and fearlessly as *they* did, "We will not serve thy gods, nor worship the golden image which thou hast set up. If it be so, our God whom we serve is able to deliver us from the burning fiery furnace, and he will deliver us out of thine hand, O King''. Daniel Chapter 3 verses 16 to 18.

I believe that True Christians all over the world, and all Believing Jews, will find themselves being confronted with a repetition of exactly that kind of situation. And they will have to be prepared to go through the flames, the fires of affliction, rather than bow down and worship that Anti-Christ's, Anti-God's image, and to receive his mark, and rather than deny their Lord and Saviour Jesus Christ, King of Kings and Lord of Lords, who is soon going to Come Again, and Reign as King over all the earth. They must be prepared to be martyred rather than deny their Lord.

Now Finally, as to the time *WHEN* this Anti-Christ Person and World-Ruler shall appear, and also as to the time *WHEN* The Lord Jesus shall return to destroy him, and then to reign on earth.

We must not be guilty of date-fixing. But God has given us some strong indications as to *WHEN* this will be. For once again, He has revealed in the Bible that He is Working to His Divinely Revealed and Pre-Stated Programme.

Concerning the Return of Our Lord Jesus Christ to Reign, which He refers to in 2 Thessalonians Chapter 2 verse 2 as The Day of Christ, He says, in the following verses:-

"Let no man deceive you by any means: for that day shall not come, except there come a falling away first, and that Man of Sin be revealed, the son of perdition; who opposeth and exalteth himself above all that is called God, or that is worshipped — (which is the exact description of him by Daniel in Daniel Chapters 7 and 11) — so that he, as God, sitteth in the temple of God, showing himself that he is God".

Now I notice that God, in this Scripture, does not say, "that day shall not come except there come a World-Wide Revival first, or except there come a World-Wide Harvest of souls, first". Rather the opposite.

And this agrees with what The Lord Jesus Himself said, when He said, "When the Son of Man comes, shall He find faith on the earth?" Which implies that He wouldn't. Luke's Gospel Chapter 18 verse 8. And again when He said, "Because iniquity shall abound, the love of many shall wax cold". Matthew 24 verse 12.

No, rather. 2 Thessalonians Chapter 2 verse 3 says, "that day, the Day of Christ, shall not come, except there came a falling away first". That means a falling away from the Faith, from the *Christian* Faith. And we see it happening all around us. So That Day must be fast approaching.

It is also all too true that iniquity and extreme wickedness literally *abounds* in the world today. And because of it, "The love of many is, indeed, waxing cold." Christians are being overwhelmed by the influences of iniquity and are being seriously affected by it. Some are even giving way to it, and giving in to it.

So all the "ingredients" are there for that Day of Christ soon to come. And those "ingredients" are rapidly increasing every day.

As 2 Thessalonians Chapter 2 verse 7 so rightly says, "The mystery of iniquity doth already work". And then it goes on to say, "Only he who now letteth (or holds it back) will let, (or hold it back) until he be taken out of the way, and *"THEN"*, it says, "shall that Wicked be revealed, whom the Lord shall consume with the spirit of His Mouth, and shall destroy with the brightness of His Coming, even him, whose coming is after the working of Satan with all power and signs and lying wonders, and with all deceivableness of unrighteousness in them that perish; because they receive not the love of the truth in order that they might be saved". 2 Thessalonians Chapter 2 verses 7 to 10.

Which again is an exact description of this Anti-Christ, Anti-God person as given in Daniel Chapters 7 and 11, and in Revelation Chapter 13.

But then notice this solemn statement that follows in 2 Thessalonians Chapter 2 verse 11, "For this cause *GOD* shall send them — (those who receive not the love of the truth in order that they might be saved) — *GOD* shall send *them* strong delusion, that they should believe a lie, in order that they all might be damned who believe not the truth, but had pleasure in unrighteousness".

A very sobering and challenging statement indeed. And notice it says *"GOD* will do it". *"GOD* shall send them strong delusion that they should believe a lie". And when *GOD* does it, they can do nothing about it.

But then it goes on to say in verse 13 of all True, Born-Again Believers:-

"But we are bound to give thanks always to God for you, brethren, beloved of the Lord, because God hath, from the beginning, chosen you to salvation through sanctification of the Spirit and belief of the Truth whereunto He called you by our gospel to the obtaining of the glory of Our Lord Jesus Christ".

So what I have been saying, from the Scriptures, in these last few concluding pages, is this, That sometime between now, and when those armies are brought against Jerusalem to battle and when the Lord Jesus Christ will Return and Intervene on Israel's behalf and then begin His Reign, as King, over all the earth, there is going to emerge onto the Stage of Human History this Anti-Christ, Anti-God, World-Ruler. And it will happen precisely according to God's Divinely Revealed and Pre-Stated Programme as stated in all the Bible Prophecies. And all the indications and signs are, that that may happen very soon, and if so, we haven't got much time left.

So in the interval of time that remains between now and when The Lord Jesus Christ Returns to Reign, His Word must be fulfilled that "This Gospel of the Kingdom shall be preached in all the World for a witness *unto all nations;*

and then shall the end come". Matthew 24 verse 14.

So here I need to Sound Out God's Ultimatum to all Preachers of the Gospel and Evangelists". Because you haven't got much time! There is a most urgent need to Preach The Saving Gospel of The Lord Jesus Christ in the Full Power and Anointing of The Holy Spirit with every modern means at our disposal, and even by satellite, to every nation of the world, and without any restrictions or prohibitions, in the limited time which is available before The Lord Jesus Christ Returns. And that does not mean in any sense entertaining people. It needs to be a clear-cut, straight-from-the-shoulder, totally Bible-Based declaration of The Way of Salvation, and of The Way to be Saved By Faith in The Lord Jesus Christ Alone, with no holds barred.

And it does not mean "moulding the morality" of this Nation, or of all the other Nations either. The Archbishop of Canterbury, Dr. George Carey, said yesterday, Monday, May 25th (1993), that he wanted the Church to "mould the morality of the Nation". But that isn't the job of the Church. You can "mould the morality of a Nation" through philosophy, through Platonism, and all sorts.

The job of the Church is not to "mould a Nation's morality". It is to Preach The Gospel everywhere in the Full Power and Anointing of The Holy Spirit so that people everywhere may believe and be eternally saved. In other words, the eternal salvation of souls is what the job of the Christian Church is all about; and the eternal salvation of souls of every tongue, and nation and kindred and of every false religion under the sun.

Furthermore, when the Lord Jesus Christ said, "This Gospel of the Kingdom shall be preached in all the world for a witness unto all nations," and when He said in Mark's Gospel Chapter 16 verse 15 "Go ye into all the world, and preach the Gospel to every creature", He meant it to be done, irrespective of what the results may be. The job of the Preachers and Evangelists is not to concentrate on what may be the results. The job of the Preachers and Evangelists is to be faithful in Preaching the Gospel. It is God's responsibility to bring about any results.

Again, The Lord Jesus Christ did not say "This Gospel of the Kingdom shall be preached in all the world, and to all nations, and then there will be a World-Wide Harvest of Souls, or then there will be a World-Wide Revival". He said it should be preached in all the world and unto all nations *for a witness*, which means that when it is, nobody will be without excuse.

The harvest of the End Days which Jesus Himself talked about in Matthew Chapter 13 verses 36 to 43 is the harvest of the wicked on the one hand to be cast into a furnace of fire; (Those are the words of The Lord Jesus Christ Himself) and the harvest of the righteous, the saved ones, into His Kingdom, on the other hand.

These same two harvests are referred to in Revelation Chapter 14 verses 14 to 20 and are referred to as "the harvest of the earth" in verse 15, and as that of the clusters of the vine in verse 18.

The one harvest is the harvest of saved souls; the other harvest is the harvest of the wicked to judgment under the Wrath of God.

And nowhere, either in Matthew 13, or in Revelation Chapter 14, is the language of a World-Wide Revival used, or of a Colossal World-Wide Harvest of souls at the End of the Age and before The Lord Jesus Christ Returns.

No. God's Ultimatum to all Gospel Preachers and Evangelists is to "Go into all the World and Preach the Gospel to every creature in these Last Days, and to make sure that this Gospel of the Kingdom is preached in all the world unto all nations *for a witness* irrespective of what the results may be, so that there is no one who is without excuse. And it needs to be done MOST URGENTLY, in the limited time that we have left before The Lord Jesus Christ Returns. Because all the indications and signs according to God's Divinely Revealed and Pre-Stated Time-Table in the Bible are, that we have not much time left.

We are fast approaching the Great Climax of Human History. That is where everything is Heading. And God is Sounding Out His Ultimatums. He did it before The Flood. He did it before Sodom and Gomorrah. He did it concerning Nineveh under the Preaching of Jonah.
And He is doing it NOW.

We must not, on any account, say, in a bouncy and naive manner, as some are tempted to do, and particularly those in some charismatic and spiritually effervescent circles, "Things are moving fast and it is all good," for that is to be guilty of sheer complacency. It is also to create a false sense of security, and manifests a high degree of spiritual immaturity. We must never say, "Everything in the garden is lovely" when everything in the garden is by no means lovely.

When God is Sounding Out His Ultimatums as He *is* doing, you cannot possibly say, "And it is all good".

It is *NOT* all good, not by any means. Because Judgment is coming, and maybe quite soon. Sooner than anyone expects. And it is very severe Judgment at that.

If fact, the Great Climax of Human History will culminate in a whole series of Judgments before ever The Lord Jesus Christ returns in Glory. That is what the whole Book of The Revelation teaches. And for anybody who has eyes to see, those Biblically — predicted Judgments of God are moving fast on us, and on the whole World. And we cannot possibly afford to be bouncy and naive about it and say, "And it is all good". NEVER!

However, the Glorious return of The Lord Jesus Christ could be far nearer than we think. The events in the World are telling us that. The vitally important thing is that each and every one of us be truly in line with God; be rightly related to Him by putting our trust in The Lord Jesus Christ as our Personal Saviour, and by inviting Him to come into our life.

If you do that, you will become a True Believer, and as a True Believer will become an heir of God with all other True Believers, and a joint-heir with Christ of His Kingdom. That means you will be reigning with Him at that Glorious Time when He comes to reign as King over all the Earth. See Daniel Chapter 7 and Zechariah Chapter 14 verse 9.

The Question is:- Are you truly in line with God and with His Divinely Revealed Plan and Purpose?

Are you Rightly Related to Him?

Are you trusting in The Lord Jesus Christ for your Eternal Salvation?

Are you one who has invited him to come into your life?

If not, you need to do it, NOW.

And when you do it, you will know for a certainty that your Eternal Destiny is secure.

The alternative is that you will go out into a lost eternity without God and without The Lord Jesus Christ and be lost for ever and ever. And God forbid that that should happen to anyone who has been reading this book.

LISTEN TO GOD'S ULTIMATUM TO YOU RIGHT NOW. AND ACT UPON IT, BY ASKING THE LORD JESUS CHRIST TO SAVE YOU ETERNALLY AND HE WILL.

INDEX

Page(s)

Abortion   5, 11, 15
Act of Settlement   3, 109
Acts of Deliverance   4
AIDS   7
AIDS education compulsory in schools 116-18
Annus Horribilis (1992)   24
Antichrist   169, 176, 190-2, 200
  Fundamentalist Islamic Ruler   179
Armed Forces
  Homosexuals   11
  Homosexuals in US   111, 136, 138
Artificial Insemination   12

Baptism   59
Believers   59-60
Believers' Baptism   59
Bible Reading   133-4
Bombing of mainland Britain by IRA   19-20
Born-Again Christians   39, 163, 198
Britain
  Bombed by IRA   19-20
  Calamity coming   142
  Christian foundation of nation   2-3
  Decadent society   105, 177
  Early Christianity   2, 100
  Early churches   101
  History of Christian Faith   164-7
  Miracles of deliverance   4
  Moral and Spiritual decline   5, 11-13
  Must not oppose Israel   189
  Nation's Leadership is silent   28-9
  Occupation by Romans   100
  Protestant Christianity Laws   3
  Reduction of defence   181

Calamity coming to Britain   142
Call for National Repentance   27, 175
Capital Punishment   5
Celebrations   10
Charismatic Movement   162, 196-7
Children
  Behaviour training   62-3
  Child abuse sponsored by
    Government   118, 119, 120
  Child criminals   31, 34, 63-6
  And Christian education   121-3

Page(s)

Ignorance of Christianity   122
In pubs   110
Thrashing by parents   63-6
Christian education
  Amongst children   121-3
  Laws   121-36, 175
Christian Faith   124-3
  And Christian education   132
  History in Britain   164-7
  Removed from moral structure   135-6
Christian life   60
  Obtaining mercy   61
  Teaching and preaching crusade 61, 67
  Trusting in Jesus   60
Christain teaching resisted in schools   135
Christianity
  Arrival in British Isles   2, 100
  Early spread   69
  In schools   121-36
  Primacy within Religious Education 132-3
  Pure form proclaimed   27
  Unifying with other faiths and religions 72-8
Christmas explained to Moslem man   127-8
Church of England   70, 106
  Needs leadership of Sovereign   106
  Terms for ecumenical union   166
Church of Rome   71, 152
  Aims to overthrow
    Protestantism   162-3, 166
  Claims to be one true church   156-8
  Conversion of Europe   153-4
Churches defiled by holding multi-faith
  services   12, 25-6, 82
Churchill, Winston: *History of the English-
  Speaking Peoples*   3, 13, 101
  Call for special prayers   4, 106
Climax of the ages   176-7
Commandments   52-3
  Purpose   51-2, 54-6
  Teaching   50-1
  Violation of   13
Conservative Party and Gay Rights
  Movement   13, 111
Conversion of Europe to Roman
  Catholicism   153-4

Page(s)

Conversion to Christianity 69
Conversion to Roman Catholicism 11, 71
Coronation Oath 3, 6, 13, 15, 17, 25, 39, 72, 75, 106, 107, 109, 168
Corporal punishment 15, 62-6, 175
Crime
  Child criminals 31, 34, 63-6
  Crusade against 61, 67
  In Europe 34
  Prevention 38
Crusade against crime 61, 67
Crusade to teach Commandments 50-1

Day of Judgment, Moslem belief in 126
Day of Vengeance 186, 187, 188, 189
Death of The Lord Jesus Christ 47-8
Decade of Evangelism article 1, 68
Decade of Evangelism crusade launched 67-71
Discipline training for children 62-6
Divine Indignation 26
Divine judgment visited on Royal
  Family 15-17, 107-8
Divorce 11-12, 15
Druid worship 100

Easter, meaning of 128-9
Ecumenical Movement 160
  Terms of Church of Rome 166
Ecumenical society as cause for alarm 72-6
Elizabeth I 3
Elizabeth II
  Author's letters to Queen 18-20, 24-7, 108
  Constitutional position 106, 107
  Needs to give leadership 106, 110
  Personal conversion 10
Established Church 71-2
Establishment, loss of status 35
Europe
  Crime 34
  Roman Catholic countries 158-9
  Roman Catholic leaders 159
European Economic Community 152-4, 158
Evangelism 68, 71
  And Proselytism 68-9
  World Evangelisation Project 160, 167
False Alliances 144-7, 175

Page(s)

Fear of God 40
Floods in the US 111-12, 136-43
France, crime 34

Gambling 15
Gay Rights Movement 15, 175
  Backed by Conservative Party 13,111
  In United States 111, 140
Gay Rights see also homosexuality;
  homosexuals
General Election (1992) 13-14
George VI 109
  Calls for special prayers 4, 106
God
  Anger of 40
  Fear of 40
  Is light 41-5
  Nature of 41
  In society 36
God's common grace 14
God's Judgment on Royal Family 15-17, 107-8
Gospel of Salvation 50, 51, 55, 68
Government
  And child abuse 11, 19, 120
  Decrees sex education for children 114-21
  Divinely appointed 14-15
  Fall predicted 20-1
Greek gods 98
Gulf Wars 8

Habgood, Dr. 72-8, 103, 105, 168
Hell, Moslem belief in 126
Homosexuality 7
  Advocated by local authorities 117-18
  Legalised 11
  see also Gay Rights Movement
Homosexuals
  Age of consent 111, 112
  Conservative policy 13, 111
  In armed forces 11, 111
  In US armed forces 111, 136, 138
  Labour Party policy on age of consent 13
House of God polluted by multi-faith
  services 12, 25-6, 82

IRA bomb mainland Britain 19-20
Idolatry 78

Page(s)

Iran
  As leader of Fundamentalist Islam 178-80
  Rearming 180
Islam
  Islamic States form confederation 180-1
  Jihad 182
  Threat to world peace 178-9
Israel 8
  Invasion 183
  Liquidation by Islam 182
  And multi-faith society 77, 82
  As a nation 185-6
  Purged of multi-faith culture by Josiah 85-8
  Redemption 187
  Spiritual rebirth 189, 190
Italy, crime 34

Jerusalem 8
  At the end of the Last Days 187-8
  Beseiged 183
  Chosen by God 182-3
  Early spread of Christianity 69
  Islamic capital of the world 182
  Temple desecrated 82
Jesus
  Fulfils the Law on our behalf 56-7
  Purpose in the world 56-7
  Responsible for our sins 58
  To return to Jerusalem 190
  Trust in 59-60
Jews 8
  Return of 185
Judgment by Fire 26
Judgment of God 6, 19, 92, 96, 203
Juvenile crime 31-2, 52, 63
  Punishment 65-6

Labour Party and homosexual age of
  consent 13
Last Days 184, 187-8
Law on Religious education flouted 121-36
Lesbianism 7

Maastricht Treaty 21, 107, 108, 144-52, 158
  Public opposition 169-74
Marriages of members of Royal Family 24, 108
Medical genetics and engineering 12
Mercy 60-1

Page(s)

Monarchy 105-110
  And the constitution 106, 107
Moral and spiritual decline 5, 11-13
Moslem beliefs 126
Moslems converted to Chrisianity 129-30
Multi-faith services 175
  Need to cease 27, 72-105
  Pollute House of God 12, 25-6, 82
  Worship condemned 72-105
Murder by children 31

Nation forsakes God 144
National Calamity 32
National days of prayer 4, 106
National disasters and tragedies 9, 19
National economy collapse 19
National Society for the Prevention of
  Cruelty to Children 65
Nature of God 40-1
Nemesis 35, 36-7, 83, 84, 88, 89, 90, 92
New Government - a New Era 1, 14-15,
              17, 18, 19, 32, 69
New Testament Christian Faith 11, 164
New Testament teaching 13

Old Testament scriptures 72-98
Old Testament teaching 103
One true universal church 156-7
One world 168, 176
Only Way of Salvation 104
Ordinance of God 14
Ordination of women 16, 71, 166-7

Parents right to thrash their children 64-6
Parliament 175
  Legalises sinful acts 5
Paul
  Arrives in Britian 100
  In Athens 98-9
  On the road to Damascus 42-3, 60-1
Permissive society 15, 17, 26, 33, 35
Peter, arrives in Britain 100
Pope 153-6
  As Sovereign over all Christians
              154, 155-6, 157-8
Prayer, effect of 4
Prayer Mission 70
Preaching and teaching crusade 61, 67

	Page(s)
Preaching the Gospel	39, 101, 201
Prophets	28
Proselytism, and evangelism	68-9
Prostitution	85, 87
Queen see Elizabeth II	
Queen in Parliament	107, 108
Redemption of Israel	187
Religious education, law ignored	121-36, 175
Repentance	10-11, 27, 174-6
Right and wrong	50
Roman Catholic countries in EEC	158-9
Roman Catholic leaders in EEC	159
Roman Catholic Social Movement	159
Roman Catholicism,	
conversion to	11, 71, 153-4
Roman Empire	155
Christianity in Britain	100, 101
Roman gods	99-100
Royal Assent	5, 9, 11, 15, 17, 18, 25, 33
Royal Family	
And Divine Displeasure	26
Divine judgment visited on	15-18, 107-8
Marriages	12, 24, 26, 108
Salvation	38, 47, 49
Gospel of	50, 51, 55, 68
Only way	104
Personal	61
Saul on the road to Damascus	42-3, 60-1
Scriptures the authority in matters of faith	
and conduct	73
Sex education for children	114-21, 174
Sex outside marriage	15
Sex as recreation taught in schools	119
Sin	46-7
Knowledge of	52, 54-5
Legalised by Parliament	5, 7-8
Punishment	57
Sound Out God's Ultimatum to	
Britain	188, 189, 198, 201
Sound the Trumpet Among the	
Nations	1, 2, 8
Sovereign's role to uphold Protestant	
Church	109
Spain, crime	34
Spiritual adultery	93

	Page(s)
Springboard	67-8, 70
Storm of the Century	111-2, 136-43
Sunday Trading	15, 137, 140, 141
Switzerland, crime	34
Teaching and preaching crusade	61, 67
Ten Commandments see Commandments	
Thrashing of children by parents	63-6
Tory Campaign for Homosexual Equality	111
True Christian message	46-9
Trumpet Sounds for Britain	1, 4, 5, 100
Trusting in Jesus	59-60
Unification with other faiths and religions	
condemned	72-8
United Europe, origins	152-3, 158
United Nations Security Council	168
United States	
Homosexuals in armed forces	111, 136, 138
Moral evil	113
Reduction of defence	181
Storm of the Century	111-12, 136-43
Visitation of Judgment	111-12
Victims of crime	32
Vikings converted to Christianity	102
Visitation of Divine Judgment on British	
Parliament	114
Visitation of God on a Nation	32
Visitation of the judgment of	
God	17, 19, 26, 114
Visitation of Judgment on United	
States	111-12
Voluntary euthanasia	11
War in the Middle East	182
Warning to the Nation	1
Weather disasters	9-10, 21-4
Welsh Revival	39
Whither Britannia?	1, 11, 13
Windsor Castle fire	16-18, 24, 107
Word of truth	59, 60
World Evangelisation 2000 Project	160, 167
Year of the Lord's Redeemed	186, 187, 188

BIBLICAL REFERENCES
OLD TESTAMENT

	Page(s)			Page(s)
Genesis			11:11-12	145
2:17	57		11:31	73
			15:11-23	78
Exodus			18:4	79
13:21	44		18:19-22	79
19:9	44		18:24-39	80
20:3	72			
20:5	72		II Kings	
20:8-11	137		18:3	82
22:20	74		18:5	82
23:13	74		18:7	82
23:24	74		21	82, 83
23:32	74		22:2	83
24:3	75		23	87
24:7	75		23:4-6	86
34:5-6	34		23:25	90
			23:26-7	91
Numbers			23:36-7	91
22	150		24:1-2	91
14:43	152		24:3-4	92
Deuteronomy			I Chronicles	
4:23-6	89		5:25	177
6:14	75			
6:14-15	89		II Chronicles	
7:2-4	89		7:21-2	10
8:19-20	89		14	78
11:16-17	90		14:9-15	145
20:17-18	75		16:1-9	145
28:46	6		18:1	146
30:17-18	75, 90		19:1-2	146
			20:35-7	146
Judges			21:10-11	92
2:17	77		21:16	177
2:19	77		31:1	82
3:1-5	76		34:3	87
3:6-8	77		34:23-5	88
I Samuel			Job	
7:3	73		9:4	29
I Kings			Psalms	
3:1	144		2	137, 140-1, 142
11:10-12	73		95:10	37

	Page(s)		Page(s)
Psalms (continued)		6:3-7	95
119:126	6	6:9	96
		11:18	93
Proverbs		14	96
1	137, 142	14:4-8	97
1:24	138, 141	14:6	96
1:25	29	14:9-11	97
8:15	106	16	148
13:24	65	18:20	57
19:18	65	20	94
22:6	62	20:7-9	94
23:13-14	65	20:27-8	94
29:15	65	20:31-2	94
		22:3-4	95
Isaiah		22:8	95
1:4	37	24:14	148
5:24	8	33:1-11	1
6:5	155	36:17-18	93
8:20	144	38	8
19:11	150	39	8
19:13-14	150		
29:6	16, 17, 18	Daniel	
30:1-3	146, 147	2:37	191
31:1	147	2:39-44	191
31:3	147	3	197
36	80	3:16-18	198
37	80	7	176, 195, 199, 200,
37:15-20	81		203
37:36	81	7:11	194
45:23	104	7:25	190
59:2	47	9:16	183
63:1-6	186, 187	9:18-19	183
		11	195, 199, 200
Jeremiah		11:27-8	191
2:20	93	11:32	191
2:37	147	11:36-9	190
3:2	93		
3:8-9	93	Hosea	
5:10	147	1:2	92
10:10-11	97	4:10	149
10:14-15	123	4:12	92, 149
10:15	98	5:3-4	92
16:5	148	5:4	149
32:34	93	5:15	152
36:23	31	7:10-13	148
Ezekiel		Joel	
5:5	182	3	8

	Page(s)			Page(s)
Joel (continued)			Mark	
3:1-2	184, 185		16:15	201
3:13	183			
			Luke	
Amos			1:26-38	127
1:14	17		5:22	46
2:4	17		13	143
3:6	9		17:1-2	120
7:4	16		19:10	46
			21:24	8
Habakkuk				
1:6	181		John	
1:12	181		1:6-9	42
			1:12-13	60
Zephaniah			1:29	48,128
3:8	8, 184, 186		3:8	60
			3:16	42
Haggai			3:16-18	56
1:5-6	151		12:41	156
1:9	152		16:13	197
Zechariah			Acts	
12:2	183		2:5	69
12:9	183		9:1-2	60
14	43		17:16	98
14:1-3	187, 188, 189		18:3	60
14:4-5	189		26:13	42
14:9	133, 156, 189, 203			
			Romans	
Malachi			1	6
2:16	11		1:18	7
			1:15-16	38
			2:12	54
			2:23	55
			3:9	54
NEW TESTAMENT			3:19	54, 55, 57
			3:22	55
Matthew			3:23	55, 57
1:21	46		4:24-5	58
5:17	56		5:10	48
7:24	132		5:15	58
10:32-3	109		5:17	59
13	202		5:19	59
13:36-43	201		6:23	49,57
15:18-20	37		7:7	52, 54
24:3	34		7:13	52, 54
24:12	34		7:19	38
24:14	201		8:1-4	56

	Page(s)		Page(s)
Romans (continued)		II Timothy	
9:11-12	109	3:1	34
11	189	3:13	34
11:32	61		
13:1-2	14	Hebrews	
		9:22	48
I Corinthians		9:26	47
3:11	131	10:31	148
3:12	132	12:6-11	62
10:6	76, 78	12:18	44
10:11	76, 78, 92, 105, 149	James	
		2:10	56
II Corinthians			
5:18-19	48	I Peter	
5:21	49	3:18	58
6:17	174		
		I John	
Galatians		1:5	42
3:24	56	4:1	197
4:4-5	56	4:3	196
4:5	54	4:6	196
Ephesians		Revelation	
1:12-14	59	11:7	192
1:15	60	13	176, 200
2:8	49	13:1	192
2:9	49	13:2	193, 194, 195
		13:3	193, 194
Phillippians		13:4	194-5
2:5-11	104	13:6-7	195
2:9-11	133, 156	13:7	194
		13:11	195
I Thessalonians		13:12	193, 195
2:3	176, 199	13:13	196
2:7	199	13:14-17	193, 196, 197
2:7-11	200	14:9-11	198
2:13	200	14:14-20	187, 202
		16:10	193
II Thessalonians		17:3	192
2:2	199	17:8	192
		17:17	194
I Timothy		18:4	169, 174
1:5	46	19:16	194
1:13	61	19:20	194, 196
6:16	42	20:10	196
		21:23	43

The Trumpet Sounds for Britain
by David E. Gardner

David Gardner's central message, in his trilogy *The Trumpet Sounds for Britain*, was to call the people of Great Britain to remember their Christian heritage and turn to the Lord in repentance. Still relevant today, the re-publishing of the book in one volume has made it available as a foundational resource to all who should put the trumpet to their lips.

'David Gardner has provided us with a unique analysis of the Christian heritage of Britain, one that would take an enormous amount of study to repeat' (Dr Clifford Denton).

Available from:
Jesus Is Alive! Ministries,
57 London Road,
Southend-on-Sea,
Essex SS1 1PF.

Tel/Fax: 01702 390500

Cover price £9.99

Special offer
UK orders sent post free to readers of *God's Ultimatum*.
Please make cheques payable to Jesus Is Alive! Ministries.

Sound the Trumpet Among the Nations
by David E. Gardner

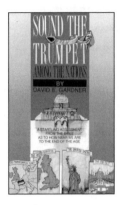

- Where are world events leading us?
- Are we heading for the finale of world history?
- How will this happen?
- When will this happen?
- What is the next stage in this great world drama?

The answers to these and many other questions can be found in this book, which reveals startling facts about the end times.

Sound the Trumpet Among the Nations will bring a challenge to all who read it and an exaltation for us to realise the imminent fulfilment of biblical truths for the end of this age.

Available from:
Jesus is Alive! Ministries,
57 London Road,
Southend-on-Sea,
Essex SS1 1PF.

Tel/Fax: 01702 390500

Cover price £3.95

Special offer
UK orders sent post free to readers of *God's Ultimatum*.
Please make cheques payable to Jesus Is Alive! Ministries.

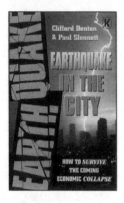

A Christian in Name Only
by David Wilkerson

 David Wilkerson, senior pastor of Times Square Church, New York and author of *The Cross and the Switchblade*, issues a challenge to every Christian. He encourages us to examine our lives and ensure that we are not just a 'Christian in name only'.

This booklet has been produced from the Times Square Church pulpit series. It is a loving word of warning to all 'wise virgins' who have begun to slumber.

For a FREE copy please send your name and address to:
Jesus Is Alive! Ministries,
57 London Road,
Southend-on-Sea,
Essex SS1 1PF.

Tel/Fax: 01702 390500

David Wilkerson's Times Square messages are available to hear at www.timessquarechurch.org